COUNSELLING SKILLS FOR
WORKING WITH GENDER DIVERSITY AND IDENTITY

also in the Essential Skills for Counselling *series*

Counselling Skills for Becoming a Wiser Practitioner
Tools, Techniques and Reflections for Building Practice Wisdom
Tony Evans
ISBN 978 1 84905 607 6
eISBN 978 1 78450 143 3

Counselling Skills for Working with Shame
Christiane Sanderson
ISBN 978 1 84905 562 8
eISBN 978 1 78450 001 6

Counselling Skills for Working with Trauma
Healing From Child Sexual Abuse, Sexual Violence and Domestic Abuse
Christiane Sanderson
ISBN 978 1 84905 326 6
eISBN 978 0 85700 743 8

of related interest

How to Understand Your Gender
A Practical Guide for Exploring Who You Are
Alex Iantaffi and Meg-John Barker
Foreword by S. Bear Bergman
ISBN 978 1 78592 746 1
eISBN 978 1 78450 517 2

Counseling Transgender and Non-Binary Youth
The Essential Guide
Irwin Krieger
ISBN 978 1 78592 743 0
eISBN 978 1 78450 482 3

Can I tell you about Gender Diversity?
A guide for friends, family and professionals
CJ Atkinson
Illustrated by Olly Pike
ISBN 978 1 78592 105 6
eISBN 978 1 78450 367 3
Part of the Can I tell you about...? *series*

COUNSELLING SKILLS FOR
WORKING WITH GENDER DIVERSITY AND IDENTITY

MICHAEL BEATTIE AND PENNY LENIHAN
WITH ROBIN DUNDAS

Foreword by Christiane Sanderson

Jessica Kingsley *Publishers*
London and Philadelphia

Contains public sector information licensed under the Open Government Licence v3.0.

First published in 2018
by Jessica Kingsley Publishers
73 Collier Street
London N1 9BE, UK
and
400 Market Street, Suite 400
Philadelphia, PA 19106, USA

www.jkp.com

Library of Congress Cataloging in Publication Data
A CIP catalog record for this book is available from the Library of Congress

British Library Cataloguing in Publication Data
A CIP catalogue record for this book is available from the British Library

ISBN 978 1 78592 741 6
eISBN 978 1 78450 481 6

Printed and bound in Great Britain

MIX
Paper from
responsible sources
FSC® C013056

CONTENTS

Part III: Practitioner Self-Care

SERIES EDITOR'S FOREWORD

The landscape of therapeutic practice is a constantly changing terrain that reflects current mental health concerns and increasingly diverse client populations. This, along with keeping up to date with the latest research in the field of mental health and good practice, poses considerable challenges for practitioners as they try to balance the demands of their practice with continuous professional development. The Essential Skills for Counselling Series is designed to provide clinicians, therapists, counsellors, health professionals, social care practitioners, and trainees with a range of tried and tested skills to enable them to enhance their practice. The emphasis is on exploring current changes in knowledge and practice which can be incorporated into their existing practice and theoretical model or orientation. The books in the series will focus on skills and techniques that are particularly useful when working either with particular client groups, such as survivors of childhood sexual abuse, or specific presenting symptoms such as complex trauma or shame.

Many practitioners are not always able to keep abreast of the latest research or be familiar with developments in practice and range of therapeutic techniques across different modalities. The handbooks in this series aim to provide current knowledge in working with particular client groups or specific mental health issues that practitioners may not have encountered in their original training. To enhance awareness and understanding the books will encourage practitioners to challenge their own perceptions and practice through self-reflection and a series of tried and tested exercises that they are invited to engage with and which can be used with clients.

The books in the series will be user friendly in using clear, accessible and easy to understand language with icons to signpost important points and good practice points. There will be boxes for experiential exercises and skills and exercises to use with clients. Practitioners will be able to dip in and out of the books as they need to enabling them access relevant information and skills without having to read extensively. To enliven the text case examples will be included to show how the skills can be employed. The focus throughout is on clear and succinct descriptions of skills, how they can best be employed and making the practitioner more aware of their own process in their work enabling them to become more sentient practitioners.

With the increased discourse on gender identity in response to estimates that around 1 per cent of the population are gender variant, it is critical that counsellors, therapists, and mental health professionals have the vital skills and information they need to be gender diversity literate and sensitive. This new addition to the series offers a timely and comprehensive introduction to how to work with gender diversity and identity. Through the unique balance of theory and practice, Michael Beattie and Penny Lenihan facilitate a deeper understanding of the complex issues in gender identity and how to work with the gendered self, gender variance, gender identity, and gender dysphoria.

Their book is packed with a wealth of clinical knowledge and a range of essential skills that will enable practitioners, trainees, and students to gain confidence when working with a diverse range of gender identities including masculinity, femininity, non-binary, trans, and cisgender. The emphasis throughout is on the need for affirmative practice in gender care and the process issues which most commonly arise in the therapeutic space, including the challenges that clients face in their daily lives and in the workplace when coming out, when transitioning, and in intimate relationships.

Through the combination of education, skills, reflexivity, case studies, and reflective exercises, the authors provide a much-needed book that equips practitioners with the knowledge and skills that facilitate good practice when working with gender diversity and gender identity that will be useful for professional development for all counsellors and psychotherapists, as well as trainees and students. It will also be a valuable addition to the literature on gender diversity and identity that would be of interest to other professionals including psychologists, psychiatrists, nurses, social workers, lecturers, and teachers, and anyone involved in mental health and well-being services.

Christiane Sanderson 2018

1
INTRODUCTION

Every part of our lives, whether we're aware of it or not, is touched by **gender identity** and the cultural and contextual meanings made of it. However, perhaps because of the very pervasive nature of gendered experience, issues of **gender dysphoria** or even reflexivity around one's own **gender** identity are rarely covered in much depth in professional trainings. Instead, gender is either taken for granted or otherwise felt to be the preserve of 'experts' and that, outside specialist gender clinics, general practitioners in the mental health field cannot or should not attempt to work with this population.

This book is about recognising that anxiety and providing practitioners with the skills and insights necessary to work effectively. It does not seek to make the reader a 'specialist'. Instead, it is positioned as part of a drive towards **affirmative practice** in gender care, focusing on reflexivity and education. It gives an overview of the subject areas and process issues most likely to come up in counselling, and aims to balance the theoretical with the practical and to point to more detailed literature, should the reader want to explore a particular area in more depth.

As the series editor, Christiane Sanderson, suggested when first discussing the idea of writing a book for the Essential Skills for Counselling series: 'What would you have wanted to know about and be aware of on your first day working at Charing Cross GIC (Gender Identity Clinic)?' Inspired by that question, we have approached the text with the assumption that, although our readership will be qualified and experienced practitioners, they may have had relatively little experience in reflecting on and working with issues of gender identity and gender variance in their clinical work.

WHY THE BOOK AND WHY NOW?

Discussions around **transgender and gender non-conforming (TGNC)** identities have become more frequent and salient in many Western societies in recent years, as reflected in the media, legislation, and social debates affecting people across the life span, in part because of several, high-profile celebrities coming out. Although often controversial, these celebrities have pushed questions of gender and gender identity into the forefront of mainstream media.

In addition, the gay rights movement has been largely successful in the West in promoting an agenda of equality. In the UK, for example, we have gone from the world of Section 28 (part of the Local Government Act that prohibited teachers to speak of homosexuality in the classroom as a 'pretended family relationship' from 1988 until its full repeal in 2003; see Nixon and Givens, 2007), to full marriage equality with the Marriage (Same Sex Couples) Act 2013, a mere ten years later. Alongside the success in sexual politics, **trans** and other civil rights activists have been actively campaigning for gender equality. Although there has been some success at a legislative level, one only has to explore the heated debate around bathroom access in the USA over the last couple of years to see that trans people's experiences in public spaces remain controversial and the fight for recognition and equality continues.

As the understanding of gender variance has evolved over time from a psychiatric disorder to a phenomenon of normal variance, a debate, currently live in the UK's National Health Service, over the future of gender services has arisen. As the question has shifted from disorder to dysphoria, there are questions around the roles of medical doctors, psychiatrists, psychologists, and the broader psychotherapeutic community in gender care. This debate exists in the context of a drive towards informed consent models inevitably limited by professional responsibilities and accountability.

Greater attention given to issues of gender, both in the public and professional spheres, means that gender identity is now more widely and more often part of public discourse. From a Foucauldian perspective, the production of differing gender discourses is part of the process by which the person accesses 'those forms of understanding that the subject creates about himself' (Foucault, 2000a, p.177). Literally, differing forms of gender identity are spoken into being as the discourse widens and language is created to reflect the rich diversity of gendered experience.

Nevertheless, despite the context of the current sociopolitical discourse around gender, the American Psychological Association Task

Force on Gender Identity and Gender Variance survey in 2009 found that 'less than 30% of psychologist and graduate student participants reported familiarity with issues that TGNC people experience' (2015, p.832). We therefore believe that it is more urgent and important than ever that practitioners 'knowledge up' and become fluent in the field in order to work more effectively and compassionately with issues of gender identity and diversity wherever they encounter them.

WESTERN CULTURAL FRAMEWORK AND UNDERSTANDINGS

This book, and much of the research and clinical practice that supports it, is situated in a modern, Western understanding of gender, and the authors are mindful that it will not necessarily speak to readers from cultures where gender is understood and performed differently. Our Western cultural framework is suffused with the binary complementarity of female and male that underpins **heteronormativity** as well as the feminist and postmodern critiques of binary that trouble it.

Heteronormativity describes the belief that people fall into distinct and complementary genders (male and female) with natural roles in life. It assumes that heterosexuality is the only sexual orientation or only norm, and states that sexual and marital relations are most (or only) fitting between people of opposite sexes. Yet, despite winning greater freedoms and civil rights in many Western countries over the last 50 years, sexual and gender minority people still need to explain and justify themselves to the **cisgender**, heterosexual majority through a process of 'coming out' and 'acceptance' (explored in greater depth in Chapter 12).

This reciprocal relationship between gender, sex, and desire creates what Butler (2006, p.23) terms 'intelligible persons'. She argues that the **gender binary** is tightly bound to the notion of heterosexuality, where 'normality' is demonstrated by desire for a complementary opposite. Drawing on the work of Wittig (1980), Butler questions the link between the discursive production of biological sex as the natural basis for heterosexual desire, suggesting that, in fact, binary gender and sex and compulsory heterosexuality are mutually productive. To accept the 'truth' of the binary nature of gender is also to accept the 'truth' of the naturalness of heterosexuality. She suggests that we are so embedded in these discursive structures that to deny them can seem nonsensical.

This book aims to focus on and unpack many of our taken-for-granted assumptions about gender and its relationship to sex and sexuality, and to encourage greater flexibility and reflexivity in our thinking and practice as mental health professionals. Nevertheless, this is the cultural framework in which both ourselves and our clients are situated, and we recognise the difficulty of maintaining this questioning and critical stance as we struggle to navigate between the binary polarities to which we are always being drawn and directed.

EPISTEMOLOGICAL UNDERPINNINGS IN AFFIRMATIVE PRACTICE

There is considerable literature (a lot of it US-based) exploring the negative impact on the mental and physical health of trans people when they cannot access affirmative care (Frederik-Goldsen *et al.*, 2014; Garofalo *et al.*, 2006; Grossman and D'Augelli, 2006) and when access to care is denied on the grounds of gender identity (Xavier *et al.*, 2012). Moreover, the literature supports the positive influence of an accepting and affirmative social and family environment on outcomes and the psychosocial well-being of trans youth (Ryan *et al.*, 2010; Travers *et al.*, 2012).

Both of the authors of this book are Chartered Counselling Psychologists and, as such, we see our work as 'a field embedded within a post-modern philosophy' (Rizq, 2006, p.614), which 'attempts to bridge the gap between research and practice and conceptualises human activity and meaning relationally' (Manafi, 2010, p.21). We are engaged in an endeavour to arrive at a 'holistic conceptualisation of human beings' (Manafi, 2010, p.22), not simply as an academic pursuit, part of a project in the human sciences that attempts to arrive at a definition of the human being, but because the field is an inherently practical one. We explore human subjectivity and relatedness because, in our roles as counselling psychologists, we work with people who come to us seeking help with their problems in living.

Our work in the field of gender care, and our approach to writing this book, are both informed by a model of affirmative practice. There is an extensive literature that describes and explores the models and benefits of affirmative practice (see Austin and Craig, 2015; Chang and Singh, 2016; dickey and Singh, 2016; Edwards-Leeper, Leibowitz, and Sang-ganjanavanich, 2016; Singh and dickey, 2016), but, at its base, affirmative practice is about practitioner reflexivity.

Singh and dickey suggest that affirmative practice is about developing 'empathy for how gender-role training and socialization affects all people – transgender and cisgender people alike' (2016, p.196). They see affirmative practice as being based on two pillars: reflexivity and education.

1. *Reflexivity*: Developing an awareness for how we are all situated within a gendered world and how we all have an experience of gender identity and gender diversity – that the problems in living are 'in here' in relationship and not 'out there' in the bounded person of the client.

As Chang and Singh (2016) suggest, 'cisgender psychologists...can work to bring awareness to their cisgender privilege or the unquestioned ways in which they have been able to move through society without experiencing anti-TGNC prejudice or discrimination' (p.141). In doing so, they are invited to 'bring a spirit of curiosity and openness' (p.141), an openness to the exploration of identity without the need to be fixed or to fix identity within normative frameworks.

2. *Education*: An ethical duty to inform ourselves about the field where our clients are experiencing distress and not leaving it to the client to educate their counsellor or therapist.

Part of that process of informing ourselves about the field in question is to look to the variety of relevant professional practice guidelines that exist and that are discussed below.

World Professional Association for Transgender Health (WPATH) Standards of Care (SOC)

The World Professional Association for Transgender Health (WPATH) was formerly the Harry Benjamin International Gender Dysphoria Association (HBIGDA), a professional organisation devoted to the understanding and treatment of gender dysphoria and named after Harry Benjamin, one of the earliest practitioners in the field. WPATH first published the *Standards of Care for the Health of Transsexual, Transgender, and Gender Nonconforming People* in 1979 and Version 7 was published in 2011. The *Standards of Care* (SOC) are available to read free online in PDF format from WPATH's website and are based on a number of core principles that assert that affirmative practice is rooted in demonstrating respect for diversity (WPATH, 2011).

British Psychological Society (BPS) Guidelines (2012)

As counselling psychologists, one of whom was an author of these, we affirm the British Psychological Society (BPS) *Guidelines and Literature Review for Psychologists Working Therapeutically with Sexual and Gender*

Minority Clients (2012). As with the WPATH (SOC), the BPS Guidelines have been written 'to engender better understanding of clients who may have suffered social exclusion and stigmatization in order to reduce the possibility of this in the clinical arena' (BPS, 2012, p.3). Once again, the focus is on both practitioner reflexivity and education, including continuing professional development (CPD), in the field as part of an ethical and affirmative approach to practice. There are 17 guideline statements in total, and these can be found online at: www.bps.org.uk/sites/default/files/images/rep_92.pdf.

American Psychological Association Guidelines (2015)

In December 2015, the American Psychological Association published its *Guidelines for Psychological Practice with Transgender and Gender Nonconforming People.* The purpose of the guidelines 'is to assist psychologists in the provision of culturally competent, developmentally appropriate, and trans-affirmative psychological practice with TGNC people' (p.832). The document distinguishes between 'standards', which it argues are 'mandates to which all psychologists must adhere', and 'guidelines', which it describes as 'aspirational' (p.833).

The American Psychological Association has issued 16 guidelines for working affirmatively, and these can be found online at www.apa.org/practice/guidelines/transgender.pdf. Although we recognise that these are American guidelines (and that both authors practise in the UK), and moreover that not all readers of this book will be psychologists, we, nevertheless, take them into consideration in our practice. In fact, with the exception of guidelines specifically focused on working with youth and children, this book explores all the issues raised in the WPATH (SOC), BPS, and American Psychological Association Guidelines.

In the *Psychology of Sexual Orientation and Gender Diversity* journal's special issue, 'Trans Affirming Psychological Practice', Singh and dickey (2016) reflect on the responsibilities that these guidelines give to practitioners. They advocate for a change in which gender variance is taught on professional training courses, arguing that, 'if trainees learn about TGNC people, it is likely that the topic will be covered in a psychopathology course', and suggesting that this unnecessarily categorises and pathologises TGNC people from the outset (Singh and dickey, 2016, p.197).

In the same way, this book aims to be part of an ongoing process of working against the stigmatisation that TGNC people have suffered for many years, particularly at the hands of the 'psy' disciplines. By unpacking the process of reflexivity and education, we hope to challenge the reader to reflect on their own process, assumptions, and experiences, while at the same time building a knowledge base from which to work in a more informed and empathetic way.

GENDER IDENTITY IS UNIVERSAL

Although this book is principally focused on trans and non-conforming gender identities, it is foregrounded with a section exploring the psychologies of femininities and masculinities and some of the process issues that arise. It is important for us that this book is not about 'preaching' from a normative perspective about how to work with people with gender identity issues 'out there' – as if gender identity is only something that 'other people' have. We all have a gender identity and we can all struggle with it to a greater or lesser degree at times.

There is a rich literature on the psychology of masculinities and femininities and our chapters present an overviw of this. It is important to foreground **non-binary** gender and trans, in particular, within the context of other, more mainstream, forms of gender identity. We do so in order to highlight that all gender is performative and that, while **cis** forms of gender have traditionally been seen as homogenous, a brief exploration of the literature will show that masculinities and femininities are every bit as heterogeneous as their TGNC counterparts. To an extent, this is about an attempt not to 'other' trans and other non-binary forms of gender identity. We wish to place all forms of gender identity and expression within the same context and to argue that managing issues of gender within the therapeutic relationship is a given – no matter what the gender identity is of those in the dyad (or group).

Often, as with sexuality, a heteronormative, cisgender lens tends to locate challenges and skills in the 'other', suggesting that gender is never really that much of an issue in all-cis dyads. We take a different view and argue that gender is pervasive and that, even when gender is not the 'problem', it is present and affecting process, transference, countertransference, and our ability to be fully present and empathic with our clients. We believe that being aware of this and choosing to work within that awareness, whether or not gender is a presenting problem, helps to deepen and enrich the therapeutic relationship, offering space for greater insight and effective ways of working.

Finally, we are aware that many books in the broader field of 'working with difference' can have a tendency to position difference as a problem that exists 'out there' in a client population. In a chapter entitled 'Use of the Multicultural Self for Effective Practice', Judith Bula writes: 'It is only with an experience of empathy, of "walking in that person's shoes", that the transformation to multicultural acceptance can occur' (2000, p.177). At first glance, this text would seem perfectly acceptable – it encourages the reader to adopt a person-centred ethic of empathy and to attempt to enter the subjectivity of a minority identity in order to work more effectively. However, it contains some very subtle (hetero) normative framing. It assumes the majority status of the reader facing the problem of the 'other' out there. It could never, for example, have been written by a non-heterosexual writer to a non-heterosexual reader so as to help that person to work more effectively with the *heterosexual* 'other'. It is framed as if there is a taken-for-granted assumption that difference rests with clients and not with therapists. Bula (2000) is not alone in her heteronormative framing, as Burman comments in reviewing a recent text on difference and diversity in counselling:

> …interestingly, and not surprisingly perhaps – given the demographic profile of most counselling practitioners – the various differences and diversities addressed in this book are assumed to be attributes of clients rather than therapists. While understandable, this equation of difference with the client is, of course, not insignificant and would have merited comment with the text, especially as it renders the position of the black or working class or gay or elderly or disabled (or all or any combination of these!) therapist very marginal indeed. (2008, pp.125–126)

We have tried to be clear, and also to write, from the perspective that gender identity is neither 'in here' nor 'out there', but instead that it is a universal experience and that all of us are positioned in the field, whether we are explicitly aware of it or not. We assert (and we hope) that our readership will have a whole range of differing gender identities and experiences and that reflexivity about those identities and experiences will help to reinforce both the heterogeneity of our difference and the importance of compassion in working with our own and our clients' gendered selves.

LIMITATIONS

As we have said earlier, the purpose of this book is to act as an accessible guide for existing practitioners (as well as for professional trainees) in the mental health field in working with issues of gender identity – in particular, gender dysphoria. It is not an exhaustive treatise on the subject and, inevitably, certain aspects will not be covered.

Our focus, from a clinical perspective, is based on work with individuals rather than with couples or groups. Many of the process issues explored in the book will be relevant in a number of settings, but the majority of our clinical practice has been one-to-one and so this book reflects that.

Second, this book is about working with adults (18+) and we deliberately do not cover the specific questions and issues around working with children and young adults. In part, this is because the overwhelming majority of our clinical practice has been in working with adults, but we also recognise that working with children and young adults brings its own specific challenges. In our view, counselling skills for working with this population would warrant its own book in order both to explore the literature in the field and the specific treatment pathways and clinical process issues.

A WORD ON LANGUAGE

For many practitioners first starting to work with TGNC clients, using the correct and respectful language can be one of their main anxieties. There are a number of terms used to describe people 'who have a gender identity that is not fully aligned with their sex at birth' (American Psychological Association, 2015, p.834), and not all of these people subscribe to those terms. WPATH suggests that practitioners can attempt to be accurate but that it's more important to be respectful (2011). They recognise that terminology is culturally and time-dependent and is rapidly evolving and argue that it is important to use respectful language in different places and times, and among different people.

We recognise that all language comes discursively preloaded with meaning and power and that the literature on the relationships between language, power, and identity is extensive. Our understanding throughout this book on discourse as productive of subjectivity has its roots in the philosophy of Michel Foucault, who suggested that discourses 'systematically form the objects of which they speak' (1972, p.49). We're not suggesting that it's possible here to take some kind of objectively neutral stance as we are always positioned within the field we're looking at. As Deutscher points out, objectivity is impossible since 'we never step out of language to touch the thing itself' (2005, p.35).

Earlier in this chapter, we touched on affirmative practice and its twin constituents of reflexivity and education. Through reflexivity, we become aware of the impact that the use of language has on the relationship and the work. We have had to make a similar choice here. Although we offer a glossary of terms that include various identity labels at the end of this book, we have decided, partly to do with ease of readability in the text and partly to do with our own epistemological stance in relation to language, to focus on the use of two terms interchangeably when referring to people with a gender identity that does not conform with the one that they were assigned at birth:

1. *Trans*: Over time, this has become an umbrella term to include people who in some way do not conform to the gender they were assigned at birth and who define as transgender or transsexual.

2. *TGNC*: An acronym for Transgender and Gender Non-Conforming people was developed in the United States by psychologists working in this field and is intended 'to be as broadly inclusive as possible' (American Psychological Association, 2015, p.832), while recognising that it is not a term that will suit everyone.

At the time of writing, the use of language within the context of LGBTQ politics continues to be a sensitive issue. In May 2017, the media reported on how a 'well-meaning' campaign to address the problem of LGBT bullying in Australian schools came unstuck because the petition urged 'tolerance' rather than 'acceptance' (BBC News, 2017). The finely nuanced meaning between the two is explored in more detail in this book in Chapter 12, but it is clear that, often well meant, language can cause offence. The seventh guideline from the BPS (2012) encourages us 'to use the preferred language of sexual and gender minority individuals'. That means exploring and checking out as part of the process of establishing a working relationship and therapeutic contract. We must be prepared to work honestly through missteps and mistakes in our language with trans clients and to openly explore the meanings that those mistakes have for them.

OUTLINING THE STRUCTURE OF THE BOOK

In contrast with some of the current psychological literature, our book has a significant focus on the management of the counselling process and guiding practitioner reflexivity around all the interpersonal and intrapsychic issues arising around working with gender identity.

The book is structured into three parts: Part I deals with unpacking gender and gender identities more generally, including looking at masculinities, femininities, and non-binary gender identities; Part II deals with gender dysphoria and other clinical phenomena relating to gender variance and gender identity; and Part III considers the importance of practitioner self-care, particularly with respect to supervision. The chapters have been constructed with the aim of balancing theory, practice, and reflexivity. Each chapter will introduce the literature around a particular aspect of gender and consider what implications this has for clinical practice, and 'break-outs' in the text will invite the reader to pause for reflection around particular topics introduced. Where possible and helpful, anonymised clinical vignettes from the authors' own experience will be used to personalise the content and provide real-world context to the issues raised.

Part I: Gender Identities

In the first part of the book, we explore the concept and notion of gender. What is it and how is it understood by us and our clients? We also explore the different forms of gender identities, from binary notions of masculinities and femininities to non-binary forms of gender identity. What are they? How are they constructed and understood? Throughout Part I, we will be balancing theory and practice. Initially, each chapter will set out research in the area and key theoretical arguments so that the practitioner becomes familiar with the field. Later in each chapter, we will look at how these theoretical ideas come to life in the clinical setting and the different ways in which practitioners might work.

Part II: Working with Gender Dysphoria

The second part of the book focuses on what has been termed in the psychiatric nosology as gender dysphoria (GD). We are aware of the problems in language that the history of the psy disciplines has had in pathologising gender diversity – indeed, we explore these issues and arguments in some depth throughout the book. Nevertheless, using GD as shorthand, Part II looks at the distress that arises for people whose gender identity is not fully aligned with their sex assigned at birth. We explore care pathways, treatment options, legal questions, the role of practitioner advocacy, and key themes in **transition**. As before, each chapter looks to balance research and information provision with reflexivity and exploration of how these themes may affect the therapeutic relationship.

Part III: Practitioner Self-Care

The book ends with a reflection on the importance of self-care. It summarises the main themes from the book and explores the use of the gendered self in therapy. It also looks at the importance of supervision and finding peer groups and supervisors experienced in the field and able to support affirmative ways of working.

Part I

GENDER IDENTITIES

2

WHAT IS GENDER?

In many ways, we are setting ourselves an impossible task in answering the question: 'What is gender?' There are many different positions taken in the literature and, crucially, there is a great variety of human experience in relation to gender that you will encounter in your practice with all clients. However, in this chapter, we will attempt to unpack some of the key theories and debates around gender as a foreground to exploring the psychology of masculinities, femininities, non-binary gender, and trans identities. As we do so, we will use a single case vignette throughout the chapter in order to illustrate some of the main themes and therapeutic implications of differing understandings of gender identities. We look at how gender is performed as well as a core identity: 'There is no gender identity behind the expressions of gender… [I]dentity is performatively constituted by the very expressions that are said to be its results' (Butler, 2006, p.33).

A NOTE ON LANGUAGE

Any book on gender diversity, gender variance, and non-conforming gender identities will inevitably have to keep defining the terms in usage and even redefining them in different places, since the more we think we know something, the less we tend to reflect on what we actually mean by it! Although there will always be disagreement around terminology (and one thing learned from experience in working in gender care is that we are always going to get the terms wrong according to someone), the questions, more importantly, are: 'To what degree is there disagreement?' and 'What are the consequences of using that term as opposed to another?'

Although *sex* and *gender* are often used colloquially to say much the same thing, it is important to differentiate more precisely in academic and professional contexts, where the difference can be key to what is being discussed. It is especially important when working with gender diversity to have some kind of common understanding of what we are referring to, since the aim, ultimately, is clarity in our communication. For our purposes in discussing what gender is, it can be thought of as more of a social entity, the cultural allocations to being male, non-binary, or female; of having a masculine, **androgynous**, or feminine gender identity, and so on (Richards and Barker, 2013). Gender is, in itself, arguably an abstract construct (despite often being treated as an absolute), culturally specific, and expressed in individual ways, with reciprocal validation from the social setting and others. It differs from sex in that sex is equated with the biological, the 'absolute', our innate biological characteristics. If gender is perceived to be social, whereas sex is biological, then how inherent, really, is the latter? This will be explored throughout the book.

Gender identity moves further towards our internal sense of personal gender, our gendered being, our sense of who we are genderwise, and the diversity is far wider than often imagined. It can include gender identities that are male, female, non-binary, androgynous, **agender**, transmasculine, **transfeminine**, and more. Therapists need to be always open to how their client defines their gender identity, by not assuming but always asking and, if necessary, unpacking and clarifying. Many people take their gender identity for granted, without even reflecting on it. But those whose gender identity is incongruent with their natally **assigned gender** and sex don't have that privilege. The world around them can be telling them one thing from an early age and their sense of self and experience of who they are can be telling them another. It can feel like their body is alien, a vehicle that lets them down by signifying that they are something that they are not. This is a feeling that can be somewhat shared by cisgender people, who may also feel misconstrued by social assumptions and reactions to the body that they present with, but in a different way. Not to the extent that the body feels like it is wrong in itself, but that fluidity in gender can become apparent in the discomfort that everyone can feel at those times in their lives when they realise that it restricts who and what they feel themselves to be.

 Remember

Someone's appearance and body may not reflect the gender that they feel themselves to be. Reflect on times when you felt consciously that you were being socially filtered through the lens of gender and felt discomfort that you were being seen in a way that wasn't who you felt yourself to be. Now, imagine that feeling as your normal experience on a daily basis and also how it could be to never feel that way.

A POSTMODERN FEMINIST CRITIQUE OF GENDER

Judith Butler revolutionised the philosophy of gender with her book *Gender Trouble*, first published in 1990. In it, she draws on the work of Jacques Lacan, Foucault, Luce Irigaray, Monique Wittig, Julia Kristeva, and others so as to advance an argument for the relationships between sex, sexuality, gender, and the body, and poses the question: 'What best way to trouble the gender categories that support gender hierarchy and compulsory heterosexuality?' (Butler, 2006, p.xxx).

One of the most well-known aspects of her thesis is the idea that gender is not a noun but is instead a speech act, a performance that takes place within a regulatory frame that has an appeal to normativity by virtue of its own self-legitimisation through an historical/genealogical narrative: 'In this sense gender is always a doing, though not a doing by a subject who might be said to pre-exist the deed' (Butler, 2006, p.34). It is these aspects of power and genealogy that she seeks to deconstruct by 'troubling' or questioning our taken-for-granted assumptions as to the 'truths' of gender, sex, sexuality, and the body: 'in particular, I opposed those regimes of truth that stipulated that certain kinds of gendered expressions were found to be false or derivative, and others, true and original' (Butler, 2006, p.viii).

Butler takes on the idea of binaries in gender discourses – opposing constructs such as male versus female, masculine versus feminine, and biological/natural versus socially constructed through culture. She argues that language itself is not somehow pre-discursively outside gender but is instead situated within it. Irigaray (1981) goes further in arguing that language itself is not only gendered but, particularly in the case of the modernist language of science and rationality, clearly masculine.

Moreover, gender is itself not outside other cultural intersections such as 'class, race, ethnicity, and other axes of power relations that both constitute "identity" and make the singular notion of identity a misnomer' (Butler, 2006, p.6), a point explored in more detail in Chapter 16. This critique, therefore, calls into question the whole notion of essential gender – in other words, the idea of man or of woman or masculine and feminine existing separately from the social, cultural and political discursive fields that they inhabit.

CHALLENGING A PRE-DISCURSIVE ACCOUNT OF GENDER

Like Foucault (1998), Butler questions the basis of our understanding of gender by first troubling notions of power and knowledge. She suggests that juridical power creates the subjects that it seeks to regulate and represent, whilst at the same time concealing that productive act in order to legitimise its own right to rule. As such, juridical power produces the idea of a pre-discursive subject who exists independently of the power structures that have, in fact, spoken it into being.

Butler challenges the notion of 'a non-historical "before"…[with] persons who freely consent to be governed and, thereby, constitute the legitimacy of the social contract' (2006, p.4). In doing so, she calls into question the notion that discourses of sex and gender have recourse to a 'prior-to-culture' truth, a natural basis that is 'God-given' and that cannot be questioned.

SEX AND GENDER

In exploring gender, Butler uncovers discourses that have sought to split the 'natural', biological 'fact' of sex from gender, which is understood as socially constructed through culture. She questions whether 'the ostensibly natural facts of sex [are not also] discursively produced by various scientific discourses in the service of other political and social interests' (Butler, 2006, p.9):

> …there is no recourse to a body that has not already been interpreted by cultural meanings; hence, sex could not qualify as a prediscursive anatomical facticity. Indeed, sex, by definition, will be shown to have been gender all along. (Butler, 2006, pp.10–11)

Anne Fausto-Sterling cites sexologists in the 1950s as being responsible for the split between gender (mind) and sex (body), reinvented by feminists in the 1970s. She also questions discrete concepts of genders and sexes versus a more continuous classification system. She argues that feedback constantly changes the brain and the body, and, along similar lines to Butler's pre-discursive argument, suggests that 'we have to stop thinking of the body as something prior…that is unchanging and that becomes the base on which some sort of cultural framework is built… [N]ot only do [bodies] generate behaviors, but they in turn are generated by behaviors' (1999, p.56).

As identified earlier, this position is not to suggest that gender is not 'real' for those who live it. Instead, it asserts that this subjective reality is constantly being negotiated and constructed in relationship. It is a position that recognises Foucault's contribution to our understanding of subjectivity as constructed in power relations as well as one that privileges the intersubjective as the space where gender identity, and all other subjectivities, are constantly being negotiated.

But, if there is no recourse to a pre-discursive truth about gender, sex, and desire, then how is it possible for the human subject to escape the discourses to which they are subject? Butler is hopeful here that troubling, questioning, and refusing to take for granted apparently settled 'truths' offers a solution. Taking a Derridian deconstructive approach to what appears essential – sex, gender, and desire – 'holds out the possibility of a disruption of their univocal posturing' (Butler, 2006, p.44).

GENDER TRANSGRESSION

It is not a trivial thing, however, to challenge gender, to transgress social assignations from birth. Historically, gender has conventionally been seen as synonymous with chromosomal and genital sex, and how you are defined can determine your legal status and rights as well as how your sexuality and its sexual and romantic expression is viewed (Biggs and Chagaboyana, 2015). The appearance of genitalia at birth leads to the natally assigned sex and the social gender identity, and the individual gender identity is automatically assumed to be the same. Individuals, by default, are expected to comply with the ascribed social gender role, and to resist this in a way that makes it clear that gender identity is *not* what has been socially assumed means coming out as *not* being cisgender.

The organised assumption that natally assigned sex leads to social gender identity and thence to assigned social gender role also includes the implicit assumption of heterosexuality. The choice faced by the person is then continued identification of heterosexuality or the requirement to come out as *not* being heterosexual. To be cisgender and heterosexual means not having to come out, since one is already assumed to be who one is. Even if one's identity is questioned in some way because of a non-conforming gender, the identities themselves are held by default. The complex issues surrounding the requirement to come out are explored in more detail in Chapter 12.

Expressions of sexuality and potential relationships are defined from early adolescence in accordance with assigned gender and biological sex. Sexual orientation is generally categorised according to discrete notions of gender – both yours and those of the people whom you are attracted to – but not everyone can easily fit into these categories and identities. People can identify as lesbian, gay, bisexual, pansexual, **asexual**, queer, and many more, some of which facilitate moving away from being defined from gender as a reference point, but never fully escape it.

It has increasingly been argued that modern binary models of sex, gender, and sexuality are, indeed, contemporary contexualisations of complex constructs (Lenihan, Kainth, and Dundas, 2015), and sex, gender, and sexuality are both biologically influenced and socially constructed (Dozier, 2005; Money, 2016). Individuals may also have sexual identities that are not easily socially identifiable from the outside. A natally assigned male who is male bodied and who is attracted to women may self-identify as lesbian, if they have a female gender identity. This may not be immediately apparent, especially if they are not open about being trans or if they are not in a relationship. Their spouse, if female, may identify as a heterosexual woman, so the relationship between the couple, especially if the other party goes through social and physical **gender reassignment** changes, may need to be redefined by them.

Whether we stay in the gender assigned to us at birth or not, what is apparent is that it requires a commitment to action and assertiveness to verge away from the prescribed path laid out for us. Clients can present at any age with gender issues, which they may have suppressed and have tried to distract themselves from for months, years, or decades, and it is in the counselling room that they may be looking towards developing a more authentic way of being.

 ## Remember

Don't assume someone's sexual orientation and sexual identity from their social gender role, the relationship they are in, or how they are embodied.

Case vignette: Jason

Jason presented at age 48 to counselling with anxiety and depression. He had been married to a woman for 18 years and had a son aged 11 and a daughter aged 13. His GP referred him to counselling as he had been treating him for depression for the last five years with anti-depressants but he seemed to be getting worse rather than better.

The therapist explored with Jason what might be the underlying causes and factors maintaining the depression. Everything appeared to be going well in his life, according to him, except he was unhappy in it. On further exploration over the course of the initial three sessions, it transpired that he had always felt himself to be female. Occasionally, he put on female clothing when the family were out, but he had never shared this with anyone. Jason had conformed to the gender role ascribed to him at birth, had joined the army, and had taken up bodybuilding when he left it. This seems to have been more 'a flight into hypermasculinity', to try and suppress the gender dysphoric feelings and to signify to the world that he was really a man, than a specific choice or preference. He was known as a 'man's man' by friends and family but that just wasn't who he really felt himself to be.

It felt very difficult, though, to disabuse others of how they saw him, but as he had moved into his forties, the dysphoria that he felt around his gender had increased and became less easy to suppress. This had become even more the case, now that he was watching his own children growing up and his daughter moving into puberty. He was torn between being the father that he thought he should be for his children, a 'good' male role model, and who he knew himself to be behind his performance of masculinity.

 Reflection

- How might your own ideas around gender get in the way of really hearing Jason's experience and empathising?

- What might his fears be here?

- Why might his age and his children developing into adolescence have brought these issues to the fore now?

It is often when we seek to move outside the restrictions of gender, when we start feeling restricted by the bonds of gender conformity, that we truly begin to experience how gendered the social environment around us is and the part that social conditioning plays in the communication of gender cues and the normative performance of gender. We start coming up against the wall of those solid, innate biological differences that are at the heart of so much of the heated debates around gender and gender identity. How men and women differ is a question that keeps being asked and researched, whether in spatial abilities (Reilly and Neumann, 2013), or in pain sensitivity and relief (Greenspan and Traub, 2013), and in many other areas, too. Whatever the answers, the asking of the question continually reinforces the existence of differences and, so, where you fit in the discourse matters.

HOW CAN GENDER BE PERCEIVED, ANYWAY?

The general default for perceiving gender in others has been to start with an appraisal of how the individual is embodied. But to assume that this is the only, or even primary, means of doing so is debatable. Social gender cues other than primary and secondary sex characteristic are a key means by which others are cued into social gender and gender roles. Gender is performed in different ways, according to the social contexts through which we move, but the performance usually communicates the social gender identity that is assumed to reflect the personal gender identity. Social gender cues might also include subtle or explicit differences in style of clothing, hair, make-up, bags, shoes, and so on. For example, jeans can be male or female, but those made specifically for women, like shirts, can differ in the tailoring. Individuals are socialised into presenting as the gender they were ascribed from birth from a very early age, so they may not even be aware of their social gender cues. They often just take them for granted, unless there is reason to do so otherwise, assuming that their body is the primary means of communication around gender, rather than simply the way in which they are presenting it.

 Exercise

Think about what you are wearing today or during this week (not how you are embodied) and what choices specifically could have cued others into your gender, such as choices of jewellery, watch, type of socks, shoes, hairstyle, etc.:

- What changes could make your presentation more masculine, feminine, or androgynous?

When meeting clients for the first time, it pays for a therapist to be attentive to the details as to how people are presenting themselves. Not considering just whether they are 'well groomed', 'presenting appropriately for the occasion', or having 'good personal care' or not, but looking more closely at the choices that they are making which might be linked to gender expression. At the same time, assumptions should not be made about the meanings of choices in self-presentation. Instead, use your observations to help you to create a closer connection with who your clients really feel themselves to be. Removing the filters and scripts around gender, based on assigned biological sex and phenotype, can help in connecting to the client in a more authentic way and may help to challenge your own gender-related assumptions through openness to looking at what is in front of you.

Is that person being who they want and feel themselves to be? Is what they are saying possibly conflicting with the social presentation and gender cues? How can you, as a therapist, make the therapeutic space one in which performance of gender can be free to be discussed and expressed differently, in which the client is not being seen through a constricted view of their presenting gender?

As explored in the exercise, above, it is also important to be aware of how your own gender presentation and social gender cues might be impacting on the therapy. Once we conceptualise gender as different to sex and, to a large extent, socially constructed in its performance, we can reflect more deeply on how gender is performed. Social conditioning starts at a young age, and it can be helpful for both ourselves and our clients to look back to when that training in social gender cues was first instilled, those first gendered items of clothing and social expectations and pressure as to what is 'appropriate' to wear.

 Exercise

Reflect on where your ideas around gender first came from:

- Who has most influenced your ideas around how you present yourself socially and your performance of gender?

- What early influences do you still agree with, and what ideas have you now moved away from or discarded?

CULTURAL REINFORCEMENT

The media constantly reinforces what constitutes a desirable depiction of masculinity and femininity, what it means to be a man or a woman, through narratives of all types. So, we aren't usually deliberately choosing the social gender cues in our presentation by the time we apparently make our own choices. We may select clothing according to our preferences or beliefs and to increase our social desirability and validation, but generally not so much to actually cue people into our gender, since that is assumed to be socially visible (unless, of course, the natally assigned gender and associated gender role and performance doesn't actually reflect who we are). Butler (2006) discusses how anatomical sex, gender identity, and gender performance are highlighted as distinct entities through drag; challenging the notion of women being parodied through this performance, she points out that drag, in itself, deconstructs the heteronormative interrelationship between them. Gender is something that we *do* rather than what we *are*; it is socially regulated, and social constructions of it are rooted in the framework of heterosexuality and heteronormativity that constantly police and 'other' any performances that challenge the 'norm'.

Case vignette: Jason *(continued)*

Jason had always presented to the therapist in what she initially assumed to be an unequivocal male presentation. In fact, she didn't even think about it being otherwise. When she looked at him more closely, she realised that the jeans he was wearing buttoned to the left, his shirt buttoned to the right, his eyebrows were slightly shaped, and his nails manicured and shaped in a way more usual in a woman's manicure. The overall presentation was male, but the clothing was predominantly specifically female and, now, when she considered it, the hair had a slightly feminine style to it. Like most people in his life, she had initially seen a large, well-built man in jeans, a shirt, and trainers, with extensive upper-body muscle mass, and assumed him to be a cisgender man without even thinking about whether he was cisgender or not, but if she had been more attentive, she might have seen that there were aspects of his presentation that were deliberately selected to be more feminine.

 Reflection

Remember that biologically assigned sex, gender identity, and social gender role are different things and be careful not to make assumptions. The therapeutic space may be the only place in a person's life where the assumed links between them can initially be challenged and explored.

How we think about gender, of course, started well before we were born, within the cultural and religious narratives of the societies that we are born into, from the medical and legal dominant discourses creating the social contexts within which we move and converse. From these narratives we learn that men and women aren't inherently assumed to be the same, and so we have had to successfully argue that they *are* equal and should both be able to vote, that special measures don't have to be taken to make women 'acceptable' beings because of their different biology to men. We learn through having to debate gender-related rights and differences that there is, indeed, something substantive to debate. The debate itself, and the attendant need to research gender differences, arguably plays a significant role in socially reinforcing the point that these differences are real and that they exist.

Mainstream religions tend to link gender with sexuality in a way that places different expectations and rules on how men and women can behave, with a binary-cisgender model usually being central. Those who don't fit in are typically then either accommodated in some way or marginalised and rejected, but rarely is gender irrelevant in the debate. As Clucas (2015) reminds us, the religious positions on homosexuality need to be put into the historical context of how sexual relations between the same sexes have been reconceptualised over time and, with these changes, increased prohibitions have been based on gender.

 Exercise

Think of five common mainstream debates around gender differences and the assumptions made behind them:

– What beliefs are the debates themselves reinforcing?

– What would it be like to live in a society where the debates didn't occur, where they just wouldn't be thought about, because the binary gender discourse within which they occur didn't exist?

Case vignette: Jason *(continued)*

In exploring Jason's sexuality and gender with him, it became apparent to the therapist and Jason that he found it difficult to imagine himself as being anything else in society other than an assumed cisgender heterosexual man. He didn't currently want to be referred to using a female pronoun or title or to make any significant changes in his life, seeing himself as a father and husband, with roles to play that he felt he couldn't fulfil being anything socially genderwise other than that which he already was.

He found it hard to reconstrue his parental role in a way that didn't gender him as male but simply as a parent. In private, and now in therapy, he could express what he called 'his feminine side' more explicitly but he became very anxious at the thought of anyone else in his life knowing. Jason felt that he really just needed the space to explore and understand who he was. He had no immediate intentions to undergo gender reassignment, and his internalised **transphobia** and homophobia, in any case, made this unthinkable for him at that time. He had been brought up in a conservative Christian family and he found it difficult to separate out his gender from his sexuality. He experienced considerable shame that he felt most sexually aroused when wearing explicitly feminine clothing and, when the family was out, masturbated in such clothing.

The therapist respected where Jason was in his journey and endeavoured to walk alongside him rather than tell him what he 'should' be doing. Neither of them knew what the outcome of therapy would be in terms of any significant life changes. But the overall therapeutic goal was to work towards reducing his gender dysphoria and to increase his sense of authenticity, rather than forcing adherence to an ideal that seemed currently unattainable.

NON-BINARY IDENTITIES

Much of what we have looked at so far has illustrated how core the notion of a gender binary has been to all discussions of gender. Going outside the binary challenges the very discussions themselves. How can we debate gender differences outside a gender dichotomy? What meaning can we place on people's sexuality and sexual choices if not linked to gender? How can we construe a world not filtered through there being two genders? Yet, nevertheless, we have a growing number of people identifying as non-binary and **genderqueer**, people who don't identify as male or female, or their gender identity and performance can vary, or who identify as both male and female, people who challenge the existence of the gender binary itself (Richards *et al.*, 2016).

Challenging an assigned masculine or feminine social gender role can be difficult and, as discussed so far, brings to the foreground issues around gender, sexuality, and what it means to be a man or a woman. This is even more the case when individuals step outside the gender binary altogether, challenging the whole concept of there being two genders. Not only are they then moving away from what has been assumed about them, which inevitably requires discussion with others, but they are also moving into identifying as a gender that these others may not even understand and might question its very existence. The absolute certainty with which biological sex is generally assigned on the basis of genitalia, in the absence of conflicting information indicating the possibility of being **intersex**, continues into the assignment of the corresponding social gender role and gender identity. It can therefore be very difficult to get outside the binary discourse to one where sex and gender are male/female, masculine/feminine to one where these constructs become more fluid and open, to the extent that they may even disappear. It may be that, at some time in the future, a child's parents will be asked whether they know the gender of the child yet, but that's not now, and it's a difficult idea for many people even to imagine. Imagining a time when the question isn't asked at all, since it is no longer socially relevant to do so, may be even harder to imagine!

 Exercise

To help explore your own experiences of gender and gender identity, reflect and write notes on the following:

- Is it easier for cisgender people to express and communicate gender identity or have they not reflected on it to the same extent as those who are **gender variant**?

- How would you describe your gender identity to others?

- What are your experiences of gender and being gendered?

- Have you ever felt restricted by your social gender role?

- What would be your ideal social gender role and presentation?

We have seen that gender is not a fixed construct and that natally assigned gender cannot automatically be assumed to be congruent with an individual's gender identity and preferred social gender role. Moreover, increasing scientific evidence of a biological influence on gender identity in itself challenges the simplistic sex–gender identity association that is generally assumed. The sheer diversity of how gender can be performed and the difference between what constitutes gender and natally assigned sex based on identification of genitalia at birth precludes making any assumptions in a therapeutic context if we are to facilitate clients in moving towards authenticity in gender and sexual expression.

3

EXPLORING THE PSYCHOLOGY OF MASCULINITIES

The mass of men lead lives of quiet desperation.

Walden, or, Life in the Woods, Henry David Thoreau (1908)

The study of the psychology of masculinities offers a rich and diverse literature. This chapter attempts to summarise and present some of the main themes to give the reader an introduction to the field. Not only is there not enough space here to go into any great depth, but also the focus of this book is to explore how psychological and therapeutic research and scholarship in gender applies in the field. As such, this chapter and the one that follows introduce themes around the psychology of masculinities and some common content and process issues that present in therapy. Along with the section on the psychology of femininities and non-binary gender identities, it acts to foreground Part II in the book, which explores trans and non-binary in more detail.

As the title of this chapter suggests, contemporary gender theory argues that there is no such thing as a singular masculinity. Instead, a plurality of masculinities is understood to exist that varies enormously both within and between different cultures and times (Kimmel and Messner, 2007). As such, all the models that we explore in this chapter should be seen as 'scaffolding', a way of looking at the world that can help practice while we are trying to make sense of what is happening in the human encounter in the counselling room. As both authors espouse a somewhat anti-essentialist view of the world (including gender and its constructs and models), we do not subscribe to the idea that what follows constitutes the 'truth' about gender or that it is in any way 'complete'. Instead, everything we do to explore and unpack is always an imperfect attempt to describe and capture a complex phenomenon.

UNPACKING GENDER

The focus of this brief exploration of some of the literature on the psychology of masculinities is heavily informed by feminism and postmodernism and attempts to trouble a determinist–realist account of gender. Given that most of what follows challenges accepted notions of gender, it is perhaps important to start with a realist caveat. Although a postmodern critique of gender does much to question our assumptions about gender identity, it is important to recognise that the vast majority of the population – including those who engage with post-structuralist debate – act in the world as if gender were essential. For most of us who work outside of specialist gender clinics, our clients will come to us and exist in the world as if their biological sex were synonymous with their gender. This is not intended to suggest that there is no such thing as gender. Instead, troubling the essential nature of gender identity is intended to cast a light on how embedded we are in our assumptions about ourselves and others and to encourage us as practitioners to question how these may be unconsciously affecting the relationships that we form with our clients every day.

DISCOURSES OF MASCULINITY

Hegemony and heteronormativity are two pervasive discourses that have influenced the way in which men understand and perform their gender. They have been powerful in defining normative gender identity for men in Western (and, in particular, English-speaking) culture over the last two centuries. Hegemonic masculinity is a theory of masculinity first put forward by Raewyn W. Connell in her seminal work *Masculinities* in 1995. The theory is underpinned by two philosophical concepts: Antonio Gramsci's theory of hegemony and Foucault's ideas around 'dividing practices' and the disciplinary forces discursively produced in power relations.

Gramsci, the Marxist philosopher, developed his theories about power and its operation while in prison in Italy in the 1920s. He was interested in why people seem to conform to norms in the absence of an overt compulsion to do so, and he created a framework to explain it based on what he termed 'hegemonic society' (1971). Drawing on Greek notions of the 'hegemon' – leadership by an individual or a group – he argued the leading group or class uses its power in society to discursively create embedded value systems and norms so that their view becomes *the* worldview. Everyone who is stratified in the group comes to accept their place as naturally and morally right – usually with recourse to the God-given right of those in power to rule. The right to power is something that is consented to by those who are ruled, and those in authority do not need to resort to oppression or violence. Because we have a belief that the structure of society is 'natural', it then seems simple 'common sense' that the status quo does not need to (indeed, should not) be questioned. It is this consent to be ruled that makes hegemonic cultures or societies distinct from authoritarian ones.

Foucault developed the concept of 'dividing practices' in his work on understanding the relationship between the 'subject' and 'power'. He argued that power in cultures and societies works to objectivise individual subjects such that 'the subject is either divided inside himself or divided from others. This process objectivizes him. Examples are the mad and the sane, the sick and the healthy, the criminals and the "good boys"' (2000b, p.326). Foucault suggested that there was a kind of 'disciplinary gaze' in society and drew on the idea of Jeremy Bentham's 'Panopticon' as a utopian form of discipline. In the panopticon, one always has the sense that one is being watched over and one's behaviour and work is being scrutinised by an observer. It's what he termed 'a constant supervision of individuals by someone who exercise[s] a power over them – schoolteacher, foreman, physician, psychiatrist, prison warden – and who, so long as he exercise[s] power, ha[s] the possibility of both supervising and constituting a knowledge concerning those he supervise[s]' (Foucault, 2000c, p.59). For Foucault, there did not actually need to be a *real* person supervising the subject – the supervisory role is played by norms, by culturally accepted ideas, 'in terms of what was normal or not, correct or not, in terms of what one must do or not do' (Foucault, 2000c, p.59). Once these norms are internalised and accepted as 'natural' and 'right', the disciplinary gaze is turned inward and the subject begins to observe him or herself and carry out that disciplinary and punishing work without the need for external action.

These two philosophical theories came together in Connell's thesis for what she termed 'hegemonic masculinity' (1995). Thus, there is a normative way of being masculine and all men are organised and organise themselves in relation to that ideal, accepting their place in the hegemonic structure. What follows is the belief that keeping to these norms will help a man to meet 'societal expectations for what constitutes masculinity in…public or private life' (Mahalik, Locke *et al.*, 2003, p.3). Tharinger defines it as 'an idealised form of masculinity by which boys and men can be measured by themselves and by others, to determine the extent of their "manliness" [and is] signified…by the extent to which they can demonstrate power over women and other men' (2008, p.224).

At the top of the pyramid is the idealised man whom all others aspire to be and in reference to whom they accept their position in the group. Erving Goffman famously described this idealised man in an American context as:

> A young, married, white, urban, Northern heterosexual, Protestant, father, of college education, fully employed, of good complexion, weight and height, and a recent record in sports. Every American male tends to look out upon the world from this perspective… Any male who fails to qualify in any one of these ways is likely to view himself…as unworthy, incomplete, and inferior. (1963b, p.128)

Connell (1995) suggested that there were three forms of masculinity created by the hegemonic process that divide and discipline all men: complicit, subordinated, and marginalised masculinities.

Complicit masculinities describes a group of men who, although not exemplifying Goffman's idealised perfection, nonetheless gain advantage from male privilege through what she calls the 'patriarchal dividend':

> A great many men who draw the patriarchal dividend also respect their wives and mothers, are never violent towards women, do their accustomed share of the housework, bring home the family wage, and can easily convince themselves that feminists must be bra-burning extremists. (Connell, 1995, p.80)

Because the man at the top of the hegemonic pyramid is so idealised as to be more or less impossible, she argues that the majority of men are in the complicit group.

Subordinated masculinities describes a group of men who are excluded. Gay masculinity was, for Connell, the most conspicuous form of subordinated masculinity, with gay men subordinated to straight men by a variety of cultural practices, including 'political and cultural exclusion, cultural abuse…, legal violence…, street violence…, economic discrimination and personal boycotts' (Connell, 1995, p.78).

Marginalised masculinities describes a group of men who are marginalised and excluded from all the benefits of male privilege because of race or class. For example, although working-class men may embody a kind of toughness and stoicism that is prized, they do not benefit as greatly from that privilege as those in the middle and upper classes do. For Coston and Kimmel, 'working-class men are the male equivalent of the "dumb blonde" – endowed with physical virtues but problematized by intellectual shortcomings' (2012, p.107).

 Exercise

Paule Zajdermann made a film with and about Judith Butler for ARTE France in 2006.[1] In it she talks about a young man in Maine who had recently been targeted and harassed by other men and boys in the town for having a perceived feminine way of walking – what she describes as a 'swish'. In the end, the boy was violently attacked and thrown from a bridge and killed. In the film, Butler asks why it is that the way a young man walks could be so offensive and disturbing to his peers that they would want to attack and kill him – simply to eradicate his walk.

– On reading about this story from Butler (or hearing about it in more detail in the film clip), what comes up for you?

– How do you relate it to your own experiences of having your gender performance 'policed' by your peers when you were growing up?

– Do you feel that it is still policed even now?

– To what extent is the policing of gender performance an issue for your clients?

NORMATIVE MASCULINITIES

Building on Connell's work, Mahalik and his colleagues were the first to attempt to ground research on masculine gender norms in the broader social psychological literature. The Conformity to Masculine Norms Inventory (CMNI) developed by Mahalik, Locke *et al.* (2003) suggests that there are 12 norms: winning, emotional control, risk-taking, violence, dominance, playboy, self-reliance, primacy of work, power over women, disdain for homosexuals, physical toughness, and pursuit of status. Cohn and Zeichner (2006) took these norms and simplified and grouped them to argue that hegemonic masculinity is comprised of four principal dimensions: competitiveness and dominance, emotional non-expressiveness, gender role stress, and homophobic and misogynistic attitudes.

---

1   Available on YouTube at: www.youtube.com/watch?v=ALx1MEW2P3U – accessed 06 December 2017.

Encoded within these norms is an implication that 'real men' avoid self-care and avoid seeking help, a phenomenon that has been extensively explored in the literature (Andrews, Issakidis, and Carter, 2001; Courtenay, 2001; Shepherd and Rickard, 2011; Vogel *et al.*, 2011). As Bunton and Crawshaw suggest, 'a key element of hegemonic masculinities is a direct rejection of bodily maintenance and self-care in order to assert masculinity. To "be" or act like a man is to show lack of concern for care of the self' (2002, p.192).

DISCOURSES OF HETERONORMATIVITY

As we have seen in our earlier exploration of Butler's thesis, gender does not exist in isolation from sex and desire. Orthodox masculine gender performance in Western culture is therefore also strongly influenced by the discourse of heteronormativity. This is 'an ideology which presumes the normality and superiority of heterosexuality and which requires any other form of sexual expression to be explained, justified or defended against' (Beattie and Evans, 2011, p.10).

Already encoded into the hegemonic masculinity discourse through 'disdain for homosexuals' (Mahalik, Locke *et al.*, 2003, p.6), hetero-normativity is a discourse that produces an 'unspoken identity…from which deviation is abnormal' (Weber, 2008, p.44). Corbett suggests that 'the only "honourable" male sexual behaviour consists in being active, in dominating, in penetrating and in thereby exercising one's authority' (1993, p.352). This is a discourse that regulates all men, whether gay or straight, and is arguably the source of anti-effeminacy discourse in gay male culture (Taywaditep, 2001). Therefore, 'from the perspective of gender, homoerotic desire is transgressive. Desire between men is haunted by hegemonic masculinity and the gender relations that govern it. Male same-sex desire is fraught with this dilemma: how do I desire another man without diminishing my sense of myself as male?' (Frommer, 2002, p.681).

Some authors, such as Kimmel, have even gone so far as to suggest that masculinity *is* homophobia. He argues that masculinity is a homosocial enactment for the benefit of other men: 'manhood is demonstrated for other men's approval…and its overriding emotion is fear' (2007, p.78). Because of this fear of one another and the constant danger that a member of the male tribe will shame us and cast us out, masculine gender performance is riven with homophobia:

Homophobia is the fear that other men will unmask us, emasculate us, reveal to us and the world that we do not measure up, that we are not real men. We are afraid to let other men see that fear. Fear makes us ashamed, because the recognition of fear in ourselves is proof to ourselves that we are not as manly as we pretend…our fear is the fear of humiliation. We are ashamed to be afraid. (Kimmel, 2007, p.79)

In his book *Guyland*, Kimmel goes on to suggest that homophobia is fear of other men – 'that other men will perceive you as a failure, as a fraud… that others will see you as weak, unmanly, frightened' (2008, p.50).

Hegemonic and heteronormative masculinity discourses are interrelated, and it is not a simple matter to keep an exploration of the literature on gender and sexuality separate from one another since both concepts require one another's existence because both of their reference points and discourses are permeable. Heteronormativity is part of the discourse of masculinity just as a binary notion of gender is at the heart of a discourse that privileges the 'normality' of heterosexuality.

Particularly important in the context of therapy and counselling is the normative assumption that emotionality itself is binary-gendered along heteronormative lines. As Moon asserts, 'heterosexuality, taken as the bedrock of social and sexual relations, is used to structure and organise the knowledge or understanding of an individual even at the level of emotion, and regardless of the sexuality of that person' (2008, p.40). In this architecture of feelings, not only are men expected to control emotions as part of the hegemonic masculinity discourses of self-reliance and physical toughness, but also, to the extent that feelings are expressed, they, too, should be gender normative.

The literature would suggest that 'women generally report more sadness, fear, shame and guilt, whereas men report experiencing and expressing more anger and other hostile emotions' (Fischer *et al.*, 2004, p.87). Indeed, as Cohn, Seibert, and Zeichner (2009) argue, men can often use anger as a form of emotional regulation, releasing it precisely because it is the only permissible emotion under the policing of hegemonic masculinity.

As we have seen, a core part of what Anderson (2012) has termed 'orthodox masculinity' has its bedrock in not doing, saying, or being anything that might be seen as feminine. As Brannon (1976) argued, the first rule of being a man is 'no sissy stuff'. Instead, these sexist and misogynistic constructs at the heart of orthodox masculine gender performance are understood as helping to shore up the theory of men's 'natural' dominance over effeminate men and women. Men who fail to live up to the standards set, as Connell (1995) argued, are excluded or marginalised to the extent of their transgression. The fear of the loss of power and male privilege lies in the rejection of masculinity's apparent binary and complementary opposite, femininity.

GENDER BINARIES' NEED FOR ONE ANOTHER

As Mahalik, Locke *et al.* (2003) and others have suggested, masculinity is often defined in opposition to femininity – to be authentically male, one must not be in any way feminine. This 'boy code' (Frosh *et al.*, 2002) informs the way young boys grow up, and to fail to live up to it is to be cast to the other end of the binary, in what Corbett calls 'girlyboyhood' (1999, p.108). Straight-acting gay boys who can 'pass', therefore, have access to orthodox masculine subject positions that are denied effeminate straight boys. The issue at hand, therefore, is not sexual orientation but, rather, apparent effeminacy in masculine gender performance, irrespective of sexuality.

Tharinger refers to this naming and shaming discourse as 'a kind of "gender police" to ensure that not too many boys challenge the existing gender order [and] that both heterosexual and homosexual boys who do not conform to the requirements of hegemonic masculinity always have the potential to be subordinated within the social organisation of masculinity' (2008, p.225).

Corbett suggests that the homosexual male is often constructed as equivalent to the heterosexual female, since both are seen as having a 'passive mode of sexual satisfaction', and that 'male homosexuals are thereby removed from the realm of masculinity and recast as counterfeit women' (1993, p.346). There is almost a 'cast out of heaven' quality as punishment for betraying the masculine gender, something that he suggests has its roots in early psychoanalytic literature. Freud, in describing Leonardo da Vinci's homosexuality, lays the blame at his mother's door: 'like all unsatisfied mothers, she took her little son in place of her husband, and by the too early maturing of his erotism robbed him of a part of his masculinity' (Freud, 2001, p.117).

This conflation of 'erotism' with 'masculinity' seals the normative construction of a teleological relationship between sex, desire, and gender. According to Freud, therefore, not only did his mother rob him of 'part of his *masculinity*', but she also left him 'to play the part of the *woman* in sexual relations' (Freud, 2001, p.86, our italics).

Interestingly, while the literature on masculinity would suggest that hegemonic masculine discourses need the feminine in order to define the masculine, the same would appear to be true in discourses of femininity, particularly those affected by contemporary feminist thought. Butler suggests that 'the universal person and the masculine gender are conflated' (2006, p.13), while Irigaray argues that the feminine is always created in contrast to the 'dominant phallic economy' (Irigaray, 1981, quoted in Loewenthal and Snell, 2003, p.131). Drawing on the work of Lacan, Butler suggests that language is 'phallogocentric' and exclusionary, aiming always to exclude the 'unconstrainable and undesignatable' (2006, p.13) feminine 'other'. She goes on to agree with Irigaray that the binary nature of gender where each constantly has recourse to the other is 'a masculinist ruse that excludes the feminine altogether' (Butler, 2006, p.36).

Exercise
The Male Privilege Checklist

Barry Deutsch was inspired by Peggy McIntosh's essay, 'White privilege: Unpacking the invisible knapsack' (1989) to create the Male Privilege Checklist. His edited introduction to the checklist reads as follows:

> McIntosh observes that whites in the U.S. are 'taught to see racism only in individual acts of meanness, not in invisible systems conferring dominance on my group'. To illustrate these invisible systems, McIntosh wrote a list of 26 invisible privileges whites benefit from. As McIntosh points out, men also tend to be unaware of their own privileges as men. In the spirit of McIntosh's essay, I thought I'd compile a list similar to McIntosh's, focusing on the invisible privileges benefitting men. Due to my own limitations, this list in unavoidably U.S. centric. I hope that writers from other cultures will create new lists, or modify this one, to reflect their own experiences.
>
> An internet acquaintance of mine once wrote 'The first big privilege which whites, males, people in upper economic classes, the able bodied, the straight (I think one or two of those will cover most of us) can work to alleviate is the privilege to be oblivious to privilege.' This checklist is, I hope, a step towards helping men to give up the 'first big privilege'.

What follows is an edited list from Deutsch's original 45:[2]

---

2   The full list can be downloaded at: www.cpt.org/files/US%20-%20Male%20 Privilege%20Checklist.pdf – accessed 06 December 2017.

1. My odds of being hired for a job, when competing against female applicants, are probably skewed in my favour. The more prestigious the job, the larger the odds are skewed.

2. I am far less likely to face sexual harassment at work than my female co-workers are.

3. If I choose not to have children, my masculinity will not be called into question.

4. If I have children and pursue a career, no one will think I'm selfish for not staying at home.

5. As a child, chances are I was encouraged to be more active and outgoing than my sisters.

6. If I have sex with a lot of people, it won't make me an object of contempt or derision.

7. If I'm not conventionally attractive, the disadvantages are relatively small and easy to ignore.

8. I can be loud with no fear of being called a shrew. I can be aggressive with no fear of being called a bitch.

9. I can ask for legal protection from violence that happens mostly to men without being seen as a selfish special interest, since that kind of violence is called 'crime' and is a general social concern. (Violence that happens mostly to women is usually called 'domestic violence' or 'acquaintance rape', and is seen as a special interest issue.)

10. I will never be expected to change my name upon marriage or questioned if I don't change my name.

11. The decision to hire me will never be based on assumptions about whether or not I might choose to have a family sometime soon.

12. If I have children with a wife or girlfriend, and it turns out that one of us needs to make career sacrifices to raise the kids, chances are we'll both assume the career sacrificed should be hers.

13. Complete strangers generally do not walk up to me on the street and tell me to 'smile'.

14. On average, I am not interrupted by women as often as women are interrupted by men.

15. I have the privilege of being unaware of my male privilege.

- What comes up for you in reading this checklist?

- Do the statements seem familiar to you?

- Have they been part of your 'script' when growing up?

- Are they part of your clients' scripts?

- What effect, if any, do you think that they have had on your sense of self and your identity?

- How do they come into play in the work between you and your clients?

WHERE IS ORTHODOXY PRODUCED?

Clearly, orthodoxy, by its nature, is the pervasive gender discourse in society and is likely to be reproduced in the media you consume, the advertisements you watch, and your day-to-day encounters in the world. Nevertheless, schools represent particular disciplinary institutions in which the heteronormative discourse is promulgated and a particular time at which children are taught and instructed by powerful adults about what is and what is not acceptable. It is a time at which rewards are produced and punishments threatened and during which attempts are made to condition a generation of children to uphold the discourse that has been handed down to them.

Moreover, adolescence is a time in one's life when the need to be normative is more urgently felt (Korobov, 2005). Adolescence is a crucial transitional period during which the child bridges the space between family and the outside world, making sense of who he is and how he fits into that wider world. The adolescent is subject to considerable peer pressure, has a deep need to belong, and is significantly more sensitive to public shaming and embarrassment. As Mills points out, 'it is clear that schools are a major social site within which masculinities and femininities are formed and contested' (2001, p.77).

Frosh, Phoenix, and Pattman (2002) explored the ways in which adolescent males take up subject positions in school environments, looking at the significant influences on boys to fit in and adopt the mainstream and dominant subject positions on what it means to be a man, or a boy. They considered how this 'boy code' is policed via an external panopticon-like gaze (Foucault, 2000c) and, indeed, how this gaze is internalised to create the young boy's own policeman, which he constantly uses to check the extent to which he's fitting in and living up to the 'boy code'. Moradi, van den Berg, and Epting (2009) explore the effects of this internalisation of prejudice and its relationship to a particular kind of stress and problems with identity formation.

Pollack (1998) argues that it is this 'boy code' that forces boys to 'man up' from an early age. The emotional flexibility and vulnerability of small boys soon changes as they enter school and all-male groups, ultimately leaving 'boys with a whole host of psychological disorders that follow them into adulthood' (p.46).

MASCULINE GENDER ROLE STRESS

It was Joseph H. Pleck's hugely influential text *The Myth of Masculinity* in 1981 that first described what he called the *gender strain paradigm*. The paradigm 'describes the strain men experience when they attempt to live up to what they perceive as the normative male role, which inevitably is an impossible and traumatic task' (Addis, Reigeluth, and Schwab, 2016, p.83). Along with Pleck, O'Neil (1981) was among the first to explore the idea that men are conflicted about following masculine norms when pursuit of these norms provides external validation at the cost of betrayal of internally experienced transgressive feelings and desires. So-called 'Masculine Gender Role Conflict' (O'Neil, 1981, 2008; O'Neil *et al.*, 1986) has been linked to depression, anxiety, health-risk, low self-esteem, and problems with intimacy (Betz and Fitzgerald, 1993).

The argument goes that if you use masculine capital to purchase privilege amongst other men, then it comes at a cost. Moreover, the problem with performance alone is that it doesn't get you everywhere. There are certain variables that are just down to chance – race, age, class, height, good looks, and so on. Which is one reason why sports have traditionally been seen to be such an important constituent of an authentic masculine gender performance (see Anderson, 2012). Athleticism acts as a bolster for masculinity and is one of the reasons why, traditionally, rugby players have been given greater cultural permission to engage in homoerotic play than, say, table-tennis players.

Not only is it acknowledged in the literature that it is stressful for men to 'keep up the act', but it is also understood that this performativity needs constant maintenance in homosocial relations. As Kimmel points out, 'masculinity must be proved, and no sooner is it proved than it is again questioned and must be proved again – constant, relentless, unachievable, and ultimately the quest for proof becomes so meaningless that it takes on the characteristics, as Weber said, of a sport' (1996, p.74). You have only to look at the masculinisation of a great deal of popular culture to see that this is true.

At the time of writing, BBC Two is featuring a series called *Bake Off: Crème de la Crème*. It is a baking competition featuring teams of professional pastry chefs who are pitted against one another through a series of patisserie-focused tasks. The chefs are given ever more ridiculous and impossible challenges and then roundly criticised by the judges for failing to complete a task that was more or less impossible to complete in the first place. This kind of hyper-competitive, relentless requirement to prove oneself over and over again seems, to these authors at least, just one way in which orthodox masculinity is constantly being reproduced through culture. Its reproduction is irrespective of the genders of the people involved – in this case, both the men and women in this competition are equally subject to it. For them, success is defined as participating in and triumphing despite a hyper-competitive and relentless game.

TROUBLING HEGEMONIC MASCULINITY

Although discourses of hegemonic masculinity and heteronormativity still circulate widely in Western culture, in particular in schools and male-dominated or all-male environments like the prison and the army, there is some evidence from recent research that this 'macho-man' stereotype is being eroded by other ways of performing masculine gender identities. As Evans points out, 'Men are not tied exclusively to one spectrum position. Most will express aspects of different positions depending on context, company and age' (2010, p.230). Moving away from an idea of fixity and essentialism allows us to understand gender performativity as something fluid and contingent.

Eric Anderson (2012), too, has suggested that dominant forms of masculinity are being challenged in contemporary Western culture. His research has looked at the attitudes of White, college-educated young men in the UK and America and has found that so-called 'orthodox masculinity' is on the retreat. He argues that orthodoxy is gradually being challenged and replaced by 'inclusive masculinities', which he describes as 'an archetype of masculinity that undermines the principles of orthodox (read hegemonic) masculine values, yet one that is also esteemed among male peers' (Anderson, 2012, p.93). Importantly, however, he points out that more inclusive ways of 'doing male' that are less homophobic or misogynist do not necessarily mean a reduction in **heterosexism**. He argues that heterosexism is a phenomenon independent of homophobia and that a decline in overt antagonism towards gay men need not necessarily mean that heterosexuality is no longer seen by straight men as the dominant and 'natural' orientation. It is simply that denigrating other forms of sexual orientation is no longer socially acceptable.

Anderson wonders why, when orthodox masculinities are so socially harmful, not least for those who succeed in performing them, they have been so persistent in Western culture. He examines the argument by Connell (1995) and others that orthodox masculinity is constantly reproduced 'as a way of symbolically justifying and retaining patriarchy' and male privilege (Anderson, 2012, p.76). He suggests that this is only partly true and instead argues that orthodox ways of doing masculinity wax and wane relative to the level of what he calls 'homohysteria' in society.

Anderson points to a range of qualitative and quantitative studies over the last 25 years or so that 'have shown a significant decrease in cultural and institutional homophobia within Anglo-American cultures' (2012, p.81). In the culture of a relative decline in homohysteria (at least amongst White, college-educated men), he suggests that 'multiple masculinities will proliferate without hierarchy or hegemony, and men are permitted an expansion of acceptable heteromasculine behaviours. In such a zeitgeist, the gendered behaviours of boys and men will be less differentiated from girls, and the symbolic meaning of soft physical tactility and emotional intimacy between men is consumed with a heteromasculine identity' (Anderson, 2012, p.97).

Although more inclusive ways of performing and understanding masculinities may be less prevalent than orthodoxy, their existence points to a certain amount of resistance against the dominant discourse and the opportunity for agency by men in taking up a range of different subject positions with respect to their own gender identity.

Mark McCormack (2012) researched homophobic discourse in a range of secondary schools in the south of England and found strong evidence that the ways in which young men are policing gender and sexual identities is changing. He suggests that it is no longer the case that gay boys are automatically shamed by straight ones and denied power in homosocial relationships.

On the contrary, he suggests that hegemonic stratifications of power, which previously relied on domination and exclusion, are increasingly being seen as outdated. He argues that boys in his research value charisma, authenticity, emotional support, and social fluidity (McCormack, 2012, pp.100–107). This is an astonishing volte-face in masculine gender performance away from the emotional control, dominance, and pursuit of status exemplified in Mahalik, Locke *et al.*'s (2003) 12 norms. Instead of valorising emotional control, boys in his research suggest that they value emotional support from their male friends and see it as important to form friendships with boys across different social groupings in the school.

If the phenomena that he sees in his research sites are beginning to be replicated elsewhere, then it is likely that the ways in which young men understand themselves and their relationships with other men – gay or straight – have the opportunity in the future to be less polarised, less binary, and more inclusive. And that can only be a good thing for all men.

INTERSECTIONALITY

Although the focus of this chapter has been a brief exploration of some of the main themes and arguments in the psychology of masculinities, we are aware of how all gendered subject positionings are both intersectional (e.g. Cole, 2009) as well as dynamic and fluid. In other words, subject positionings are influenced between domains – for example, subject positionings of class and race will influence subject positionings of gender and sexuality and vice versa – as well as constantly negotiated within relationship. For example, men are unlikely to adopt one single way of being male in childhood and simply reproduce that subjectivity in all places and at all times, henceforth. Instead, they are more likely to take a position with respect to dominant discourses and adjust their relationship to those discourses, depending on the context in which they find themselves. As Addis *et al.* point out, 'the construction of gender can rarely be separated from the social meanings of race, ethnicity, class, sexuality and disability' (2016, p.88).

Bilge (2009) explores the relevance of intersectionality in researching masculinities. She suggests that, although 'all members of society are located within the systems of social relations...from an intersectional perspective, individual accounts need to be analysed as located within simultaneous power relations...without separating different dimensions of social life into discrete or pure strands' (Bilge, 2009, p.3). Yet, as Bowleg (2008) acknowledges, this is a delicate balancing act since the researcher must make sense of these coincidentally experienced intersections, even when participants may not explicitly reference them. We would, once again, recommend practitioner reflexivity over intersectional identity categories when considering how gender impacts both on you and your client's life experiences and, indeed, on the therapeutic relationship in the room. In order to help in this exercise, intersectionality is explored in more depth in Chapter 16.

 Exercise

Imagine three British men. One is 68 years old, a retired teacher, Black, and gay, and living in Peckham in South London; another is a 19-year-old, White, heterosexual factory worker, living just outside Aberdeen; and the third one is a middle-aged, South Asian, Muslim accountant, who uses a wheelchair and lives in Nottingham:

– How might their ideas about masculinity differ from one another?

– What would it be like for them to meet?

– What ideas about masculinity might they have in common that transcend the class, race, age, sexual, or regional differences between them?

IMPLICATIONS FOR TRAINING

Clearly, the issues above have implications for the way in which counsellors, therapists, and psychologists are trained. Mahalik, Good, and Englar-Carlson (2003) consider some implications for training and practice when working with what they call 'masculinity' scripts. Drawing on Mahalik, Locke *et al.*'s CMNI work, Mahalik, Good, and Englar-Carlson (2003) explore a number of masculinity scripts that are likely to present in the room: Strong-and-Silent, Tough-Guy, Give-'em-Hell, Playboy, Homophobic, Winner, and Independent. These scripts and how to work with them are unpacked in more detail in the chapter that follows. However, working within a counselling psychology framework, they suggest that therapists should receive training to become familiar with the ways in which men are socialised and how these socialisations affect the ways in which men might feel about seeking help. They further argue that practitioners should be reflexive about their own gender identities and how they might impact their work with men.

As we can see, there are many theoretical explorations of the 'causes and becauses' of masculine gender performance. All men are subject to a particular form of disciplinary gaze as they struggle to maintain their place in the masculine hegemon, with attendant stress and poor physical and mental health outcomes for many men as a result. Yet, wherever there is orthodoxy, there exists the possibility for resistance and the production of different ways of performing masculinity. Being aware of some of these dynamics, of the dynamics of power and privilege that are present within them, will help you to be more sensitive to and work more empathically with your male clients.

4

WORKING WITH ISSUES IN MASCULINE GENDER IDENTITIES

In Chapter 3, we explored and unpacked some of the principal theoretical arguments that underpin our current understanding of the psychology of masculinities. The aim of that more theory-heavy chapter was to foreground this chapter, which considers some of the clinical issues surrounding masculine gender identities, often embedded in judgements about fitting into normative stereotypes of what it means to 'be a man' in contemporary Western culture. In doing so, we recognise that there are many intersectional dynamics to take into account and that there is no single way of understanding and performing masculinity. This will be contingent on an individual's experience of their gendered self in the context of other subjectivities such as age, class, race, ethnicity, sexuality, and (dis)ability, amongst others.

In focusing on process in this chapter, we are aware that there is also a significant literature on particular process content – such as men's anger and shame – as well as many books and journal articles that explore counselling skills for working with men (e.g. Englar-Carlson and Stevens, 2006; Rochlen and Rabinowitz, 2013; Wexler, 2009). Once again, we do not intend to present this chapter as a definitive guide to working with men's issues, but want to highlight the point that gender is pervasive in the therapeutic encounter, whether or not the particular presenting issue is gender diversity or dysphoria. As such, we do not cover every aspect of working with masculine gender identities, since this would inevitably require an entire book of its own.

This chapter is split into five sections, each dealing with a particular aspect of working with masculine gender identities:

- What is it with men and asking for directions?

- Restricted emotionality and shame

- Anger and aggression

- Working with masculine scripts

- Gender Aware Therapy.

We have seen that affirmative practice is about the twin roles of reflexivity and education, the importance of considering our own process and ensuring that we are aware of the field in which we're working. As such, each section both situates the phenomenon in the literature and goes on to present case vignettes, exercises, and techniques that may be helpful to the practitioner in day-to-day working.

WHAT IS IT WITH MEN AND ASKING FOR DIRECTIONS?

We have already seen in Chapter 3 that physical toughness is one of the norms in Mahalik, Locke *et al.*'s (2003) Conformity to Masculine Norms Inventory (CMNI). This idea that 'real boys don't cry' is a core part of gender socialisation and built into the 'boy code' (Frosh, Phoenix, and Pattman, 2002). Over time, this injunction to avoid the 'feminine' and instead to take risks, compete, threaten violence, and avoid care of the self becomes conflated with the delivery of an authentic masculine gender performance. Even if nowadays there is greater flexibility for boys and men to adopt different masculine gender performances (Anderson, 2012; McCormack, 2012), the subjectivity itself is arguably still defined in relation to traditional, orthodox, 'macho' masculinities.

Not only is it important to have a lack of concern for the care of the self, but it is also important to be *seen* not to care. Berger *et al.* argue that following Western masculine gender norms plays a large part in the fact that men so seldom ask for help with emotional problems. They suggest that 'men who adhere strongly to hegemonic masculine norms face a "double jeopardy" characterized by higher psychological distress and less willingness to seek help… [A]s a result, men may often suffer in silence' (2013, p.433).

Biddle *et al.* looked at the prevalence of help-seeking in younger adults in the UK and found that

> young adults experiencing minor mental disorder…had notably low rates of help seeking and were particularly unlikely to consult a GP. Even when they perceived themselves as having a mental health problem, most did not seek help… [M]en were significantly less likely to have sought some form of help…and appeared to have a higher threshold of

severity for help seeking than female cases, particularly for help from a GP. (2004, p.251)

The 'suffering in silence' script that comes with normative masculinity has also been linked to and used to explain higher rates of male suicidality. The Samaritans' *Suicide Statistics Report 2017* explored statistics for 2015 and found that 'male rates remain consistently higher than female suicide rates across the UK and Republic of Ireland – most notably 5 times higher in Republic of Ireland and around 3 times in the UK' (2017, p.6). In the USA, suicide was reported to be the tenth highest cause of death (Centers for Disease Control and Prevention, 2014), and the vast majority of those (78%) were men.

Granato, Smith, and Selwyn looked at US data and argued that conformity to masculine norms builds an 'acquired capability' for suicide:

> Individuals who are socialized to adhere to masculine gender norms are more likely to engage in impulsive, aggressive, and risky behaviors – painful and provocative life events – the consequence of which is acquired capability. Such a process is consistent with Addis' framing of masculine socialization from a social learning perspective. When men and boys' masculine behaviors are reinforced and feminine behaviors are punished, they are often done so in contexts that expose them to pain and provocation. For example, when a football player is hurt, but his suppression of physical and emotional pain and engaging in competition and aggression is reinforced, he is also exposed to and trained to tolerate further pain and provocation. The result of the accumulation of these experiences is habituation to fear and pain and an acquired capability for suicide. (2015, p.249)

Against the backdrop of the painful difficulty in seeking help of any kind and particularly with emotional problems in living and the higher risk of suicidality as a result, Mahalik, Good, and Englar-Carlson (2003) argue that clinicians need to be aware of how masculinity scripts may affect men's help-seeking. They suggest that, 'from a socialization perspective, many of the tasks associated with help seeking, such as relying on others, admitting that one needs help, or recognizing and labeling an emotional problem, are at odds with masculinity scripts' (2003, p.127).

They go on to suggest that, when we encounter men in our practice, we should first work to understand what their expectations of the process are. They might have any number of false, stereotypical ideas about what is involved, and helping to correct these at the outset may help to build an initial working alliance. They also suggest that normalising psychological distress, becoming aware of the ego-centrality of many of the issues at hand (e.g. unemployment or retirement for men whose identities are bound up with work), and exploring different and more flexible ways of being male can all be helpful.

Willingness to seek help was also found by Berger *et al.* (2013) to be linked to who it was in the first place that suggested they seek help – for example, whether it was a romantic partner, a doctor, or part of a court-mandated treatment. Research in the USA (e.g. Griffith, Ober-Allen, and Gunter, 2011) notes that spousal suggestion and support for mental health treatments, especially the talking therapies, can positively increase men's motivation.

 Exercise

Often, we begin our therapeutic encounter with exploring what it is that brings our client to see us. And why now?

This may be a particularly important question to ask when starting work with male clients. What is it that has brought them to us? Is it that some external factor has 'forced' them to be there? Do they come with resentments about why they're there? Are they doing it to please someone else?

Is pleasing someone else – a wife, husband, boyfriend, girlfriend, family member – just a mask? Does it allow them to continue to adhere to masculine norms in that it's not really ***them*** who are seeking help, they're just doing it to please X, Y, Z…

If that is the case, how might you work with your client from the outset to encourage him to own the therapeutic experience for himself?

RESTRICTED EMOTIONALITY AND SHAME

Emotional control is the very first norm in the CMNI (Mahalik, Locke *et al.*, 2003). Male mastery is part of that modern, positivist view of man as the master, through science and enlightenment, of all of nature, including even his own feelings. In his 1902 novel *The Art of Disappearing*, John Talbot Smith writes: 'At times his emotion seemed to slip from the rein, threatening to *unman* him' (Smith, 1902, p.361). This vividly conjures up not only the idea that feelings are like a wild horse, needing to be broken and tamed, but also that their free and unfettered expression is literally emasculating.

As with much of the content in this book, there is a rich psychological and sociological literature available that explores the historical context of emotional regulation more widely in society and specifically for men in the modern era. Moon explores the relationship between norms around emotional expression and 'modernity's quest for order and rationality over the chaotic and irrational body' (2008, p.41). Ian Hislop explored an Englishman's reputation for *sang froid* in a series of programmes for BBC Two in 2012 called *Ian Hislop's Stiff Upper Lip: An Emotional History of Britain*. He argued that a range of influencing factors – not least of which a horror of the apparently ungovernable emotion of the French in the revolution of 1789 – caused the English to be far more circumspect in their expression of emotions from the end of the eighteenth century, having far-reaching implications for Western culture more generally.

Moreover, American values in entertainment, produced by Hollywood, have dominated Western cultural values over the twentieth century and ensured the deep embeddedness of American myths and stereotypes such as those of the cowboy, the pioneer, and the superhero. Again and again, global audiences are presented with archetypes of masculinity informed by America's own history of conquest and the central importance of (White) man's mastery over (indigenous) nature and culture.

Although there is far greater freedom these days around emotional expression for men, arguments over what constitutes an acceptable level of emotionality in public remains controversial. The Hollywood actor Brad Pitt spoke publicly about his separation from his wife, Angelina Jolie, in an article for *GQ* magazine in May 2017. His frank admission of emotional vulnerability in the piece created a media sensation for some time after, famously occasioning an acerbic Tweet from the journalist Piers Morgan on 5 May in reply to Jonathan Heaf, the Features Director of *GQ* magazine:

> *I'm not convinced by this new trend of male public soul-bearing. Time for our gender to get a grip, methinks. Life's tough – man up.*

Clearly, this vignette simply captures the views of a couple of male celebrities and is not meant to act as some kind of exemplar for masculinity. Nevertheless, Morgan's invitation for 'our gender' to 'man up' is exemplary of the shaming discourse that is so much part of the process by which heteronormative, hegemonic masculinity is promoted. No matter where you sit in the pecking order as a man, you will inevitably have been subject to disciplining through shame. Indeed, some time ago, Hartley (1959) found that it was repeated humiliation by other boys for violating gender norms that ensured compliance and the persistence of the norms themselves.

Chapter 13 explores the phenomenology of shame – particularly in the context of trans identities – and there is also a book in this Essential Skills for Counselling series that specifically addresses shame in far greater detail than is possible here (Sanderson, 2015). But it is worth touching on the role of shame in restrictive emotionality and the problems that this causes for men in their lives both inside and outside the therapy room.

Shepard and Rabinowitz (2013, p.451) explore the operation of shame in men who are depressed and suggest the following definition in that context, which is worth citing in full:

> Shame is a complex psychological construct, consisting of cognitive (self-attacking thoughts), affective (emotional pain), and behavioral components (submissive facial and postural expressions, as well as social withdrawal actions)…[that have] the potential to pervade the self, 'embracing our worth, our adequacy and our very dignity as human beings…leaving us feeling naked, defeated, and intensely alone' (Kaufman, 1985, p.7). Blum (2008) examined the research on the felt phenomena of shame and derived a three-part description: (a) intense emotional pain, including the possibility of anger and rage against self and/or others; (b) a feeling of wanting to hide; and (c) a feeling that the self is bad, unworthy, and somehow deficient.

Men are in a triple bind here. They are shamed by one another into normative patterns of masculine behaviour, including the need to hide normal emotional expressivity. That shaming in turn creates the possibility of anger or rage, a desire to hide, and a sense of poor self-worth; none of which can be talked about or dealt with since another aspect of orthodox masculine gender performance involves a prohibition on help-seeking.

We are not suggesting that all men will rigidly follow these edicts for all time and in all circumstances. But traces of its effects will be felt by all men at some time or another. And that's what makes it important to consider here in how it manifests in our work with men.

A fear of possible unrestricted emotionality in therapy might also explain why some men 'prefer therapies that are more directive and focused on cognition rather than emotions' (Berger et al., 2013, p.434). Some authors have even suggested that constructing psychological help as 'coaching' rather than 'therapy' or 'counselling' could help some men overcome the shame and stigma associated with help-seeking and to reassure them about the level of emotionality and vulnerability required to take part. There is limited research in this area, but Gale *et al.* (2002) have suggested that gender imbalance is less pronounced in coaching, with men making up 52 per cent of reported clients. McKelley and Rochlen (2007) argue that offering coaching might be one way of further engaging counselling-resistant men in psychological interventions.

Case vignette: Simon

Simon is in his mid-40s. His parents divorced when he was 6 and he went to live with his mother. An only child, he was often overwhelmed by the needs of his depressed mother, whom he often took care of. Early on in the sessions, he says, 'I became an adult at 7,' and professes not to remember anything else about his childhood from before the age of 7 – it's just a blank. Moving to a strange town as a child, he was often bullied, isolated, and 'othered' at school and he found it hard to make friends and connect with others.

He has come to therapy because he is worried that he is having too much casual sex and it seems to his therapist that Simon uses sex to manage most of his feelings. Although he presents as charming, stylishly dressed, and smiles a great deal, his therapist has the sense that, underneath, Simon is frightened and confused.

Five sessions in, during a pause in their interaction, Simon looks out of the window and confesses to a fantasy of curling up and crying in the therapist's lap. A key theme of the work starts to centre around his desire to ask for things – both in therapy and in the world in general – but being terrified to do so. He appears very self-reliant and strong and often suggests to the therapist that he can 'take it' and that she can be as brutal as she wants to be in her feedback to him.

The therapy is limited to 12 sessions and Simon will need to miss the last session for a work commitment. This need to miss the last session is explored in session eight in the context of Simon's tendency not to allow himself to ask for what he needs. When he finally asks if he can have his final session the following week and his therapist agrees, Simon bursts into tears. As the session ends, Simon and his therapist explore what it feels like to be able to ask for what he wants and to get his needs met in relationship – rather than meeting them all himself.

 ## Reflection

Simon's case illustrates a number of key themes around shame, restricted emotionality, and the control of feelings through sex. There is a strong relationship between orthodox masculine gender performance and the rejection of needs. Often, this can lead to men finding it hard to have their needs met in relationship. Be aware in your work with men how this can lead your clients to want to meet their needs themselves and to reject help. Sometimes, asking your clients to express their needs from you in the therapeutic relationship can be a cathartic moment and an opportunity to work on needs, shame, and vulnerability in the here and now.

ANGER AND AGGRESSION

We have seen that the way in which men are socialised to feel that they *should* be able to handle everything that life throws at them can trigger feelings of inadequacy and shame in help-seeking and that this can, in turn, lead to feelings of anger and aggression in some men. We also know that therapy is a site of considerable power imbalance and that those who value the orthodox norms of autonomy and control may be highly attuned to this power differential. Their response to the power imbalance may therefore instinctively be 'fight or flight' – either aggressively battling for 'top dog' position with their therapist or withdrawal and refusal to engage. Moreover, researchers such as Fischer *et al.* (2004) and Cohn *et al.* (2009) have found that not only are men more likely to express anger and hostility in therapy than women, but they are also more likely to use it more frequently in order to regulate their emotional life.

Case vignette: Kevin

Kevin is a 36-year-old father of two young girls who has presented for therapy ostensibly because he is experiencing periods of intense sadness and low mood. He has the sense that he has missed out somehow in life; that the potential he dreamed of when he was younger has not been realised. In his initial intake assessment, he meets with the female supervisor of the service. However, the therapist he works with is a young gay man.

When they first meet, the therapist is struck by his physical size and immediately picks up on a very palpable sense of anger in the room. He wonders if it's because Kevin is finding it hard to show sadness and vulnerability with him and is instead showing him anger. This is particularly difficult for the therapist, as he has had a history of being bullied and marginalised by physically large, angry men.

The work gets off to a difficult start and the therapist feels like he and Kevin are constantly taking up positions against one another. Often he feels controlled and manipulated by Kevin, but doesn't feel that he should rise to this invitation to play 'top dog'. He also feels that Kevin is playing his cards close to his chest – keeping a lot of his emotional process hidden. He shares his feelings with Kevin, saying, 'Sometimes, it feels like we're playing poker with each other.' This only serves to make Kevin angrier, as he feels like he's being told that he's not taking therapy seriously – not working hard enough.

The therapy continues in a way that the therapist characterises as a form of a dance to his supervisor. At times he is active and gives Kevin something to think about, at others he retreats, with both of them alternating between closeness and getting frightened by that closeness and pulling back. The therapist acknowledges that both he and Kevin are getting frightened for different reasons, but that both are mirroring the other.

 Reflection

   – Do you think that there might be a gendered reason why the supervisor/assessor experienced Kevin as 'sad', while the therapist working with him experienced him as 'angry'?

   – How does the therapist's fear of anger work to help bring anger into the room?

   – Or, is it simply the fact that orthodox masculinity makes it hard for Kevin to be vulnerable with another man?

   – To what extent are attempts to work within the restrictive bounds of orthodox masculinity making it hard for Kevin and his therapist to work together in the early stages of therapy?

Strokoff, Halford, and Owen (2016) carried out a meta-analysis on 15 studies, exploring outcomes in therapy with men, and found that all modalities – from cognitive behavioural therapy (CBT) to psychodynamic, person-centred, and existential approaches – have benefits to offer and that it is not necessarily the modality or technique used that is predictive of positive outcomes. Citing McCullough *et al.* (2003), they looked at a variety of emotions and their functions as well as at the functions served for men by their inhibition. They suggested that expression of anger helped to affirm the self and maintain boundaries, but also guilt, shame, self-blame, and hatred/disgust were used in order to inhibit a range of emotions such as sadness, fear, closeness, and love.

Mahalik *et al.* (2012) looked at what practices were helpful in work with men and boys and, inter alia, suggested that many of their participants found being able to unpack the role of gender socialisation on emotional expression for men was very helpful. They suggested that therapists 'work with clients to help them understand the effects of social prohibitions against men showing emotions – other than anger – and needing to be strong and in control of their feelings' (Mahalik *et al.*, 2012, p.596).

Given the longstanding nature of socialisation, they emphasised the importance of taking things slowly and respecting the amount of time that it might take for a boy or man to increase their range of emotional expression. One participant in their research noted:

> I think anytime I've acknowledged a man's intense anger/rage, which has been scary for others, as a possible sign of depression/sadness, it has opened the path to acknowledging those more vulnerable feelings. It's generally been more helpful than assuming 'anger management' is the way to go. (Mahalik *et al.*, 2012, p.596)

The way in which men are socialised can also make it more acceptable for anger to be expressed physically as well as verbally (Courtenay, 2000). In their study of coping mechanisms in African American men, Thomas, Hammond, and Kohn-Wood (2015) suggest that aggression can be a way back into hegemonic masculinity after a perceived infraction. For example, a man may have feelings of anxiety and depression and perceive this as a lack of self-mastery. For many men, losing control can make them feel weak and 'less than'. They can have the fear that other men will notice this and that they'll be called out for it and, even if they hide it successfully, they can feel themselves slipping away from the male tribe. In that context, an act of violence or aggression expresses a core tenet of masculine gender norms and acts to restore them to the tribe. The problem for men is that this act of violence or aggression does nothing to actually deal with the anxiety/depression and probably just makes things worse.

 Exercise

On 12 June 2016, Omar Mateen, a 29-year-old security guard, killed 49 people and wounded 53 others inside the Pulse nightclub in Orlando, Florida. This violent and murderous attack was the deadliest mass shooting by a single shooter, the deadliest incident of violence against LGBT people in US history, and the deadliest terrorist attack in the United States since the September 11 attacks of 2001. *The Guardian* (2016a) reported the following day that 'Omar Mateen's former wife says the man responsible for America's deadliest ever mass shooting was physically abusive towards her, had mental health issues and was "obviously disturbed, deeply, and traumatised"'.

The following month, on the evening of 14 July 2016, a 19-tonne cargo truck was deliberately driven into crowds celebrating Bastille Day on the Promenade des Anglais in Nice, France, resulting in the deaths of 86 people and injuring 434. *The Guardian* (2016b) reported that the perpetrator, Mohamed Lahouaiej-Bouhlel, had been troubled and often violent. His father remembered him as being 'always alone, always depressed'. But he insisted that, as a teenager, had shown no jihadi tendencies, only self-destructive ones: 'He would become angry and he shouted,' Bouhlel said. 'He would break anything he saw in front of him.'

These two incidents obviously attracted a great deal of attention in the media at the time and there are clearly many other acts of male violence that go unreported but which, nevertheless, have devastating impacts on those who experience them. Consider the following:

– What learnings are there for us practitioners in working with men?

– How do we work effectively with anger?

– How can we encourage the men we work with, who might be at risk of acting out violently, to explore different and more flexible forms of masculine gender performance?

– What role do we play as mental health practitioners in advocating for mental health support for vulnerable men?

– How do we ensure that informed and sensitive discourses around men, mental health, and help-seeking are circulated?

We have seen that gender role socialisation makes it hard for men to seek help, that doing so can trigger feelings of weakness and shame that might result in withdrawal and aggression. One way of conceptualising the unique bind that gender role socialisation causes for men is through the lens of affect regulation/dysregulation as explored by Schore (2003a, 2003b) and Gerhardt (2004), among others. These authors and others in their field consider maladaptive adult behaviours through the lenses of developmental neuroscience, attachment theory, and infant psychiatry. They argue that early relational trauma – of which overly harsh gender role socialisation could be one – can be a contributory factor in the development of antisocial ways of being as an adult. They suggest that failures to help children and young adults to manage affect are at the root of much of the disordered behaviours that present in later life for psychological support. A socialisation that charges boys and men to suppress normal affect and to refuse to ask for help is the perfect recipe for unhealthy sublimation and the development of maladaptive strategies for coping with the fallout.

WORKING WITH MASCULINE SCRIPTS

Of course, not all men will present in therapy with all of these challenges. Mahalik, Good, and Englar-Carlson (2003) consider a range of masculine scripts that different clients might adhere to and consider an approach to working with them. We explore them here as a model that you might find helpful to consider when working with male clients. They identify seven different scripts, all in some way related to their development of the CMNI (Mahalik, Locke *et al.*, 2003):

Strong-and-Silent Script – This script is all about stoicism, control of feelings, leading to what Levant (1998) termed 'alexithymia' – literally 'without words for emotions'.

Tough-Guy Script – Like the Strong-and-Silent man, Tough-Guy is about restricted emotionality. However, more than Strong-and-Silent, it's important in Tough-Guy's self-image for him to be aggressive, fearless, and invulnerable.

Give-'em-Hell Script – For men who follow this script, being aggressive, fearless, and invulnerable is not enough. They must also prove it through violence. These men are likely to either have committed acts of violence, including domestic violence, or at least to strongly express attitudes supportive of others that do.

Playboy Script – Gender role socialisation often prizes the lack of emotional connection and vulnerability in sexual relationships. Men who present with this script often boast of their multiple sexual exploits while complaining of how difficult it is to 'meet the right person'.

Homophobic Script – Research suggests that men who see the world in very binary ways are likely to employ 'more immature psychological defenses, such as projection and turning against the object, and report greater paranoia, psychoticism, and feelings of personal inadequacy' (Mahalik, Good, Englar-Carlson, 2003, p.126).

Winner Script – Western culture's obsession with 'Type A' behaviour is typified by this script's competitive drive, impatience, perfectionism, and the need to control.

Independent Script – There is a whole literature on the importance of a secure attachment style and its role in helping to develop a strong sense of an interdependent self. Men with this script style are likely to be obsessively self-reliant and uncomfortable asking for or accepting help or care from others.

In approaching work with men who present with scripts such as these, Mahalik and his colleagues suggest following a four-stage process:

1. *Identify the script* – This may not be immediately obvious as the client may be following a number of different scripts at once and is unlikely to be fully aware of what their script patterns are. Once you have a sense of the script, you might like to try out sharing your impression with your client: 'It sounds to me like it's important for you to be a winner – does that resonate with you?'

2. *What are the upsides?* – Once the client is ready to hear and take on board their typical script decisions with respect to their gender role socialisation, you can work with them to explore how those scripts have helped them in the past: 'Being a tough guy must have helped you defend yourself in fights when you were growing up.'

3. *What are the downsides?* – Once you've had an opportunity to work out the upsides of your client's script decisions, you can move on to explore some of the costs they've experienced in following those scripts consistently over the years: 'It sounds like being a bit of a playboy has been fun and exciting and made you popular with the other guys, but has caused a lot of pain to your girlfriend who you love.'

4. *Flexibility* – By going through all these steps you now have a chance to explore how your client can be more flexible in his relationship with his script(s). Just because he's always done this in the past and in all circumstances doesn't mean he needs to continue to do so in the future. 'I wonder what it would be like to continue to compete at work, but to cut yourself a bit more slack with your friends and family?'

Of course, all of this is not to say that you will not meet men in your practice who are emotionally literate and able to engage with the therapeutic process pretty easily. Not all men will have these scripts and not all men automatically have maladaptive ways of coping with emotions. We recognise that this paper was written some time ago and in a US context and that, although it may provide a helpful schema and heuristic in your work with male clients, it is, of course, not a comprehensive and complete solution to all work with men.

 ## Exercise

Thus far, this chapter has focused on the experience of cisgender men and the ways in which gender socialisation is productive of norms that might create problems in living for some men. However, these norms will also have had an effect on your TGNC clients in a number of ways. Consider the following:

– How will the injunctions to compete, be independent, and in control affect your clients assigned male at birth and socialised as men when they start the transition process?

– Might they feel anxious about losing control to medical professionals, might they overemphasise the importance of having a 'perfect' transition?

– What will your clients assigned female at birth, transitioning to a male role, make of masculine gender role norms?

– Will they feel obliged to adopt many of those orthodox behaviours, or will they feel more open to take a more flexible approach to the way in which they express their masculinity?

GENDER AWARE THERAPY

A great deal of research has been undertaken on the centrality, function, and nature of the therapeutic relationship. As Safran and Muran have commented, 'after approximately a half century of psychotherapy research, one of the most consistent findings is that the quality of the therapeutic alliance is the most robust predictor of treatment success' (2003, p.1). Clarkson identified what she called 'an integrative psychotherapeutic framework containing five possible modalities of the client-psychotherapist relationship as being present in any effective psychotherapy': the Working Alliance, the Transferential Relationship, the Reparative Relationship, the Person-to-Person Relationship, and the Transpersonal Relationship (2003, p.1).

Much has also been written about the first of these – forming a working alliance – when working with men. Bedi and Richards (2011) and Richards and Bedi (2015) explore how vital it is in working with men that early alliance formation is effective. They cite therapist openness and clarity around the issues to be worked on as the most important of all variables. For men often sensitive to the need to be able to 'handle' themselves, they found that alliance formation was helped by preparing men to know what to expect and by setting clear boundaries around 'scheduling, time management, fees, treatment approach, mannerisms and behaviors of the clinician' (Richards and Bedi, 2015, p.179).

Robertson and Williams have taken this idea one step further and developed a framework that they have called Gender Aware Therapy (GAT), specifically designed to work with 'highly skilled men [who] may engage in disruptive or explosive behavior, cross sexual boundaries with clients or patients, abuse substances, or have other psychiatric problems that compromise their workplace performance' (2010, p.316). Built on the foundations of work by Good, Gilbert, and Scher (1990) as an extension of feminist therapy with men, GAT suggests that therapists should:

1. view gender as an essential aspect of psychotherapy

2. examine presenting problems in larger societal and systems contexts

3. address the negative consequences of gender bias

4. develop collaborative rather than directive therapeutic relationships

5. encourage clients to develop their own understandings of their histories, behaviours, and emotions.

The GAT Model uses a number of quite active and collaborative tools and is broken down into three parts as follows.

Part One: Self-understanding
Like Mahalik, Good, and Englar-Carlson's (2003) script model, the GAT approach starts with helping (mainly professional) men to discover and recognise their own patterns of behaviour. They suggest that creating specific tasks for clients like those explored below can help them to engage with the process:

Summary of Themes from Early Memories (STEM) – This is a public domain tool developed by the GAT authors to help clients recall and organise key memories that have helped to build their self-concept, relational patterns, and ways of coping.

Family genograms – Taking a Systems Theory approach, this technique involves gathering and organising information about the last three or four generations of the family, along with their attitudes, values, rules, and ways of coping with their feelings.

Bibliotherapy – Although the research on this appears to be mixed, the authors found that giving reading homework to high-performance men helped in their process of self-understanding and increased engagement with the therapeutic process.

Part Two: Self-regulation

The second part of the work is all about acquiring new, more adaptive skills such as 'emotional competency, disruptive behavior management, interpersonal skills, professional boundary awareness, and substance recovery skills' (Robertson and Williams, 2010, p.320). In keeping with the collaborative approach of GAT, it is suggested that the therapist engages the client in articulating his own goals.

Skills development work is also supplemented with group work, stress management (including mindfulness techniques), individual therapy, psychophysiologic training (exploring how emotions are felt and experienced in bodily sensations), self-help recovery groups, and Eye Movement Desensitisation and Reprocessing (EMDR) Therapy. This exhaustive battery of programmes and techniques ends with a final project, a lengthy written assignment that can take several weeks to complete. In it, the client reflects back on the process of GAT and creates a plan for implementing all the new skills and insights that he has learned in the future.

Part Three: Self-monitoring and aftercare

The final part of the programme looks to ensure that clients can sustain their progress. Typically, GAT is administered in an in-patient setting, and so it's important in the model that men ensure that they have plans and systems in place to avoid relapse once they re-engage with their day-to-day lives.

Case vignette: Kiran

Kiran is a straight, British-Asian man in his late 30s who has come to therapy in order to be able to feel more comfortable with his emotional life and to be able to be more spontaneous in his emotional and sex life with his partner. A significant schema for Kiran is that strong emotions are felt to be uncontrollable and dangerous – he has even referred to experiencing such emotions in the therapy room as 'like riding a wild beast'. A lot of his effort and energy goes into controlling such emotions in any way he can – usually by splitting them off and locating them in another person, predominantly his partner, where they can be more easily managed.

His desire to control the external world is manifest in therapy, too, where he invariably arrives each week with a well-thought-through agenda of what will be discussed. He is psychologically aware enough to know that this is what he is doing and he and his therapist wrestle with his ambivalence around control and letting go.

As they work together, his therapist encourages Kiran to allow himself to feel whatever arises in his consciousness for him and to be curious rather than controlling. When first suggested in the second session, Kiran appears open enough to the idea, only later admitting that, at the time, he thought it the most facile and ridiculous notion – just to allow his feelings to 'be'. However, he tries to let go of the need to control and is finding the experience to be both frightening and liberating.

This kind of radical acceptance of and curiosity about all emotions also suggests a radical acceptance of self as self is experienced. A well-known mindfulness practitioner, though by no means one on the counselling psychology end of the scale, who writes extensively about this kind of acceptance, is Oriah Mountain Dreamer. In her book *The Dance* (2001, p.43), she poses a question: 'What if the question is not why am I so infrequently the person I really want to be, but why do I so infrequently want to be the person I really am?'

 Reflection

Our male clients can come into the room with very clear and fixed ideas of 'what it means to be a man'. These ideas often transcend race, ethnicity, age, and sexuality. Although Kiran may see himself as a sensitive and gentle man – in no way buying into the 'macho' stereotype of normative masculinity – he still struggles with the need to control his emotional life.

Mindfulness and a kind of radical acceptance of 'what is' – informed in part by modalities of compassion-focused therapy (Gilbert, 2013) – has been helpful in Kiran's case. Using his case as an example, consider the following:

– In what ways could you encourage your male clients to let go of their need to control themselves, their emotional expression, and the therapeutic process itself?

THE STRUGGLE FOR COMPLETENESS AND PERFECTION

In a parallel process with many of the men whom you might encounter in therapy, we ourselves struggle with wanting to give you, the reader, a complete or 'perfect' account of the topic we're exploring and writing about. But there's only so much that could be written about here and we've had to leave out a great deal. We wanted to write about the Jungian notion of the mid-life crisis and its role in driving men to greater self-reflection and often ultimately to therapy (Hollis, 1993). We wanted, too, to explore men's complex relationships to their own bodies, to ageing and how it affects those bodies and men's sense of self; to explore sexual dysfunction and what meanings men make of it (McDermott and Schwartz, 2013); to write about the process of healing the narcissistic wound created by gender socialisation through Kohuttian ideas and processes (Johnson, 1987).

But, as with so much of life, we have had to be content to leave this chapter incomplete and to instead invite the reader to continue to read, explore, and engage in their quest to become ever more affirmative practitioners.

5

EXPLORING THE PSYCHOLOGY
OF FEMININITIES

The study of the psychology of femininities, like masculinities, gives us a greater understanding of the gender discourses within which we operate and through which we accept and dispute 'truths' and the means by which social functioning is controlled and policed. As we have seen, masculinities and femininities are sociocultural categories, gender identities, constructs, and behaviours culturally positioned as 'masculine' or 'feminine'. Individuals within different cultures are generally socially conditioned towards performing masculinity or femininity in accordance with their society's norms, or, failing that, towards adopting a social role where deviation is accepted or at least tolerated.

Performing gender outside of social norms and prescribed roles can attract considerable pressure to conform and there are often heavy social sanctions for continuing to position oneself outside them. As always, we should be wary of 'universalising gender theories' and always be ready to consider reviewing gender theory for ourselves as critical practitioners, of all therapeutic approaches. Our understanding and awareness of gender, like our therapeutic maps, which help us negotiate the therapeutic encounter, whilst remaining open-minded and present to the individual client, can be experienced as a changing evolving entity, with areas foregrounded as relevant and useful for the space being explored and the desired destination.

In this chapter, we briefly explore some of the main themes in the psychology of femininities, looking specifically at the hegemonic stratification of femininities and the pervasive role of heteronormativity and the binary in creating and policing feminine norms. Finally, we briefly look at the role of feminism, not only in the construction of what it means to be a woman in modern Western societies, but also in how it has shaped both psychology and its approaches to and understanding of gender and identity. In doing so, we once again assert, as with our chapters on masculinities, that there is no such thing as a singular femininity. Instead, a great number of different ways of performing femininity are understood to exist, contingent, as always, on culture, time, and social setting.

HEGEMONIC ORGANISATION OF FEMININITIES

Our earlier chapter exploring the psychology of masculinities unpacked the philosophical idea of the *hegemon* and its importance in organising and stratifying masculinities according to their relative power. Those with the ability to deliver a stereotypically normative performance have greater social standing and power over those that are less successful. We have also seen that one of the defining processes in hegemonic masculinity is the constant need for it to be performed and for one's position in the hegemon to be defended. Authors such as Vandello and Bosson (2013) have further suggested that this relentless defence is something unique to masculinity and that somehow femininity is more essential and less performative. Chrisler hits back against this and suggests that 'both manhood and womanhood are socially constructed, and thus people must perform their gender role as expected (or nearly so) to maintain their gender status' (2013, p.117).

Chrisler identifies the same hegemonic processes in femininities, suggesting that normative feminine performance is organised around two main themes – motherhood and beauty:

> There are two main ways that women perform gender to demonstrate their womanliness: both ways are difficult – not 'essential' – and they require both achievement and restraint. The first is the pursuit of beauty and demonstration of sexiness: the second is the 'good' mother. (Chrisler, 2013, p.118)

The 'motherhood mandate [is defined as] the belief that all women "should" become mothers and that "real" women "yearn" for the experience' (Chrisler, 2013, p.117). By appealing to nature and the so-called 'maternal instinct' – itself historically popularised by psychological research and discourse – normative femininity is, in part, defined by an ability to be 'of use' to men as child-bearers. Moreover, it is not enough simply to *be* a mother – one must also be a *good* mother. Chrisler and Johnston-Robledo uncover the ways in which media 'portrayals of happy, calm, and confident mothers' perpetuate this stereotype and to discipline so-called *bad* mothers (2000, p.118). As Chrisler goes on to point out:

> Any mother who is annoyed, angry, impatient, loud, frustrated, bored, turned inward, or otherwise unapproachable is considered to be a 'bad' mother...to be labelled a 'bad' mother...is a clear loss of status, an indication that she is not a 'real' woman [punishable] by mocking... divorce, loss of child custody and social isolation. (2013, p.118)

By appealing to the archetype of the 'good' mother, women are socially policed into self-sacrifice, self-discipline, and self-silencing, while at the same time having these traits reinforced as essentially feminine and 'natural'.

Nowhere is feminine beauty more essentialised, idealised, and at the same time positioned as ephemeral and capricious than in modern Western popular culture. We are more and more aware of how impossible these ideals of beauty are to live up to, and yet, at the same time, the pursuit of an idealised form of beauty and sexiness is once again pursued through considerable 'work', self-sacrifice, self-discipline, and self-silencing:

> If womanliness is indeed essential and ascribed, it would not be necessary to exaggerate the womanly aspects of the body through diet, exercise, foundation garments, body sculpting, and cosmetic surgery. If women did not believe that they would 'lose' feminine status and be punished for it (e.g., be mocked and harassed as fat or ugly, lose their lovers, be denied job opportunities that require 'front office appeal') if they gave up these activities, why would they ever engage in 'body work' that feminist theorists have described as oppressive (Dworkin, 1974), misogynistic (Jeffreys, 2005), and as ways to control women and maintain the power hierarchy (Wolf, 1990)? (Chrisler, 2013, p.118)

HETERONORMATIVITY, COMPLEMENTARITY, AND THE PERVASIVE BINARY

Heteronormativity is as pervasive a discourse in femininity as it is in masculinity. What is considered appropriate gender performance is generally rooted in heteronormative discourses, so strongly so that only those who seek to critique it are even aware of it. It is in the very nature of mainstream discourses that they seem 'normal' and that anything outside them is clearly 'abnormal', 'untrue', or 'mad'. As we have seen, heteronormativity refers to the privileging of heterosexuality, the norming of it such that it is unquestionably assumed as the default, the norm (Berlant and Warner, 1998). It is structured, institutionalised, and contextualised in a way that its performance and practices are socially supported and promoted with a power of which those who benefit from it are not even aware.

Heterosexuality brings together gender and sexuality in a prescriptive, normative way that imbues everything that is experienced related to these areas, while at the same time defining what is normal, permitted, and accepted, and also what is seen as variant and unacceptable. At its heart, there is the theory of complementarity, a belief that there are two complementary sexes with 'natural' procreative and bonding drives, which, in turn, give rise to 'natural' gender identities and normative social roles and behaviours by which they can be identified. In this binary model, in which we are all positioned, femininity is the 'natural' opposite to masculinity and vice versa. To be feminine is to be 'not masculine', and to be masculine is to avoid 'the feminine'.

Glick, Wilkerson, and Cuffe (2015) looked at how men who hold stereotypical views of masculinity also hold complementary stereotypical views of femininity. Self-identified 'career men' and 'masculine men' demonstrated complementary favouritism towards the traditional feminine stereotypes 'stay-at-home mothers' (exemplars of motherhood) and 'feminine women' (typically, valuing passivity and physical beauty). Masculine and feminine social roles not only help to create and sustain the binary, but they can also legitimise a coordinated division of labour (Eagly, 1987; Eagly and Wood, 1999) – the so-called 'boys' jobs and girls' jobs' made famous by UK Prime Minister Theresa May, in her BBC television interview (*The Guardian*, 2017) with her husband in May 2017 – as well as providing each of the sexes the opportunity to bolster their gender performance. 'Masculine' men have passive 'damsels in distress' to rescue and 'feminine' women have men to seduce and appear appropriately attractive towards.

It is clear that cultural performances of gender are strongly influenced by the normative expectations of sexualities and transgressions of these. Therefore, the way in which an individual performs femininity will often give rise to others' speculation around their sexuality and sexual orientation and lead to defensive behaviour on behalf of the individual designed to change the way in which their identity is being construed. For example, the historical equation of passivity of women with femininity can mean that those who challenge this with a more active way of being can be described as 'tomboys', ensuring that this way of performing femininity is clearly positioned as deviating in some way from gender norms. 'Pseudo-masculinity' can be seen as acquired through performing gender within the discourse of masculinity for women, but the deviation from the social constructions of femininity is often construed as reflective of a deviation from heteronormativity and heterosexuality.

TRANSGRESSING NORMATIVE FEMININITIES

To be a masculine woman can lead to being positioned as 'like a man' or heterosexuality being questioned where it might otherwise have been assumed by default. Within LGBT culture, various terms have evolved to describe certain 'types' of gay men and women; these include names such as 'lipstick lesbian', 'studs', 'otters', and 'bears'. Whilst perhaps functioning as positive identities for those who adopt them, they are still arguably reflective of heteronormative femininities and masculinities that position a feminine or very masculine-presenting gay woman as usefully categorised, reinforcing that gay women who wear lipstick and have a feminine appearance are a specific category of the generic group 'lesbian'. The 'lipstick lesbian' is also arguably construed out of male heterosexual desire, identifying the gay woman of sexual fantasies as opposed to the one who is experienced as rejecting male desire in reality and fantasy. The very masculine gay woman might have gone beyond what is considered the norm of being lesbian to a specific type of femininity equated with a very male signifier ('stud'). We don't have such descriptors for heterosexual women, generally; even 'tomboy' has the implication that it is a childhood phase. Adult women can't really be 'tomboys', and a 'lipstick straight woman' is unlikely to catch on, since wearing make-up is construed as a 'natural' state of being for women within heteronormativity. A very masculine straight woman is also not generally referred to colloquially by terms that reference her as being straight and masculine; more likely, any such descriptor indicates or implies a non-heterosexual orientation.

Likewise, femininity in the male sex has long been associated with a gay sexual orientation in the psychological literature (Freud, 1922). Early Freudian theories around boys identifying with their mothers and becoming more feminine and 'homosexual' are well known. Whilst they may not be so entertained as they once were, there still seems to be that all-pervasive social gaze determining how feminine or masculine gay men are. Like all men, gay men also trade between themselves and other men the social privileges associated with a more normative masculine gender performance (see Chapter 3). Femininity, therefore, whilst not being contingent on being female, is often equated with being female-bodied, being seen as both an expression of that embodiment as well as an ideal to be aimed towards (Mills, 1992).

PERVASIVE DISCOURSES AND DECONSTRUCTION

Masculinity and femininity discourses influence our lives across all the areas and even in our understanding of time itself. Kristeva, Jardine, and Blake (1981) contend that cyclical/natural time and eternal mystical time is associated with femininity, and linear/historical time with masculinity, reflecting the cyclical biology of women (de Beauvoir, 1949). In contrast, the more masculine notion of linear, historical time has an end point moving towards new achievements, controlling biology, and overcoming nature. Whether or not you agree with Kristeva *et al.*, the very discussion illustrates how the scope of gendered phenomena in discourses and how the impact of notions around femininity and masculinity go far beyond what colour and type of toys are in the aisles of Toys R Us aimed at 'boys and girls'. And this is undoubtedly where the expectations of future social gender roles all starts. Social conditioning and its plasticity were recently explored by Javid Abdelmoneim in a two-part series for BBC Two, entitled *No More Boys and Girls: Can Our Kids Go Gender Free?* (2017). He explored ideas around how the different treatments of boys and girls in childhood may be behind a lack of equality in adulthood. That subtle (and less so) stereotypical messaging – 'girls are pretty' and 'boys are strong' – alters self-concepts and ambitions. Although these questions and experiments help to challenge the binary, they do so in the context of an environment that is overwhelmingly 'blue and pink'.

We therefore try to deconstruct femininity within the discourse that creates, recreates, and supports it, sometimes feeling like we are flailing in the dark, hoping to increase the areas of light through which we can expand our awareness of gender. Science is not immune to this either; for example, the male gamete is described as pursuing and latching onto the female gamete in human fertilisation, taking the gendered language and stereotypes right to the way in which we understand and describe the moment of conception. For a full discussion of this, see Emily Martin's paper (1999), titled: 'The egg and the sperm: How science has constructed a romance based on stereotypical male–female roles'. This early identification of biological sex leads on to the social conditioning of the individual into what is appropriate gender performance and strengthening of the gender identity assumed to be associated with that biological sex. The significant others in the developing child's life influence that development both in reinforcing what are seen as 'appropriate' gender role behaviours, possessions, and attire, and in reducing the likelihood of other 'inappropriate' behaviours reoccurring, with the shaming being frequently used by peers, and often family members, too, to support this process.

Policing gender is a family-and-friends activity, as well as that of the media and total strangers in our social worlds. It starts in early years and becomes internalised such that the other's gaze is always with us, like Bentham's *panopticon* explored in the work of Foucault (see Chapter 3). The power of the male gaze and the effect on women is powerfully illustrated in Roman Polanski's 1965 film *Repulsion*, where the main female character moves into psychosis under it, with the disturbing increasing paranoia of never being able to escape it. She is undoubtedly expressive of socially desirable femininity and descends into insanity as the film progresses, and she increasingly rejects the attention of men responding to her appearance.

 Exercise

A *Guardian* newspaper article published on 14 July 2015 (*The Guardian*, 2015) discussed how female athletes often face 'the femininity police', giving the example of Serena Williams, an athlete whose treatment reflects not just gender but also the effects of intersectionality of race and colour.

She has been described on social media as an 'ape' and 'gorilla', and a Russian tennis official in 2014 made reference to her and her sister as 'the Williams brothers'. Her size has been mocked and she has been declared unattractive in sports commentary. All women athletes seem to be fair game for discussion around their 'womanliness', and being described as 'like a man' if successful is an occupational hazard. Tennis players have long had to endure this; for example, when Martina Navaratilova was playing (generally considered one of the best female tennis players of all time), it was common for her to be subjected to conversations around her masculine appearance and queries of whether she 'was a man'.

It seems to be that a successful woman in sport is often perceived by association as more masculine, or, indeed, in many other fields such as politics. On 14 July 2016, *The Telegraph* (2016) ran an article on how Jo Pavey is 'the 42-year-old mum on the way to her 5th Olympics' from her book *This Mum Runs* (2014). Her overriding identity in these writings is as a mother and, whilst that is her choice, it is not one that would work in the same way for male athletes in relation to being a father. Her achievements are seen as all the more impressive *because* she is a mother. In contrast, male accomplishments are often not seen as significantly more worthy of comment simply because those men are fathers, too.

Reflect on how you feel your achievements and interests might have been restricted by discourses around femininity, whatever gender identity or social gender role you have:

- Can you identify incidents of 'gender policing' around your expressions of femininity?

- What effect did they have on restricting your behaviour and presentation?

- How might your achievements and goals in life so far have been affected by these discourses?

NORMATIVE FEMININITIES

We have seen, therefore, that femininities are constructed around certain 'norms'. Lehman (2000) developed the Feminine Ideology Scale (FIS), which is itself part of the Gender Role Strain Paradigm (GRSP), a feminist framework first theorised to explore how gender role socialisation creates stress and a variety of negative outcomes. Alongside models such as Traditional Femininity Ideology (TFI) (see Levant, 1996; Levant *et al.*, 2007), feminine gender norms are seen as being socially and culturally produced and reinforced through social conditioning, including rewards for conformity and punishment for transgression. For Lehman (2000), there are five subscales to FIS:

> *stereotypic image and activities* (the belief that women should maintain a particular physical image and engage in traditional activities); *dependency/deference* (the idea that women occupy subordinate roles in relationship to their male partners); *purity* (value should be placed on women's chastity and passive sexual role); *caretaking* (the ideal of motherhood as women's ultimate fulfilment); and *emotionality* (the notion that women should be emotionally sensitive and expressive, and perform traditional roles). (Levant *et al.*, 2017, p.2)

Although research (see Levant *et al.*, 2017) continues into testing the validity of such models, we have seen that certain discourses are highly productive of normative femininities. One of the most powerful and pervasive of these is the image of women as mothers. This seems to be reinforced across all areas of society, with women often being defined by having or not having children and, as we have seen, defined as 'good' or 'bad' mothers. For Il'iyink (2012), motherhood is the foundation on which all of the other normative traits are built and with which they are inextricably entwined. The argument put forward in the paper explores a range of proposed femininities: 'infantile', 'inversion', 'deformed', and 'androgynous':

> In our opinion, normative femininity corresponding to the female habitus with orientation to female values that are deemed traditional in the public conscience can be distinguished. Family and maternity belong to these in the first place. All models of female behavior are built in accordance with these values. The orientation to family and maternity in one way or another impacts on the traits of character: conformity, empathy, kindness, simplicity, carefulness. *Infantile femininity* can be called another type. Females of this type take the initiative in their hands, try to occupy an active leader position and be self-sufficient. Absence of conformity, desire to control other people, lack of empathy, elements of intolerance can be observed in the traits of character. But the main feature of infantile femininity is that family and maternity values are not at all dominating. *Inversion femininity* can be considered one more type. Females with this type of femininity possess excessive masculinization. In this case it is more appropriate to use the term 'inversion' but not 'masculine' femininity in order to focus attention on the drastic changes of normative femininity. Thus, inversion femininity is life in compliance with a habitus of independence, sense of purpose, non-conformity, self-confidence, businesslike approach, work addiction, professionalism, pride, ambitiousness, aggressiveness, competitiveness (including that with men). *Deformed femininity* is another type in our opinion. Females with this type have behavior models that are accompanied by alcohol addiction, drug addiction, child abandonment and other destructive patterns. These females can even have traits of character that apparently correspond to normative femininity but are opposite to them in their content. And, finally, such type as *androgynous femininity* can also be distinguished. The behavior models in this type of femininity are characterized by a rather high level of combination of both 'female' and 'male'. Women with androgynous femininity prefer such qualities as even temper and common sense. (Il'iyink, 2012)

This argument is particularly interesting as it appears to be so certain and so reductive. It seems that, for Il'iyink at least, to be a woman is to be maternal. Where family and maternity values are not prioritised, in the model above, femininity is deemed 'infantile'. Forms of femininity described as 'inversion', 'androgynous', and 'deformed' use highly emotive language to starkly highlight deviations from the 'norm' of 'empathy, compassion, passivity, gentleness, maternally, and family-oriented and kind'. To hand over the care of children or 'abandon' them is depicted as 'deformed'. Yet, what does this mean for those women who choose not to have children, not to be the primary carer, or for those who don't fit these norms of femininity? In the next chapter, we will be looking at how these normative expectations might adversely affect our clients in therapy and what we can do to facilitate positive changes.

Normative femininities, whilst placing women on a spectrum of femininity and marginalising some altogether as being deviant, nevertheless allows for their existence as feminine beings. Men, by virtue of being men, fall outside normative femininities; to be a feminine man is to be rejected and subordinated by hegemonic masculinity and excluded from normative femininity. It is hard to find positive discourse around being a feminine man; the heteronormative discourse dominating discourses around gender positions the two terms pretty much as a contradiction. The more feminine a man is perceived to be, the less of a man he will be considered to be. Femininity in itself is considered less desirable than masculinity, so the social contradiction becomes: Why would a man want to give up male privilege in order to be more feminine?

Women are deemed to be feminine by default and not through choice; their biology makes it so through the linking and justification of ideas around femininity to motherhood and the maternal instinct. In essence, acting in a way that is contrary to the norms of femininity is then constructed as being 'unnatural' or 'resisting nature'. Masculinity, by contrast, is constructed of innate socially desirable traits. There isn't the same discourse around biology being resisted by being a feminine man, more a deficit of masculinity and masculine traits that allows this to be possible.

Feminine power is a positive to the extent that it is a poor relation of masculine power, and subordinate to it. There is equality but not superiority of abilities, unless in an area of endeavour that, in itself, is seen as being of less value. Childcare, for example, may be asserted to be a high-value activity in relation to women. However, social norms have yet to change for it to be considered not just acceptable for men to look after their children full-time, but also a socially desirable way of life, with widespread validation of the skills and traits making them particularly suitable for this. As Jay Hanshaw, a 16-year-old Bronx-based teen, says when explaining why he is not afraid to be called feminine: 'Want me "to act like a man"? I already am' (Hanshaw, 2016).

THE IMPORTANCE OF FEMINISM

One of the main ways in which all forms of gender identity have been resisted, contested, and questioned has been through the various waves of feminist activism from the end of the nineteenth century to the present day. So-called first-wave feminism came out of a movement for social justice and equal rights for women at the ballot box. The idea that somehow having a female body made it impossible for a particular kind of human not to be able to participate in political discourse had its roots in 'the natural'. Sex differences were seen as constitutive of different kinds of persons with fixed traits, including the infamous example of ungovernable emotional excess in *hysteria*, a female-only condition, driven by the mysterious 'wandering womb'. With fixed and embodied differences between the sexes, men were seen as more 'naturally' suited to politics and governance and women to duties in the home, lacking as they did the suitable intellect or emotional control to be trusted with the vote or social leadership roles.

Building on a movement that questioned these innate differences with respect to gender equality in voting and property rights, second-wave feminism opened up the debate to a wider range of issues, including sexuality, family, the workplace, reproductive rights, and the question of domestic violence and legislation around rape and reproductive health for women. Started in America in the 1960s and with its roots in men's response to taking back women's roles in society occupied in the West during the Second World War, second-wave feminism formed a central role in informing the debate in the psy disciplines.

Rutherford and Pettit explore this reciprocal relationship between psychology and feminism, arguing that 'the psychology of women deserves equal scrutiny as a scientific field that has real world effects on the lives of ordinary women and men' (Rutherford and Pettit, 2015, p.226). They point to how the feminist Betty Friedan drew on Maslow's ideas of self-actualisation in order to argue for women to be given the opportunity and the right to pursue their own potential as human beings, just as much and as fully as any man. In doing so, feminists were battling against a field traditionally dominated by men. Nowhere can it be seen more starkly than in the statement in 1965 by the psychoanalyst Bruno Bettelheim:

We must start with the realisation that, as much as we want women to be good scientists or engineers, they want first and foremost to be womanly companions of men and to be mother. (1965, p.15)

The essentialist social myths, such as 'maternal instinct', were used again and again by psychologists and psychiatrists to justify discrimination and unequal treatment. A paper by Feldman and Aschenbrenner about twenty years later shows that things had not gone forward a great deal as they explore 'Sex Role Behavior' and 'Sex-Related Personality Characteristics':

Sex Role Behavior

This is typified by the division of labor into masculine and feminine tasks or by the exhibition of interest in areas deemed appropriate to the roles commonly assigned to women and men. For instance, in line with her childbearing and childrearing roles, a woman is expected to be interested in and nurturant towards babies. Correspondingly, a man is expected to exhibit interest in economic conditions and business practices, in accord with his breadwinner role.

Sex-Related Personality Characteristics

There is a general consensus that masculine behavior involves an instru-mental, outward-oriented function and feminine behavior an expressive, interpersonally directed function... (Feldman and Aschenbrenner, 1983, p.279)

The relentlessly pervasive presence of binary sex roles and gender identities, embedded in a recourse to the 'natural' and 'self-evident' in psychological literature, even as late as 1983, shows the enormous impact that feminist thought, activism, and research has had on gender politics and identity politics as a whole in the time since. Eagly and her colleagues point to an astonishing statistic that, 'in 1960, women constituted 17.5% of PhDs awarded in psychology...and in 2009, 75.4% of PhDs and 78.8% of PsyDs' (2012, p.226). Clearly, not only has feminism contributed to expanding research and scholarship on gender and identity, but it has also significantly widened the number of women working in the field and setting the agenda for enquiry and debate.

Moreover, feminism and feminist activists have had a significant role to play in changing attitudes towards sexual violence – particularly in how that violence is constructed in the diagnostic literature. It seems extraordinary to us now from the perspective of today, but in the mid-1980s, the American Psychiatric Association (APA) proposed three new disorders for inclusion in the *Diagnostic and Statistical Manual of Mental Disorders* (DSM): Paraphilic Coercive Disorder (PCD), Self-Defeating Personality Disorder (SDPD), and Late Luteal Phase Dysphoric Disorder (LLPDD). For an excellent exploration of the history of this incident and its meanings for gender identity and politics, especially femininity, see Dodd (2015).

In promoting the diagnostic category of PCD, its authors attempted to frame rape as a hormonal issue. They argued that men's drive towards sex with women was, in itself, 'natural' and it was simply that, in the case of PCD, hormones were out of balance, driving the poor, unfortunate man to non-consensual sex. There was considerable outrage expressed – not only by feminist psychologists – over the sexist, androcentric view of rape as PCD, not least on the grounds that it could, by the back door, give rapists a psychological defence for their actions, potentially minimising the wrongfulness of the perpetrator's conduct. As a result, PCD was quietly shelved and failed to be included in the diagnostic nosology.

In the case of SDPD, a 'disorder' oriented towards a form of learned helplessness in women, feminist activists again succeeded in having the category kept out of the DSM (it was relegated to an appendix). They did so by lampooning a diagnostic category embedded in female socialisation with one that was embedded in male socialisation, the so-called Delusional Dominating Personality Disorder in men. By holding up a mirror to the DSM committee, the activists offered a broad critique of the unconscious sexism and double standards operating both in psychology and psychiatry as well as in society more generally.

 Exercise
Privileges of femininity

We have already seen in Chapter 3 how discourses around masculinities serve to restrict and oppress men alongside the privileges outlined in the Male Privilege Checklist. As with masculinities, so, too, has it been argued that there are equivalent female privileges. Whilst not necessarily agreeing with all or most of these (some of which seem somewhat misogynistic in the Female Privilege Checklist), what can be acknowledged is that discourses around masculinity and femininity create bars around both genders, restricting lives and perpetuating inequalities.

As discussed in the Female Privilege Checklist,[1] female privileges include men being told not to hit women, but women not instructed in

---

1   The Female Privilege Checklist can be accessed online at: https://mensresistance. wordpress.com, accessed 06 December 2017.

kind, and having a protective status that is retained as a female, but which men lose when they reach adulthood. Women are described as being more able to access help without stigma. The ability to carry children is seen as providing women with an 'essential' status, and fertility clinics are orientated around the needs of women to reproduce rather than men. Reference is made to perceived inequity in how the custody of children is awarded following divorce, with fathers less likely to get custody over mothers. Mothers may expect facilities in larger public female toilets for changing infants, whereas these are unlikely to be provided in men's toilets. Of direct relevance to gender diversity and presentation, men encounter more social prejudice if they wear feminine clothing than women do when they wear masculine clothing. Women may also benefit from being seen as more approachable to talk to than men and potentially less threatening.

What thoughts come up for you when considering these privileges? Have any of the items been part of your experience in the past? Are there more than you can think of? If a woman, what occasions might you be aware of where you relied on female privileges? For all genders, consider times where your values/beliefs have conflicted with your socially conditioned expectations. An example of this might be in equality of paying: Does it feel more uncomfortable to you if paying for dates in a heterosexual relationship is done more by a man or a woman? How feasible is it to be exactly equal in contributions, and which gender would feel more comfortable to you to be contributing more financially to a heterosexual relationship? What difference does sexual orientation make to how these privilege checklists apply, and are they themselves reflective of heteronormativity?

INTERSECTIONALITY

In Chapter 16, we spend some more time exploring intersectionality as it relates to gender. However, it is worth acknowledging here the diversity of experience within what we have discussed, even if it is not immediately apparent. Intersectionality has been part of a third-wave feminist critique of categories, such as the psychology of women, arguing that they crudely bundle all women together without explicitly recognising the heterogeneity of people, experiences, and identities within that category.

Normative femininities vary cross-culturally, and assumptions made about others in regard to femininity may themselves be rooted in racism, class, religion, expectations around disability, or what it means to be trans.

A **trans woman**, for example, can find herself even more under pressure to conform to ideals of femininity, whilst feeling biologically unable to do so in some areas. She may want to present in a quite androgynous way but feel judged for not 'looking feminine enough'. There may be a pull towards hyper-femininity to compensate for not meeting the gender norms in some areas, which can also attract criticism, leaving a narrow path to walk for social validation as a woman. Discourses around femininity also assume able-bodiedness, and the Alison Lapper 2005 statue *Pregnant Woman in Trafalgar Square* was widely feted as a 'powerful piece', partly because it challenged social expectations around disabled women and pregnancy.

Case vignette: Miriam

Miriam is a trans woman in a long-term relationship with a cisgender male heterosexual-identified partner, Jack. They live together, but she has only met a few of his friends and hasn't met his family as yet. Jack is currently unemployed but looking for work; Miriam supports them both as she has a relatively well-paid job as a retail manager. She doesn't seem to be particularly happy in this relationship but keeps saying that Jack 'accepts' her as a woman and loves her. Recently, she came to a session rather upset that, when arguing, Jack had said that she was fortunate to be with him and that, if he wanted, he could be with a 'real' woman. This is not the first time that he has said this, and she is now wondering if he might leave her, but she also feels uncomfortable that she is supporting him. She wonders, though, if anyone else 'would want her'.

 Reflection

– What do you think are the issues here that relate to the discourses around femininities?

– How might both women and men be complicit in creating the constructs of what constitutes a 'real woman' and what doesn't, such that Miriam may accept Jack's premise that she isn't one?

– How threatening might it feel to let go of some of the ideas around what a woman is and how can you, as a therapist, facilitate Miriam in creating a relationship in her life where she feels affirmed and supported rather than in some way deficient in her identity as a woman?

GENDER AND POWER: A FUTURE LESS BINARY?

Throughout this chapter (and, indeed, in Chapter 3 as well), we have looked at how those marginalised by the patriarchy and binary structure of heteronormative gender performance – women, gay people, people of colour, and others – have consistently troubled and questioned taken-for-granted notions of identity. They have attacked the privilege and power that come with a (White, able-bodied, middle-class) male identity and attempted to redress the power imbalance in gender relations. In doing so, the rights and roles of women (and other previously marginalised groups) have changed dramatically for the better over the course of the last century. While there is clearly much more that can still be done to change attitudes in society, and to bring about real equality (not just equality under the law), rigidly held beliefs over the differences between the sexes (and the implicit denigration of women in that equation) are far less common now than they were even 30 years ago.

And in that societal change there is hope. Hope for a future, less binary world, where there is greater freedom of gender expression for all, regardless of birth sex, gender identity, or sexuality. Already we are seeing, for example, that femininity can be performed by men, women, and people who are non-binary and **gender-fluid**, and it might vary from day to day for the same individual. Moreover, the attributions around sexuality and sexual orientation made in relation to femininity where the tie to sex has been loosened are changing, such that the gender binary seems increasingly inadequate to reflect social identities, roles, and lived social experiences.

6

WORKING WITH ISSUES IN FEMININE GENDER IDENTITIES

In this chapter, we move away from psychological literature around femininities to look at how these theorised experiences and discourses might emerge in the clinical setting and some useful ways of working with them. The clinician's awareness of their own gender identity, performance of gender, sexuality, and assumptions around gender and sexuality, especially the heteronormative bias in these, is considered key in influencing the emergence of the gender discourse in clinical settings. As in the chapter on working with men's issues, we are not aiming towards producing a definitive guide to working with women's issues here either, but instead to facilitate raised awareness of how gender presents and some of the ways in which it may influence the therapeutic encounter.

The reader is invited to read widely around working with women in therapy and gender issues in psychology (e.g. see Dow and Wood, 2012; Kopala and Keitel, 2005). There are also many useful publications referenced in this book, including Nadal's (2017) *The Sage Encyclopedia of Psychology and Gender*, which covers many different aspects of women's lives seen through multidisciplinary lenses that explore the intersection of gender and psychology. This chapter will focus specifically on five themes that help to unpack ways of working with feminine gender identities:

- Speaking with 'my woman's voice'

- Validation

- Expressing emotion

- Working with feminine scripts

- Feminist therapy.

SPEAKING WITH 'MY WOMAN'S VOICE'

One of the authors (female) and her colleague (also female) often used to joke, when they felt that they hadn't been heard properly in various work environments, that they 'were speaking with their woman's voice'. It may be that the conversation continued unchanged after their contribution and on occasions the same point or suggestion would then be made by a man and acknowledged as insightful and useful. Another variation might be that their idea or argument was later credited to a man. The joke was particularly apposite since both are quite assertive women who don't adhere to normative feminine scripts of passivity, and they recognised that women who are more overtly feminine in their presentation and interaction were observably talked over altogether on occasion or more quickly interrupted.

But surely all this is now changing as we enter an era of greater and greater gender equality? Not according to the opinions expressed by women writing to the *New York Times* (2017b) in response to their piece 'The universal phenomenon of men interrupting women' (2017a). As Mary Conroy from Madison, Wisconsin, put it: 'Gender inequity is not going to fix itself, but I wish I had a dime for every time someone tried to "mansplain" this problem for me.'

The one place that women really do need to feel heard in is in the therapeutic encounter. Techniques to encourage this might be to start the consultation with an open mind, take a phenomenological approach, and actively avoid moving too quickly to interpretation or a solution focus – valuing the process of exploration, empathy, reflection, understanding, and connection over the allure of being 'solution focused', 'moving forward', and 'effectively treating' whatever the 'defined problem' is (arguably a more masculine response from friends, family, and partners that may already be familiar to women entering therapy).

As we come to define the therapeutic issue and goals, we can also reflect on whether the referrer's formulation dominates our thinking, or whether it is our own experience and knowledge. We can question how open we really are to listening to what the woman in front of us is saying. To what extent are we filtering her voice through our own femininity scripts and what room is there in those scripts for gender experiences outside the binary? For example, we might be working with a non-binary individual, who is female-bodied and who may be both feminine and non-binary in their varying presentations, or feminine in appearance and have a non-binary gender identity.

Case vignette: Nathalie

Nathalie has been referred for therapy by her GP for treatment for depression. The GP has also mentioned in the referral that Nathalie has 'poor parenting skills', based on what he has observed when she visits him with the children at his practice.

On receiving the referral, the therapist keeps an open mind, as until she has met and discussed her situation with the client, it will not yet be clear what the problem is and for whom it is a problem. For example, the children's behaviour appears to have been an issue for the GP and he also feels that his patient has depression, which needs addressing, but Nathalie herself has yet to be heard.

At Nathalie's first session, it is evident to the therapist that she is underweight and expressing symptoms of depression. She does not raise any of her own concerns around parenting and the therapist is aware that, as the mother, Nathalie has been assumed to be responsible for the children's behaviour, whereas they do also have a father at home. He was not mentioned in the referral but attended the therapy centre and was asked to wait in the waiting room, rather than attend the therapy. The young children (ages 3 and 5) were being cared for by a neighbour.

The therapist noticed how friendly Nathalie's partner was when they arrived, thanking her for seeing Nathalie and showing concern around her welfare, presenting very much as the protective, supportive male figure. Nathalie herself said very little until about halfway through the session. She explains how her partner usually accompanies her to appointments and talks for her, with much of her time otherwise being spent at home.

The therapist spends the initial sessions with Nathalie, listening and facilitating her in telling her story. She moves at Nathalie's pace, until Nathalie tells her that what is most problematic in her life is her relationship with her husband, the children's father. The children get bored as they spend most of the time at home with few toys and play activities, and her husband is not comfortable with her going out without him. As this session (4) develops, it becomes clear to both Nathalie and the therapist that she is in a relationship that is coercive and sometimes violent. They are now able to work together on what is most significant in Nathalie's life and Nathalie says that she feels truly heard for the first time, without being 'told what to do', before truly communicating her situation and how she feels.

 Reflection

Often, when a situation brings up an emotional response in the therapist, it can be hard to stay with it and listen to the client. In the same way, as clients try to avoid emotional pain, therapists may feel drawn to move away from the 'stickiness' and negativity of difficult emotions and on to a quick solution, where all the parties feel happier as a result.

'The woman's voice' could be applied to any client characteristic, where they are more likely to feel less heard, such as, but not exclusive to, disability, accent, gender non-conformity, sexuality, race, and mental health history. Giving space to that voice is not only essential to good therapy but can also be practised in everyday situations such as with colleagues, at dinner parties, in shops, with friends and family, or anywhere where we can consciously choose not to be compliant in privileging some voices over others.

VALIDATION

Following on from effective communication and hearing the voices of all others, not just those with more social privilege, comes validation. In seeking to be heard, the client also seeks validation – validation of who they are and how they feel. In the last chapter, we explored how feminine identities and discourses around femininity are tied up with expectations of presentation and performance that can be associated with degrees of social validity as a woman. Not uncommonly, we see trans people in clinical settings who have made what we have previously described as flights into 'hyper-masculinity' or 'hyper-femininity' before settling into the way of performing gender in society that is most congruent with their gender identity. There can be a period, though, of varying lengths, when validation as a man or a woman is sought for self and others through aspiring to what is presented as the ideal feminine or masculine social script. In achieving social validation, many clients hope that personal peace of mind will follow. What tends to happen instead is that a disconnect begins to be felt between the social persona (reinforced and validated) and internal identity (that can still be experienced as shameful, bad, and 'other'), further increasing the sense of gender dysphoria.

In the same way, cisgender clients might present looking for a way forward where their personal identity is congruent with their gender performance, whilst at the same time feeling invalidated as a woman. We have seen some of the social rules on what men and women are expected to be and do and the potential consequences of being seen to transgress these. Women are often policed into certain roles through the threat of being seen as 'less of a woman' if they fail to do so. But there can also be a freedom in the intersections of being other, of being transgressive, in that, as previously discussed, one can become 'that kind of woman' with revised expectations, though generally at the cost of reduced social privilege and status. A very feminine-presenting woman who decides not to shave her legs any more is likely to attract more attention and comment than a more masculine-appearing one. The more the appearance conforms to heteronormative cisgender discourses, the more tightly the prison bars might be felt to keep one within the ideal or restrict one from achieving goals not seen as congruent with that presentation.

Validation starts with active listening, understanding, and reflection. It also requires a shared understanding of what is being relayed, and this is particularly important for social groups, where their experience may be marginalised or seen as less valid. If the client does not have to educate the therapist, then there is already some common ground of knowledge which serves to validate that they are not so outside the norm, not so 'other'. Although women have traditionally been seen as expressing their feelings more, being more 'in touch' with their emotions, and constructed as more empathic, alongside that has run invalidating stereotypes relating to their biology, their 'sensitiveness', and their supposed 'irrationality'. So, as a woman, it may be socially acceptable to show your feelings but that does not necessarily mean that those feelings will be validated and responded to in the way that the person wants them to be.

 Exercise

On first viewing the humorous video cited in footnote below,[1] the initial reaction might be: 'it's obvious' that the nail needs to be removed! But its very 'obviousness' invites further reflection on the verbal and non-verbal interaction between the man and the woman, in which he moves from advising her to take the visible nail out of her head when she talks about her discomfort to attempting to validate her feelings of distress.

Consider the following:

– How often do we so obviously see 'the nail in someone's head' and think that we know the answer to all their problems?

Trans women can feel invalidated as women on a daily basis in a society that sets unachievable norms of femininity for women generally, but seems to expect even more of those who are trans. The norms are further reinforced by the never-ending debates around what constitutes a 'real

---

1   See the video at: https://queerguesscode.wordpress.com/2013/05/29/validation-or-solution-navigating-feelings-with-women-and-men, accessed 6 December 2017.

woman' – whether it's Janice Raymond's (1980) *The Transsexual Empire* or journalists Julie Bindell and Jane Fae (2017) discussing whether or not trans women are 'real women'. As in all questions around gender differences, the very question communicates that trans women may not be 'real women'. Their identity and very selves are open to discussion and 'up for debate'; their personal identities as women cannot be fully validated externally without question. Fae makes the point in the discussion that trans women may feel uncomfortable with an interviewer who has expressed views questioning their identity as a woman; Bindell responds that she would never be interviewed if she avoided interviewers who disagree with her. Our right to exist as a defined being with a particular identity is generally not questioned when our opinions are disagreed with, though when our very right to exist *is* directly questioned, it can feel that we are being invalidated as a person.

In the therapeutic encounter, it is therefore particularly important that the therapist has a well-thought-out and informed understanding of trans so as not to invalidate trans clients, either consciously or unconsciously. This raised awareness can then extend beyond trans to cover a range of women clients' experiences, where they may feel less socially validated as women, for example due to infertility, post-hysterectomy, post-menopause, with ageing, changed facial and body appearance, and loss of hair, amongst many others.

 Exercise

Reflect on your own gender identity in the context of femininity:

- Can you identify any heteronormative assumptions underlying your beliefs around what it means to be feminine and the expression of your femininity?

Gender identity can be confusing for some clients because they find it difficult to separate out shame around their sexuality and desired social role presentation when it deviates from heteronormativity from their experience of their own gender. Consider how you can help them gain understanding and self-acceptance and work with these issues:

- Do you have the knowledge and understanding of feminist and queer psychology to better enable you to do this?

> – How might a trans woman feel in your therapy room, and what could you say and do to be validating of her femininity and female gender identity?
>
> – What knowledge might you need to acquire to better enable you to do this?

EXPRESSING EMOTION

Emotional expression socially associated in relation to women has changed over time, arguably not as a linear progression of a social shift towards self-development and individuality but more in waves linked to politically dominating discourses around empowerment and oppression (Cancien and Gordon, 1988). Women have become increasingly encouraged to express anger as well as love, but the responsibility for maintaining intimate relationships tends to remain with them. And if they do express anger, they risk being described as 'aggressive' and being seen as less feminine if this results in conflict. This can lead to the double bind of the pressure to 'be real' and 'honest' in relaying angry feelings to others but at the same time trying to maintain a non-conflictual, cooperative situation and to avoid upsetting others. The expression of anger by their male counterparts already has the underlying threat of aggression built in, and women's role has traditionally been to appease them, de-escalate the anger, and make things right. Men's anger has been more socially perceived as linked to external circumstances, whereas women's anger is more essentialised as a reflection of internal characteristics, possibly indicating a lack of emotional control. Some studies have even shown that angry professional women will be attributed lower status than angry professional men, regardless of rank (Brescoll and Uhlmann, 2008). There is also substantial international data on the gendered nature of bullying in the workplace, with women being more likely to be victims (see Leo et al., 2014).

In therapy, we can work with all clients to manage anger by identifying triggers, connecting these with past and present and looking into the future, so as to develop strategies to manage the anger and look at changing behaviour, where it is self-destructive, in order to promote more constructive reactions to stressors. Underlying this work, though, should be an understanding of the influence of gender and the impact that it has on the client's experience. Exploring what emotions are felt to be permissible as well as those positioned as less congruent with a feminine identity, and questioning these together with the client, may help facilitate desired therapeutic change.

In our clinical setting, trans women have often expressed concerns around how they can express anger as a woman with concern around the increased risk it may place them at. This includes, for some, taking into account the increased risk of situations where they feel victimised and subject to abuse, with their instinct being to react angrily with violence, yet they fear the potential conflict and the legal implications of harming others. In the therapy room, this is a space where these feelings can be explored without judgement and unpacked in relation to social discourses and stereotypes around femininities, masculinities, non-binary, and what it means to be a man, a woman, or non-gender. Hearing the client means also not dismissing the real concerns being expressed around being trans in an environment where the person may be at increased risk and subject to discrimination.

WORKING WITH FEMININE SCRIPTS

Femininity scripts exist in opposition to, rather than interwoven with, scripts of masculinity, allowing fluidity of all genders. To be a 'tomboy' means a rejection of femininity (Paechter, 2010), while hegemonic masculinity simultaneously defines and constructs femininity. Third-wave feminism aims to address this and achieve not only equality of the genders but also a definition of femininity as something more than the foil and opposite pole to masculinity.

Ideally, we would like to see society move towards the integration of femininities and masculinities such that the question of being a 'real woman' or a 'real man', or a 'feminine' or 'masculine' person, no longer arises; the question instead being what kind of individual you are in the world. It is difficult within a binary, cisgender, heteronormative, dominant discourse to envisage a world where gender becomes an expression of self and our bodies at birth do not lead to such a mountain of assumptions about who we are and what we can do and be – a world where gender can be fluid, change, or be fixed but where our biology does not constrain or define us because of the way we construe and categorise gender.

The reality is, though, that we are still operating within stereotypical gender scripts, and those associated with women and femininity tend to be nurturing, maternal, loving, caring, compassionate, and calm, and, if otherwise, possibly a little emotionally unstable. Anger, as we have seen, is not positively reinforced in women, and trying to meet the other expectations of femininity whilst assertively expressing angry feelings can be a challenge. The social role expectations of mother and wife can act as barriers to progressing in work, having personal achievements outside the home, and being self-directed to meet one's own needs rather than always those of others first.

 Exercise

Reflect on how you can adapt your therapeutic approach to facilitate your clients in both addressing issues relating to gender, but also in order to escape the restrictive scripts around gender and the performance of femininity within masculine scripts to support and reinforce them.

FEMINIST THERAPY

In the previous chapter, we briefly explored the impact of feminism on psychology – specifically the psychology of women – and gender, more generally. It would clearly be beyond the scope of this chapter to write a detailed account of what constitutes feminist therapy. Books, journals, and series of publications are written on this alone, but it would also be an omission not to mention it when discussing femininities and feminine gender identities.

Feminist therapy, as a specific discipline within psychology, developed as part of the women's movement dating back to the 1960s, challenging traditional views of mental health that were deemed damaging to and not therapeutically supportive of women. Gender Aware Therapy (GAT) or gender sensitive therapy was developed by Good *et al.* (1990) as an extension of feminist therapy with men. Central to feminist therapy was challenging the power that men had over women to assess, diagnose, and decide the solutions for their lives, rooted in sexism and gender bias. Through feminist therapy, clients were encouraged to express their anger, make choices about their own lives, enter egalitarian therapeutic relationships, and connect with other women in therapy and elsewhere. The new model of feminist therapy questioned the assumptions underlying more androcentric, gender-centric, heterosexist, positivist models of therapy that located pathology within the individual rather than something mediated through external social factors (Worell and Remer, 2003). Feminist thinking continues to move forward through third- and now into fourth-wave feminist ideas, with authors already mentioned in this book and more (see, e.g., Cochrane, 2013; Penny, 2014). Current feminist theory prioritises intersectionality (see Chapter 16) and, in discussing gender, gender scripts, masculinities, and femininities, therapists are reminded of the complexity of the individual in front of them beyond the lens of gender, of the importance of knowing how to work in an empowering way with clients with feminine gender identities, and also of navigating beyond gender altogether.

7

NON-BINARY FORMS OF GENDER IDENTITY

In this chapter, we are going to look in more depth at non-binary forms of gender identity, what it means to be positioned outside of a binary model of gender, and how that model needs to be expanded to include gender as not being fixed but more fluid and diverse than simply men and women, male and female, and masculine and feminine. We will be moving into a world beyond these dichotomies and exploring it from the outside and inside, discussing the possibilities it offers and the challenges.

By their very nature, non-binary forms of gender identity are many and varied. By no longer being bound to picking one or other of two sides, a multiplicity of varied identities might be imagined. It is beyond the scope of this chapter to cover all forms of non-binary identity, but we will explore some of the main forms that you are likely to encounter in your practice to get a sense and better understanding of the territory and the potential diversity and similarities of our clients' unique and shared gender identities.

NON-BINARY AND GENDERQUEER

'Genderqueer' is an adjective that can be used to refer to people who deliberately 'queer' or trouble and transgress taken-for-granted distinctions within our traditionally binary understanding of gender. For some people, the words 'genderqueer' and 'non-binary' are and can be interchangeable since they have similar meanings. They can both be used to describe a range of gender identities other than man/male/masculine or woman/female/feminine that do not fit the male and female binary.

Some people use the words non-binary or genderqueer to describe their gender identity, while, for others, identifying as non-binary or genderqueer is too broad and they might wish to identify as another gender identity within the wider spectrum of non-binary, using some of the terms unpacked below.

There is no fixed structure in non-binary and genderqueer and you may find that some people wish to identify as trans as well as non-binary. They may also choose to explore transition, either medically or by changing their name and/or pronouns so that their gender expression more closely reflects their internal, felt sense of gender identity. For some non-binary people, it's important to appear androgynous and to adopt unisex names and gender-neutral titles such as Mx and/or gender-neutral pronouns such as 'them' and 'they', while others prefer to express themselves in ways that are traditionally seen as masculine or feminine or to mix aspects of the two.

As we assert throughout this book, gender identity and sexuality are different and separate parts of identity, though they are often conflated in general discourse. As such, non-binary and genderqueer people can have any sexual orientation, although if they have a primary attraction to a single gender within the binary, they may prefer to use gender-specific terms to express this, such as **androsexual/androphilic** or gynesexual.

UNPACKING SOME OF THE MAIN FORMS OF NON-BINARY IDENTITIES

Non-binary, as discussed, takes us outside the dichotomous model of two discrete genders to where things are not as clear-cut. To be non-binary means that the assumption of being cisgender is challenged. The individual is no longer content to remain within the crude social development pathway that posits that observable genitalia at birth equates to sex, and that sex determines both gender and the associated social gender role. This schema does not fit their innate sense of who they are, or their preferred way of being in the world.

It can be helpful to see non-binary and genderqueer as a kind of panoply of different combinations and intersections of identity that both draw from the binary as well as deliberately positioning themselves outside it. In addition to a multiplicity of combinations and intersections, there are also variations in intensity of feeling in relationship to those aspects of identity such that there might be many different points along a continuum of the felt sense of masculinity or femininity in any number of different combinations.

It may be that they feel themselves to be more mixed gender, pan, polygender, or androgynous, mixing elements of being a man or a woman but neither, or that they see themselves as neutrois, gender neutral, agender, gender free, genderless, or having no gender. Perhaps their gender identity is fluid so that they move between genders, describing themselves as such or as **bigender** or trigender. A non-binary individual might see themselves as a third gender, not just outside men and women or integrating aspects, but as a new gender (Richards and Barker, 2013). Many of these terms, like pangender, might mean more than one category, so it is always essential to establish what the person themselves means by the terminology they use.

Inclusive identities

There are forms of non-binary identity that reference the binary but, rather than choosing one or another identity, instead feel that they are both. People with this form of gender identity will assert that they are both masculine *and* feminine, both man *and* woman.

People with inclusive non-binary identities may choose terms such as androgyne or androgynous and can express this identity by dressing in a way where others are not able to tell if they are male or female. Some may be happy with their bodies as they are, while others might wish to pursue a degree of physical transition in order to support their social transition and to align their embodied self with their felt sense of identity.

Other forms of inclusive identity might include **intergender** – the sense that one has an identity somewhat between male and female – or bigender, trigender, or polygender – the sense that one can hold both identities or multiple gender identities simultaneously. Pangender is specifically a very expansive term that recognises and includes anything and everything along a wide spectrum of gendered identities.

Exclusive identities

There are forms of non-binary identity that reference the binary but, rather than choosing one or another identity, instead refuse to choose either. People with this form of gender identity will assert that they are *neither* masculine nor feminine, *neither* man nor woman.

People with exclusive non-binary identities may choose terms such as genderless, agender, or neutrois. In a similar way to people with an androgyne identity, they may choose to dress in a way that makes it hard for an external observer to identify them as male or female. They may also choose to pursue some form of physical transition.

Xenogender identity is a specific form of exclusive non-binary identity, where the person is so far removed from the binary that they may choose to identify simply as their first name or as a real or imaginary animal. Their sense of self is so far removed from ideas of male or female that they choose to reference ideas and identities outside of gender altogether in order to describe themselves. Some researchers have linked these forms of non-binary identity to synaesthesia, a condition where people's senses become linked and fluid and where, for example, sounds and words might bring up specific colours in their minds. In this instance, synaesthesia-like perceptions might cause non-binary people to describe their gender identity in terms of texture, size, shape, time, light, sound, or other sensory characteristics that most people don't attribute to gender at all.

Fluid identities

There are forms of non-binary identity that reference the binary but, rather than choosing one or another identity, instead feel that they move between them in a way that is not fixed or certain. People with this form of gender identity will assert that they are *at times* more masculine or feminine, and *at times* feeling more like a man or woman.

People with fluid non-binary identities may choose terms such as gender-fluid and may vary their presentation over time and in different situations to match their identity at the time. They may be less likely than other forms of non-binary to pursue physical transition due to their desire not to fix their identity in a particular form of gendered body.

In addition to fluidity in gender presentation and identity, gender-fluid people may experience an overlap of, or blurred lines between, gender identity and sexual orientation.

Other or unnamed identities

There are forms of non-binary identity that do not reference the binary at all and instead choose either to assert a so-called 'third' or 'other' gender. Alternatively, they may refuse to name or identify their gender at all. People with this form of gender identity will assert an identity that does not position itself as more or less masculine or feminine but is different from either.

Third gender identities are explored in a little more detail below in the section titled 'Culturally specific forms of non-binary', and are often used to describe socially or legally recognised other gender roles outside the binary.

Unnamed identities refer to those forms of non-binary expression that individuals find that they cannot or will not name or place. They experience themselves as broadly non-binary or genderqueer, but do not have the language to express that experience in a fixed identity or form of words. Their desire to be unnamed may also extend into their self-expression through ambiguous or ambivalent gender markers in terms of clothing, hairstyle, and so on.

 Exercise

– Having read through this initial unpacking of some of the forms of non-binary identities, what comes up for you?

– Do you feel confused by the variety?

– What other feelings do you have?

– Why do you think that you are having this emotional response?

– Are some of the categories more or less familiar to you?

– Have you felt yourself at times to have had one or more of these identities?

– Have you worked with clients with a non-binary identity?

– Given the difference and variety of identities, how do you think that you can work therapeutically with a non-binary or genderqueer client in order to affirm an identity that may itself be positioned as a deliberate choice so as not to have a clear or fixed gender identity?

CULTURALLY SPECIFIC FORMS OF NON-BINARY

Some non-binary people may have a form of gender identity that is specifically culturally located, either in their own experience or as part of a culture that has been inherited through ancestry.

People with these forms of identity will reference specific cultural identities – for example, they may describe themselves as '**two-spirit**'. Two-spirit is a culturally specific gender identity that describes someone with one of many mixed gender roles that have traditionally been found amongst Native American and Canadian First Nation people.

The English-language term was coined at the Third Annual Inter-Tribal Native American/First Nations Gay/Lesbian American Conference in Winnipeg in 1990. It is a direct translation of an indigenous term that is suggestive of a person whose body simultaneously houses a masculine spirit and a feminine spirit. Although your clients may use this language to describe themselves, using the term outside of a Native American identity or ancestry is now seen as a form of cultural appropriation.

Similarly, other cultures around the world have incorporated a legally or socially sanctioned form of gender identity outside the binary. The Hijras of India have often been referred to as an example of transgender people who don't fit the physical or psychological binary but have inspired trans people across the world as to the diversity of social gender role and identity possible, reflected in cultures worldwide.

 Exercise

– Reflect on the many different genders that you are aware of across the world.

– Take some time to briefly research historical gender diversity in India (Hijra), Hawaii (Mahu), Australia (sistergirls and brotherboys), Indonesia (Waria), the Philippines (Bakla), Mexico (Muxe), and Samoa (Fa'afafine) in order to get a sense of how limited the idea of the binary gender model as being 'natural' is and to gain more of an understanding of a wider international perspective of what it means to be a man or a woman, or to hold a non-binary gender identity.

THE LIVED EXPERIENCE

For the non-binary person themselves, having that identity might be exciting and freeing, giving them a sense of authenticity and the relief of finally being able to make sense of who they are and how they want to be in the world, but also perhaps it can be a lonely place. They may encounter many kindred spirits in forums and social groupings, whilst still feeling outside the world of many family, friends, and work colleagues. They are likely to have to constantly explain and assert their identity in a way that many others take for granted.

In a sense, the binary, though experienced as tyrannical by some, can be an easier identity to inhabit. There is considerable effort that goes into positioning oneself outside such norms, and non-binary people may have to struggle with pressure from society to move away from a non-binary identity to one that maps more simply on the normative binary framework. For the therapist, too, it can be hard to maintain an open curiosity and to avoid a rush to judgement if working with non-binary people is unfamiliar. It can be helpful to hold in mind how polarities affect so much of our thinking and ways of being in the world – from freedom to isolation, and from fixity to fluidity. Acknowledging and engaging with that constant negotiation that we must all make between extremes can help provide a sense of connection and compassion for those who engage with the struggle in terms of their gender identity on a daily basis.

Case vignette: Jo

Jo is a 20-year-old natal female, with a history of chronic depression and more recently some deliberate self-harm, who was referred for counselling by the GP.

Jo gradually discloses in therapy that they don't feel female. They know that they don't feel like a woman, but neither do they feel like a man. They have been **binding** their chest and wear baggy clothing also to conceal it. They are perceived by friends and family as being rather masculine, having been described as a 'tomboy' as a child, and their partner, who is lesbian, sees them as just being 'butch'.

There are times when Jo would like to wear some feminine clothing and also not bind their chest, but finds it very difficult to see how they could vary their presentation in this way and explain themselves to others. Over the last couple of years, they have also become increasingly uncomfortable at being in a 'lesbian relationship', which positions them socially and in relation to their partner as female. Jo is concerned about discussing how they feel with their partner, who is very comfortable in her lesbian identity, only being attracted to women.

 Reflection

– What are your thoughts around the key issues for Jo here?

– What might be the goals of therapy?

– What could be the challenges for you as a therapist?

PREVALENCE OF NON-BINARY

It is probably difficult to really estimate the number of non-binary people, since many of them have been able to and still do integrate into society without being visibly non-binary in settings where they might be counted. Indeed, the binary gender choices given on most forms and legal documents actively make them invisible even where they are 'out' more visibly in their own society. Van Caenegem *et al.* (2015) found across two large studies – one Flemish-population-based and the other amongst sexual minorities in Flanders – that prevalence of non-binary gender identity or 'gender incongruence' was 4.8 per cent in natally assigned females and 1.8 per cent in natally assigned males.

It is hard to compare prevalence studies due to the differences in the sample populations, but Joel *et al.* (2013) found that over 35 per cent of their sample (2225 participants in the general population in Israel) identified as 'other gender', 'both genders', or 'neither gender'. Surveys of specifically trans participants have found from 5 per cent in the UK (Metro Youth Chances, 2014), 13 per cent in the USA (Harrison, Grant, and Herman 2012) to 25 per cent in Scotland (McNeil *et al.*, 2012, reported in Richards *et al.*, 2016). Anecdotally, in our clinical practice, we have been finding an increasing number of people presenting as non-binary, of all age ranges, but particularly between the ages of 18 and 30 and amongst those natally assigned female.

NON-BINARY AND INTERSECTIONALITY

Non-binary and genderqueer people, of course, have additional multiple identities that intersect, such as age, race, sexuality, ethnic origin, religion, class, work and professional identities, disability, mental health, and more, all of which affect their experience of their social and global world and the microcosm of the therapeutic relationship.

It is important for the therapist both to know and understand the diversity of gender identities and social gender roles, but also to be able to engage with the unique experience and identity of the client themselves. One way of doing this is to ask preferred titles and pronouns rather than to make assumptions and then use the client's own language in describing their identity (Richards and Barker, 2013). It requires an openness to what the client brings, to put aside assumptions around gender and sexuality, whilst having 'good enough' knowledge so that your client doesn't have to educate you about what it means to be non-binary per se. The therapy room can then become a safe, albeit somewhat challenging, place, but not a place where the client feels othered and different in an 'exotic' sort of way.

Moreover, as we have asserted elsewhere, it can often be assumed in texts such as this book that it is always the client who is non-binary;

however, it is equally possible that the therapist is non-binary. It is therefore important that non-binary practitioners also reflect on how their non-binary identities might impact on the therapeutic dynamics and how they might work with more binary individuals who might be struggling with their gender identity.

 Exercise

Reflect on your own feelings around non-binary and the different forms explored in this chapter:

- How fixed is your own gender identity, and what might acting in a gender role different to your usual one feel like?

- How are you able to contain your own feelings around gender whilst working with others?

- What feelings might it bring up working with someone much younger, living without the restrictions that you've historically experienced in your social gender role, perhaps challenging those that have been self-imposed?

Much of the process of working with non-binary clients, where the therapist has a more binary identity, involves sitting with and getting comfortable with not knowing. This practice is part of all therapeutic work for all practitioners and is not limited to working with questions of gender identity, specifically non-binary ones. But it can be helpful to reflect on how an experience of fluidity that challenges normative assumptions can drive a desire for closure, fixity, and certainty. Kurtz writes about that pull toward knowing and certainty:

> Knowing, understood as a state of mind, is a condition of reasoned assuredness: a state of closure that structures further experience. Unknowing, by contrast, is a state of openness that does not foreclose experience through predetermined structure. Reaching for that openness and maintaining it are the analyst's chief and lifelong work. (1983, p.245)

Those practitioners who are binary situated may consciously or unconsciously work from a position of anxiety and attempt to move their client to a more fixed sense of self, even if that is not congruent to their felt sense of self. Evans writes about 'that period of chaos' and suggests that, 'to most human beings, a great expanse of the unknown is always a little terrifying, even as it may pump us full of adrenaline and generate the excitement of anticipating what is about to come' (Evans, 2015, p.218).

In the psychoanalytic tradition, sitting with not knowing, while being supported by the therapeutic frame, is the goal of analysis. The practitioner is encouraged to become ever more comfortable with the uncomfortable and to actively resist the rush to closure, to certainty, to the application of psychological knowledge and insight as a kind of *techne* to 'fix' the client. As Bion (1967) famously advocated, the therapist should approach each session without desire, memory, or understanding. Gottlieb writes about 'the retreat to knowing what to do' and suggests:

> Reaching for professional knowledge is a way for each of us to feel less vulnerably alone in our response. Turning to the knowledge and skills of one's field is, of course, a necessary part of learning and practicing any profession, but is worth noting the way that every participant in my research acknowledged the relief of being able to rely on this received wisdom (such as a model, technique, back up plan, theory, ethical principle or legal guideline, evidence base, mantra, or instruction from a supervisor), and the discomfort of remaining without it. (Gottlieb, 2016, p.144)

In a very real way, working with non-binary clients can be both a challenge to those with a more binary mindset, but also a very useful and helpful reminder to our own practice to remain open and comfortable with discomfort.

RESOURCES

Finally, there are a number of resources available to non-binary people that may be helpful for you to access and for you to signpost your clients towards if they are unaware of them. UK-based examples include:

Beyond the Binary – A UK-based magazine for non-binary people that celebrates diversity. Available at: www.beyondthebinary.co.uk (accessed 06 December 2017).

The Non-Binary Inclusion Project – A grassroots organisation fighting for the inclusion of non-binary people in law, media, and everyday life in the UK. Available at: www.nonbinary.co.uk (accessed 06 December 2017).

Part II

WORKING WITH GENDER DYSPHORIA

8

AN INTRODUCTION TO GENDER DYSPHORIA

This chapter prefaces the next and largest section of the book, dealing with trans identities and how they give rise to treatment modalities and legislative protections as well as in trans people's experiences in work, social spaces, and intimate relationships. In prefacing Part II of the book, we look briefly at gender dysphoria as a diagnostic category, unpacking trans and the language of gender identity and diversity as well as the role of the medical profession both in articulating the phenomenon as well as in developing a range of treatments to deal with it.

GENDER DYSPHORIA AS A DIAGNOSTIC CATEGORY

Chapter 10 explores diagnosis and transition in more detail, but it makes sense in this introduction to gender dysphoria to explore how it is understood as a diagnostic category. In diagnostic terms, gender dysphoria refers to a discongruity between the body, the internalised sense of gender, and the gender socially assigned at birth. It is not a psychiatric disorder and the term is often used more loosely in reference to anyone who has dysphoria related to gender. As in all diagnoses, certain criteria need to be met for it to be given. It requires significant clinical distress or impact on social functioning and, from the way in which it has been framed, can be applied to people who are outside the gender binary.

A diagnosis of gender dysphoria in adolescents and adults involves a difference between one's experienced or expressed gender and assigned gender, and significant distress or problems functioning. It needs to have lasted for at least six months and has at least two of the criteria listed in the DSM-5 (APA, 2013).[1]

---

1   The criteria are listed online at: www.psychiatry.org/patients-families/gender-dysphoria/what-is-gender-dysphoria, accessed 08 January 2018.

As we have noted in Chapter 1, this book addresses the issues and processes typical to working with adult clients, but therapeutic practitioners should be aware of the childhood criteria for diagnosis of gender dysphoria as it can contribute to the adult client's personal gender narrative, whether through reflecting on what was experienced at the time or in retrospective creating of meaning around childhood. In children, gender dysphoria diagnosis involves at least six of the criteria listed in the DSM-5 (APA, 2013) and an associated significant distress or impairment in function, lasting at least six months.[2]

We can generally assume that many of our clients are familiar with professional diagnostic criteria due to the easy accessibility of information through the Internet and even more so for our gender diverse clients who have often had to do considerable research to make sense of and acquire language to express their experience in the world. At some stage, a confused sense of 'not fitting in' can develop into an awareness of their distress being gender-related (often with the onset of puberty, if not before). Subsequent reading, research, and talking to others within the trans community can then lead to labelling the experience with terms such as 'gender dysphoria' or 'gender variance'.

WHAT DO WE MEAN BY 'TRANS'?

'Trans' is a label frequently used to refer to gender minorities (Lev, 2004) and to describe individuals who are transgendered or gender variant. It can be used to refer to trans men (natally assigned female) and trans women (natally assigned male), or as a description of more nuanced identities such as 'transmasculine' and 'transfeminine'. Transgender, often used interchangeably with trans, can cover a range of gender identities, including genderqueer, transsexual, drag king/queen, **transvestite**, androgynous, third sex, gender-fluid, gender variant, and so on. As we have seen in Chapter 7, people with non-binary identities may choose to align themselves as trans or transgender in some way, or may be more comfortable positioning themselves outside the trans framework.

The word 'cisgender' was developed to describe people whose gender identity is *consistent* with the gender they were assigned at birth. Nevertheless, although cisgender people may be comfortable living in the gender they were assigned at birth, they may still experience the

---

2   The criteria can be found online via the web link cited in footnote 1 above.

social roles associated with the cisgender identities assigned to them as restrictive.

From a diagnostic point of view, simple gender non-conformity is not seen in the same way as gender dysphoria and would be considered by clinicians as a differential diagnosis.

Case vignette: Peter

Peter is a 20-year-old university student who has been referred by his university medical centre to counselling at his university counselling service in order to address anxiety and depression. He presents to the counsellor, talking about how he has lost his motivation for his studies and has become increasingly anxious around other people. On exploration over subsequent sessions, it becomes apparent that Peter generally feels better when he is at university than when he is at home during breaks. The referral was made just after the summer break. Peter becomes more open with the counsellor and tells her that he sometimes likes to present as a woman, which is now known by his friends. He is feeling increasingly that he wants to do this all the time but hasn't said anything to his family. He would like the counsellor to assess whether he has gender dysphoria. The counsellor has no specialist background in gender but suggests to Peter that the medical centre refer him to the nearest NHS GIC and, whilst he is waiting for an appointment, that they use their sessions to explore how he feels about his gender and what would make him feel better, rather than focus on a diagnosis at this stage.

 Reflection

- What are the pros and cons of the counsellor's approach?

- Why might Peter feel better in his university environment than when he goes home?

- How might the counsellor best support Peter in a non-judgemental, open way but also validate his identity and experience around gender?

LANGUAGE AND IDENTITY

As we have seen, there is a rich and diverse language that is used to describe variance in gender identity. Some of it, like the word 'transsexual', has its roots in medical discourse and, like the word 'homosexual' before it, has been overtaken by a wide variety of words created by the trans community themselves, taking on the power to name and describe their experience outside of what was previously seen as a medical condition or psychiatric disorder. The domain of language can thus be a key site for many TGNC people, where power is exercised and fought over, and claimed and reclaimed. Previously derogatory terms and past 'disorders' are assimilated to become simple variance, and eventually the words just *are* without having to be *other than*, or described as varying from an assumed norm.

We cannot escape the fact that the overriding mainstream discourse within which discussions around gender and sexuality take place is heteronormative and cisgender. It can be difficult for practitioners as well as the friends, family, and allies of TGNC people to think outside the related assumptions inherent in everyday language. Reading and engaging with LGBT and queer psychology can be one way in which therapists new to the field can 'knowledge up' and get more familiar with language that is less restrictive. Similarly, engaging with other questioning practitioners and with ideas that might be initially uncomfortable without being too quick to jump to evaluation and judgement can help in our affirmative practice.

The 'acceptable' language in the TGNC field can change at such a rate that therapists might at times despair at keeping up with what language they should be employing. The professional guidelines and standards of care referred to in this book can be helpful in that, but be mindful of the importance of keeping up to date with revised and new versions. As we have said before, it is always useful to remember that the client can be asked what terms they prefer when relevant, and sometimes this might mean resisting imposing on them what we see as the 'correct terminology'.

Each gender identity expressed through an associated social gender role may require its own particular pronouns and titles, and part of affirmative practice is to work to understand and respect those differences. It is therefore generally good practice to ask what a client's preferred form of address is and what their pronouns are in order to respect and affirm their gender identity and expression. It is not a legal requirement that someone is living in their desired social gender role or for them to have changed their name to refer to them as Mr, Ms, Miss, Mx, or Mrs, according to their preference.

A DIVERSITY OF EXPERIENCE

Clients can present with mild gender dysphoria, a desire to explore their gender presentation, or simply want to work out where they fit in on the gender spectrum. They may not have taken any action or had any gender-related treatment. They might have moderate or severe gender dysphoria and express a desperate need to access hormonal and/or surgical interventions. Alternatively, they could have undergone hormonal and/or surgical interventions and be living in their reassigned gender role without any issues, but have lost their confidence in their presentation or be having relationship or sexual issues. The latter are no longer gender dysphoric but their gender history could be relevant to their therapy. For others, it really isn't because they aren't gender dysphoric, and having gone through gender reassignment treatment, dysphoria is a footnote in their history now. They might identify as being trans or say that they are just a 'man', a 'woman', or 'themselves', perhaps, with no trans identification. Others may retain a strong trans identity.

Case vignette: Julia

Julia has been referred to a GIC for counselling, and has now been given an initial appointment, having waited a significant amount of time. She went through gender reassignment about 20 years before and has been living continuously as a woman ever since. The referral was made because she had been diagnosed with depression and her GP was concerned that she should receive the appropriate specialist help. The assessing psychologist discussed with Julia why she had been feeling depressed and it transpired that there had been a number of significant changes in her life in the last few years. Her relationship of five years had ended a year and a half ago, her father had died two years ago, and, at age 59, she was now thinking about retirement. They both agreed that Julia was, indeed, depressed but also that it did not require the services of a gender specialist. Her self-esteem had reduced, her confidence in her appearance was quite low, but she still came across very much as a woman presenting with depression related to the issues above rather than her specific gender history being a primary factor. It was the case that what she was experiencing was affected by that history, but only because her depressive thinking was permeating how she felt about all the areas of her life.

Reflection

- How do you think that you, as a professional, would have reacted to Julia when she first sought help?

- Would her gender history have been the most salient factor for referring her on, or would you have considered all factors and directed her towards quicker, effective local services?

- Would you, as a therapeutic practitioner, have felt comfortable just seeing her, or would you have thought that she might be better seen by 'a specialist'?

- It is useful to reflect, when foregrounding identities with prospective clients, which identities are most currently relevant for them, as opposed to us.

MEDICAL AND PSYCHOLOGICAL INVOLVEMENT IN TRANS

As we explore further in Chapter 10, medical discourse has certainly dominated the rise of trans as an acknowledged social phenomenon. Furthermore, the association between hormonal and surgical interventions and gender reassignment has interested the public since at least the early 1950s, with Christine Jorgensen's surgery and subsequent 'outing' in 1952 (Meyerowitz, 2009).

From an historical perspective, TGNC identities were seen as the sole preserve of psychiatry and medicine. The early pioneers of gender reassignment came from the medical field and, while responding to distress and acting out of a genuine desire to help, reinforced the notion of gender diversity as a medical and psychiatric problem that needed a medical and psychiatric solution. Nevertheless, they did help to advance the options available to trans members of society in order to treat distress around their bodies and assigned gender roles.

The Harry Benjamin International Gender Dysphoria Association was set up in 1978 in the USA, becoming what we know today as the World Professional Association for Transgender Health (WPATH). They have been instrumental in helping to move the discourse along from a pure medical perspective to one that is more multidisciplinary and that privileges the trans person's needs and goals at the heart of an informed consent model of treatment. In more contemporary times, queer psychology has continued to make a contribution to the ways in which trans identities are discussed and understood. As queer psychology has grown roots and flourished, consensual sexualities expressed other than through heterosexuality and heterosexual partnerships have been decriminalised and have moved away from being labelled as psychiatric disorders.

 Remember

As general therapeutic practitioners, as well as specialists in particular areas, good professional practice is to develop raised awareness and knowledge across areas that might be outside our usual practice. Whilst we may not want to set ourselves up as specialists in those areas, it can be very invalidating for clients to be perceived as so far outside our experience that they cannot be accommodated at all, where perhaps they are not looking for specialist treatment. Reflect on what types of clients you may feel are outside of your experience and knowledge in order to see and then identify how you can increase your understanding and awareness in those specific areas so as to provide an affirmative, validating service to all clients, even those whom you may need to refer on.

CISGENDER PRIVILEGE

In Chapter 3, we looked at male privilege. We will end this chapter by looking at the privileges associated with being cisgender, which are often taken for granted. Like heteronormativity, the privileges of being cisgender can be so assumed as to be invisible, until it appears that they are no longer there. It is important to think about how strongly gendered the society you live in is and about your own assumptions around gender, especially if you are cisgender.

Cisgender people can usually assume that they will be gendered by appropriate titles and pronouns. They generally don't have to 'assert' them or engage in arguments as to why they are 'legitimate'. Their gender isn't questioned on the basis of their history regardless of their presentation and identity. When they change their name, whilst people might take time to adjust, they generally don't use the old name 'to make a point' or because 'it's difficult' to use their new name.

Trans people are often concerned around what might happen if they are hospitalised, or sent to prison, just on the basis of which sex facilities they will be allocated to and potential humiliation and embarrassment. Cisgender privilege means that changing rooms and toilets can generally be used without fear of being challenged or threatened with the police being called.

In developing relationships, there can be many reasons to fear rejection, but gender history is likely not one of them when cisgender. There is no 'coming out' or 'disclosing' past assigned gender or aspects of one's body to a new date or perhaps a long-term partner, fearing not just rejection but perhaps a violent reaction. There is no expectation that their genitalia should be changed surgically, or other body parts, to fit their social gender role and gender identity. Pressures to look physically and aesthetically a certain way are still experienced somewhat as choices, rather than expectations, which may lead to one's gender being completely invalidated if not met.

Cisgender women, unless informed otherwise, will generally assume fertility and the ability to carry their own child. Cisgender parents can comfortably be called mum or dad without having to address the challenges that may arise for parents who have transitioned gender, one of which may be to be inadvertently 'outed' publicly by one's own children. In fact, to be cisgender brings the privilege of 'outing' in relation to gender not being an issue.

Although we have only touched on it briefly here, cisgender privilege permeates society just as universally as heteronormativity. In your work with TGNC clients, especially if you are a cisgender practitioner yourself, it is vital that you work from a position of awareness of cisgender privilege and how it operates both in your own life and that of your clients.

9

TRANS IN THE UK

Having explored and unpacked non-binary identities and gender dysphoria, this chapter looks at the current situation for trans people living in the UK from a legal, employment, and medical perspective. As we do so, we are aware that this is a snapshot in time and that the ways in which legal and medical discourses understand, protect, and proscribe TGNC people has changed over time and will continue to do so. Indeed, at the time of writing, the UK is starting the process of negotiations to leave the European Union (EU). Brexit's impact on our laws in the medium to longer term, in particular those laws that flow from and are affected by EU-driven human rights legislation, remains to be seen.

We recognise that the readers of this book will encompass practitioners working from different modalities across the field of mental health and gender care. Requirements to get involved with and advocate for clients as they engage with and navigate the legal and medical pathways that accompany a typical transition in the UK will vary enormously. Some of you will work with trans clients without the need to get involved in letter-writing or advocacy, while others may be called on to write letters and statements on behalf of your clients. By becoming aware of the legal and medical processes affecting TGNC people in the UK, you can work in an informed and affirmative way. As this book is primarily aimed at a UK readership, and given that the authors all work within this UK framework, this is the focus of our chapter here. If you are working elsewhere, it is just as important for you to make yourselves aware of the frameworks that exist in your own countries and territories.

There are three sections in this chapter:

- The UK legal framework – An overview of the Gender Recognition Act 2004 and the Marriage (Same Sex Couples) Act 2013, as well as the importance of existing UK and EU equality legislation.

- The UK employment framework – This will be covered in more detail in Chapter 15, but a brief overview is provided here, exploring the implications of the Equality Act 2010.

- The UK medical framework – The main focus is on the treatment pathways in the NHS, but private treatment options are touched on as well.

THE UK LEGAL FRAMEWORK
Background to the Gender Recognition Act 2004

The decision in 1971 in the case of *Corbett* v. *Corbett* set a legal precedent regarding the status of trans people in the UK until the Gender Recognition Act in 2004 was passed. Arthur Corbett, the plaintiff, sought to dissolve his marriage to the model April Ashley on the grounds that Ashley was legally a man despite her change of gender identity. At the time, the Court made a distinction between sex, which was deemed impossible to change, and gender, which could be changed. Marriage was identified as only being possible between a man and a woman, and, furthermore, that those identities were defined according to sex rather than gender.

This ruling was challenged in the 2002 decision by the European Court of Human Rights in the case of *Goodwin and I* v. *United Kingdom*. In the decision, it was found that the UK was in violation of Articles 8 and 12 of the European Convention on Human Rights (ECHR). As a result, two trans women, Christine Goodwin and a person who chose to be identified as 'I', were given the right to have their gender changed on their birth certificates.

Having been found to be in breach of the ECHR, the UK Government had to introduce new legislation to become compliant, and so the Gender Recognition Act 2004 was drawn up and enacted.

Main provisions

The Gender Recognition Act 2004 is the primary piece of UK legislation that sets out the rights and protections for TGNC people in the UK. One of the key benefits that it confers is to give trans people the right to change their gender legally. While it is not necessary for them to get legal recognition of their expressed gender in order to be protected by the Equality Act 2010, the Gender Recognition Act 2004 allows trans people to gain legal recognition of their **acquired gender** by registering for a

Gender Recognition Certificate (GRC) with the Gender Recognition Panel (GRP).

Gender Recognition Panel process

The Gender Recognition Panel is a branch of the HM Courts and Tribunals Service that considers paper-based applications from trans people looking for formal legal recognition of what the Gender Recognition Act 2004 refers to as their 'acquired gender'. As *The General Guide for All Users (Gender Recognition Act 2004) (T455)* leaflet from the HM Courts and Tribunals Service states:

> Under the laws of the United Kingdom, individuals are considered by the State to be of the gender – either male or female – that is registered on their birth certificates. The Gender Recognition Act 2004 enables transsexual people to apply to the Gender Recognition Panel to receive a Gender Recognition Certificate (GRC). If you are granted a full GRC you will, from the date of issue, be considered in the eyes of the law to be of your acquired gender. You will be entitled to all the rights appropriate to a person of your acquired gender. This will include the right to retire and receive state pension at the age appropriate to your acquired gender. (2016, p.2)

Applicants must be over 18 and must have lived in their chosen gender for more than two years. They must satisfy the provisions of the Act and provide the GRP with evidence of a diagnosis of persistent gender dysphoria, as well as demonstrating their intention to live in the new role for the rest of their lives. Details of medical treatment and relevant dates are required and, although genital surgery is not a requirement for receipt of a GRC, where it has taken place, applicants must supply details.

Although the acquisition of a GRC is an important step for many trans people, it can also be a bureaucratically demanding and stressful one. There is a fair amount of paperwork involved – although the civil servants working in the tribunal service can offer helpful advice with this – and the process can typically take three to four months to complete.

Gender Recognition Certificate

Once a GRC has been issued, the recipient is considered legally to be his or her acquired gender. As a result, they can acquire a substitute birth certificate with the acquired gender and be subject to the same rights and restrictions as those that apply to that gender in law. There are some particular, arcane provisions relating to inheritance of title, but these are so specific as to be unlikely of any interest or importance to the majority of the clients whom you will encounter.

Confidentiality

The Act safeguards the privacy of trans people by defining information in relation to the gender recognition process as protected information. Disclosing that protected information without the consent of the trans person involved is classed as direct discrimination under the Equality Act 2010, and can result in a criminal charge under the Gender Recognition Act 2004 and a fine. Obviously, there are exceptions that allow information to be disclosed for valid public policy reasons without consent, such as to prevent or investigate a crime. Nevertheless, the Act is clear about the right to privacy of those who have gone through the gender recognition process.

 Remember

The provision of confidentiality under the Act is absolute. If you are working with a trans person who has a GRC, or you have reason to believe is applying for one, it is an offence to disclose that person's status to anyone else. Both you and any supervisor you are working with on behalf of your client will need to observe strict confidentiality. Although not all of your trans clients will have a GRC, it is good, ethical practice to maintain confidentiality as if they did.

The Marriage (Same Sex Couples) Act 2013

One other main effect of the Gender Recognition Act 2004 is to change a trans person's status with respect to the legislative framework surrounding marriage. This was of particular importance during the period of the Civil Partnership Act 2004 and before the advent of the Marriage (Same Sex Couples) Act 2013. At that time, because marriage between people of the same sex was not possible, a married trans person wishing to obtain a full GRC would have had to divorce their spouse or use an Interim GRC to apply for annulment. If they wished to stay together, the couple would then have needed to 'convert' their marriage into a civil partnership under the provisions of the Civil Partnership Act 2004. Conversely, under current legislation, a same-sex couple with a civil partnership are required to convert their union to marriage in the event that one partner transitions and successfully applies for a GRC.

Clearly, the legislative situation with regard to trans people in receipt of a GRC is complex. Our role as therapists, counsellors, psychologists, and advocates is to be aware of how these complexities are lived and experienced by our clients. We do not need to understand the law and all of its provisions in detail to do this. But we are required to be aware that navigating such complexities is one part of the experience of our trans clients in the UK.

The HM Courts and Tribunals Service Leaflet, *The General Guide for All Users (Gender Recognition Act 2004)* (2016, which is downloadable), discussed above, provides further details and links to organisations providing support and advice.

 Exercise

In Chapter 8, we looked at cisgender privilege and identified that one of the main features of privilege is the privilege of not being aware of your privilege!

For cisgender people, one of their privileges is to live in a way that is in accord with their gender identity without needing to ask anyone else's permission, approval, or assistance to do so:

– For cisgender readers, imagine how life would be if you needed to navigate through a complex legal and medical process simply to have your identity recognised – to have to put at least part of your ability to live an authentic life in the hands of others, of professionals, of a panel of people whom you might never meet.

Take some time to reflect on how that would make you feel:

– Think about how you would be required to give up power that you might automatically take for granted.

– What impact do you think that this could have in the therapeutic relationship?

THE UK EMPLOYMENT FRAMEWORK
Employment and the Equality Act 2010

The issues that trans people face in the workplace and other social spaces will be explored in more detail in Chapter 15, but here we give a brief overview of the legislative landscape currently operating in the UK. The main piece of legislation here is the Equality Act 2010, and the authors are indebted to the Law Society's (2015) practice note *Working with Transgender Employees* for a succinct summary of the principal provisions and protections of the Equality Act as it relates to trans people in employment.

The Equality Act 2010 aimed to codify and bring together a complex array of different Acts and Regulations, which formed the basis of anti-discrimination law in Great Britain (the Act does not cover Northern Ireland). It requires equal treatment in access to employment as well as private and public services, regardless of age, disability, gender reassignment, marriage and civil partnership, race, religion or belief, sex, and sexual orientation.

In 2011, the UK Government announced its *Transgender Action Plan*, one element of which was to further support transgender employees. In that document, they acknowledged that 'nearly half of transgender employees experience discrimination or harassment in their workplaces; 88% of respondents said that ignorance of transgender issues was the biggest challenge they faced in employment; [and that] transgender people highlight transitioning at work as one of the most significant triggers for discrimination' (HM Government, 2011, p.8).

The Act refers to 'gender reassignment' rather than 'gender identity' as a protected characteristic, and people are protected if they are proposing to undergo, are undergoing, or have undergone a process or part of a process to reassign their gender by changing their physiological or other attributes of gender. Importantly, the Act understands so-called 'gender reassignment' as a social rather than medical process, and previous requirements to be under the supervision of medical professionals in order to access rights and protections under the law no longer apply.

Employment rights are protected for a wide range of types of employees, including actual and prospective employees, ex-employees, apprentices, some self-employed workers, contract workers, actual and prospective partners in a partnership or limited liability partnership, and people seeking or undertaking vocational training. Under the Act, it is unlawful to refuse to work with someone with the protected characteristic of gender reassignment, even if the refusal is on the grounds of religious belief. It is also unlawful for employers to instruct someone to discriminate against trans people on their behalf, for example by asking an employment agency to reject a transsexual person.

The Act recognises that the ways in which trans people might be discriminated against in the workplace are quite broad, and it makes specific reference to six kinds of unlawful discrimination:

- *Direct* – Unnecessarily requiring someone not to be trans.

- *Indirect* – Where trans people are particularly disadvantaged by a provision or some criterion, which applies to everyone else in the workplace.

- *By perception* – Where an employer or other employee think someone is trans, and discriminates against them because of it, but they are not in fact trans.

- *By association* – If an employer or other employee discriminates because of someone mixing with, or having an association with, trans people.

- *Harassment* – Where an employer or other employee acts in a way that violates the dignity of another person or creates an intimidating, hostile, degrading, humiliating, or offensive environment for that person because they are trans (there is also protection from less favourable treatment of a worker because they submit to, or reject, sexual harassment or harassment related to sex or gender reassignment).

- *Victimisation* – It is unlawful to discriminate against someone because they have used the provisions of the legislation or have helped someone else to do so.

There is no requirement for a trans person to tell their employer about their gender reassignment status, and questions about a possible trans status should not be asked (with some minor exceptions). However, typically, a trans person undergoing transition in the workplace would engage with their employer to jointly manage that process. In some instances, a confidential memorandum of understanding may be sought between the employer and an employee, which summarises discussions about how communications on the change will take place, who will take action and when it will take place, and other matters such as time off from work, internal communications, forms of ID, name and dress changes, and access to facilities. Given that the process of transition can require employees to be absent from work from time to time, employees who are undergoing gender reassignment are protected from less favourable treatment in relation to absence from work for this reason.

One of the most controversial areas for trans people in the workplace is access to toilets and changing rooms that are appropriate to their gender identity. This single issue has resulted in more column inches and outraged political discourse in the USA in recent years than any other single public policy issue related to gender identity. In clinical practice, clients often complain that they have been asked to 'make things easier' for other employees by using disabled toilets and changing areas rather than those that are in line with their gender identity. In contrast to this common practice, the Equality Act 2010 specifically required employers to ensure that the employee can use facilities appropriate to their expressed gender identity without fear of harassment.

Case vignette: Tracey

Tracey works in administration at a local distribution warehouse where she has been for four years. About three months ago, she approached her managers and told them of her intention to pursue transition. The managers have been well meaning and have attempted to work with Tracey in order to put into place a plan that supports her in her transition and ensures that her colleagues are informed about the changes that she will make as she transitions. In the last few weeks, she has started presenting full time in a feminine role, wearing traditionally feminine clothing and some make-up. Last week, her line manager called her into a one-to-one meeting and asked if she would mind using the unisex disabled toilets rather than the female toilets so as 'to give things a chance to settle down and for the other women at work to get used to it'.

Although her employer is required to allow Tracey access to the bathroom that matches her gender identity and although the management team is keen to be as supportive as possible, Tracey feels singled out and shamed by this request. She doesn't want to cause a fuss and so goes along with this suggestion.

 Reflection

- How would you help Tracey to work through her feelings of being othered in the workplace?

- How can you help her to make sense of what is going on so that she can take a more active part in the decision-making around her rights at work?

We recognise that most of us in the mental health field are not that familiar or confident in navigating the complexities of UK legislation. And neither do we need to be – there are lawyers and legal advisers for that. What we do need to be is sufficiently informed and aware of the main issues so that we can work affirmatively and effectively with TGNC clients and their partners, families, friends, and co-workers.

THE UK MEDICAL FRAMEWORK

The treatment pathways for trans people in the UK have changed in recent years and it is possible that they will continue to change. Once again, therefore, what follows comes with the caveat that it is a snapshot in time. However, although the particular processes may change, the broad principle that trans people must engage with medical and mental health services to access treatment currently remains a constant. And the ways in which trans people make sense of their identities within a treatment framework will continue to form part of the process content of therapy.

This overview of the principal treatment pathways in the NHS is informed by two documents: the *Good Practice Guidelines for the Assessment and Treatment of Adults with Gender Dysphoria*, published by the Royal College of Psychiatrists (RCP) in 2013; and the *Interim Gender Dysphoria Protocol and Service Guidelines 2013/14*, published by NHS England, also in 2013.

For some years leading up to the publication of these guidelines in 2013, gender care in England was a tertiary care service. Trans people would be referred to the local Community Mental Health Team (CMHT) by their GP, whom, if they were satisfied of a diagnosis of Gender Identity Disorder (GID), would refer on to a specialist gender care service such as one of the seven NHS Gender Identity Clinics (GICs). Patients would typically have a local psychiatric assessment and sometimes psychotherapy before being referred for a detailed assessment process at a GIC to begin treatment. This approach to treatment has now been simplified and made easier for trans people to navigate. As the RCP guidelines state:

> We herald a new approach to care which has evolved from a linear progressive sequence to multiple pathways of care which recognise the great diversity of clinical and presentation needs. Central to the new way of working for healthcare professionals is the recognition of patient-centred care that will result in flexible treatment options, hopefully increasing the likelihood of good outcomes, reduced morbidity and improved quality of life for patients. (RCP, 2013, p.9)

New ways of working reflect and are the logical outflow from the trans affirmative legislation enacted in the UK in recent years. Central to the treatment approach is the idea of multidisciplinary and interdisciplinary care. It is acknowledged that gender care has many facets (non-psychological interventions are explored in more detail in Chapter 11), and many professionals may be involved with an individual patient:

> Gender treatment should be established on a multidisciplinary basis and may include input from GPs, psychology, psychiatry, psychotherapy, nursing, speech and language therapy, endocrinology, dermatology, surgery, social work and other related professions. Working in cooperation with other specialist practitioners or colleagues, even if on a different site, and affiliation with peer review and supervision networks, should be the goals of all clinicians. In addition to involving patients, clinicians should facilitate or provide information about assistance available to partners and families. (RCP, 2013, p.15)

Under both the RCP and NHS England guidelines, GPs (as well as other specialist services) are able to refer directly to GICs. The guidelines issued by NHS England in 2013 were acknowledged to be an interim solution whose purpose was

> to bridge the time period between the present, fragmented commissioning and provision of these services, and an agreed NHS England policy and service specification that [was being] developed through the CRG [Clinical Reference Group] in the coming months. (NHS England, 2013, p.4)

This service specification is being finalised through public and professional consultation, as this book is being completed.

The protocol flow chart (Figure 9.1) shows how an Individual Care Plan (ICP) has been envisaged to be agreed between the patient and the GIC, with the patient moving forward with a range of treatments and support programmes relevant to their needs. This chart is reproduced in full from the NHS England (2013) guidelines, not so as to ensure that the reader becomes an expert in treatment pathways but so as to demonstrate both the complexity of decision-making and the number of professional individuals with whom a trans person might need to interact and negotiate in order to achieve a 'successful' transition. Although simpler than the process before 2013, it is still potentially daunting and likely to throw up a number of issues in your work with your trans clients.

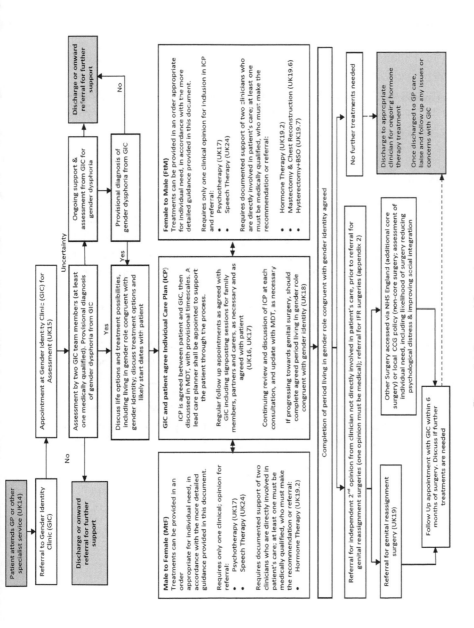

Figure 9.1 Protocol flow chart

Source: Reproduced from NHS England (2013, p.6)

Remember

Do not assume that all clients will have had the same experience of gender care. It's aways important to check your client's own, individual experience.

You can demonstrate that you are familiar with the usual processes of treatment pathways, but make sure that you're both on the same page with your understandings and that you are clear of where your client is on their journey and what their experience of that treatment pathway has been thus far (Figure 9.1).

Getting referred

Typically, a person experiencing dysphoria will first present at their local GP practice. The RCP (2013) guidelines suggest that they can also be referred, via their GP, for gender care by a psychologist, non-specialist psychiatrist, or sexual health centre. The GP is understood to be at the heart of patient care, ensuring a single point of contact, through which all patient treatment is coordinated.

Although GPs are mandated to support their patients' needs without prejudice (and with reference to the legislation explored earlier – the Equality Act 2010, Human Rights Act 1998, and Gender Recognition Act 2004), trans people can experience discrimination at the first point of contact with the NHS:

> Patients frequently find it difficult to confide their feelings of gender dysphoria to their GP, often because it is the family GP or practice, and fear of ridicule, guilt or shame as well as other pressing social factors prevent them from seeking help and treatment. (RCP, 2013, p.21)

Having a sensitive, supportive, and affirmative GP is vital if trans people are to be treated with dignity and be given access to gender care, as is their statutory right.

Case vignette: Beth

Beth is a 28-year-old natal female who has been living with her girlfriend for nearly two years. Her GP is familiar with her medical history and has been treating Beth for almost four years for a variety of day-to-day illnesses. About a year ago, Beth complained of persistent low mood and her GP prescribed an antidepressant, Citalopram 10mg per day. In her most recent consultation,

Beth has 'wondered aloud' if her low mood and some of the problems in her relationship might be down to gender dysphoria. She has always seen herself as a 'butch dyke' and struggles at times to accept her identity as female. Her GP responds by playing down Beth's concerns around her gender identity. She suggests instead that perhaps Beth should increase her dosage of antidepressant to 20mg per day and return in three months to see if anything has improved.

 Reflection

Beth's experience of her gender dysphoria not being addressed when consulting her GP is not unusual. Some GPs can feel that they do not fully understand issues of gender identity and the sociopsychological impact of trying to make sense of dysphoric feelings. Although not directly transphobic, they may feel more comfortable keeping things within areas in which they feel confident and familiar.

Getting seen by a specialist

One of the main frustrations that trans people encounter has been the wait times to be seen by a specialist in a GIC. In the past, this would have been compounded by the necessity of passing through a local CMHT assessment process, but wait times to see specialists can still be longer than many patients find acceptable. Figures published by UK Trans Info (2016) contain data for the period August–October 2015 (based on a patient questionnaire). Although these figures are only a snapshot in time, they suggest that the average waiting time for an adult patient to get a first appointment then was 47 weeks and that the longest was as much as 87 weeks. That waiting time, although being addressed at the time of writing, has since significantly increased.

The RCP (2013) guidelines acknowledge this and suggest that healthcare professionals ensure that patients have a realistic understanding of the typical waiting times for services:

> Service providers should also continually seek ways to help guarantee deadlines. Liability for 'undue delay' arising from non-clinical circumstances may fall on the commissioners. In such circumstances, private treatment undergone by the patient may also become the responsibility of the NHS (*Watts* v. *Bedford Primary Care Trust and Secretary of State for Health* [2006]). (RCP, 2013, p.18)

Case vignette: Fran

Fran has been referred by her GP to specialist gender care services, but has been waiting for more than four months for an appointment. She has finally received a letter through from the GIC and realises that she will have to wait a further four months for her first appointment. Fran and her counsellor have been meeting on a weekly basis since the time of her referral to help her work through some of her anxiety around her engagement with gender care and planned transition.

In her first session after receiving her appointment date, her relief at finally getting an appointment is tempered with anger that the process is taking so long. Her counsellor attempted to help her work through her mixed feelings and to reassure her that the process was on track. Fran had seemed to be engaged with the therapeutic process at first, but has now missed her last two sessions without cancelling in advance and her counsellor is concerned about what to do next.

 Reflection

–   What do you think could be going on for Fran here?

–   Perhaps she has started to see her counsellor as 'just another gatekeeper' – part of the daily problem that she faces in getting access to care. What do you think that her counsellor could do to help her to re-engage with the therapeutic process?

Visiting a GIC for the first time can be quite a daunting and emotional process for trans people. If you're working with someone who's attending a GIC for the first time, it will be important to give them the time and space to unpack a complex mix of emotions from excitement, fear, anger, and confusion.

Typically, patients attending a GIC will undergo multiple assessments, with the appointments taking place some months apart. After these appointments, on the opinion of the clinicians involved, a treatment plan will then be agreed with the patient. However, under current guidelines, it is now possible for a patient to be endorsed for medical treatment – such as hormone therapy – earlier than in the past. Chapters 10 and 11 look at the issues of diagnosis, transition, and treatments in more detail.

GICS IN THE UK
England
There are seven adult GICs in England. They are all commissioned by NHS England and accept referrals from any patients registered with a GP in England:

- 'Charing Cross' in London, run by the Tavistock and Portman NHS Foundation Trust from April 2017

- the Leeds GIC, run by the Leeds and York Partnership NHS Foundation Trust

- the Northamptonshire Gender Dysphoria Service in Daventry, run by the Northamptonshire Healthcare NHS Foundation Trust

- the Northern Region Gender Dysphoria Service in Newcastle, run by the Northumberland, Tyne and Wear NHS Foundation Trust

- the Nottingham Centre for Gender Dysphoria, run by the Nottinghamshire Healthcare NHS Foundation Trust

- the Porterbrook Clinic in Sheffield, run by the Sheffield Health and Social Care NHS Foundation Trust

- the West of England Specialist GIC (previously known as The Laurels) in Exeter, run by the Devon Partnership NHS Trust.

The Tavistock Gender Identity Disorder Service (GIDS) for children and adolescents is run by the Tavistock and Portman NHS Foundation Trust. They are based in London but run satellite clinics in Exeter and Leeds.

Wales
Wales does not currently have its own GIC. All adult patients in Wales are referred to the London GIC.

Scotland
There are four adult GICs in Scotland. Most of them only accept referrals from certain parts of Scotland:

- The Sandyford Clinic in Glasgow, run by NHS Greater Glasgow and Clyde, accepts referrals from throughout Scotland.

- The Aberdeen Clinic, run by NHS Grampian, only accepts referrals from patients in the NHS Grampian area.

- The Inverness Clinic, run by NHS Highland, only accepts patients from the NHS Highland area.

- The Chalmers Clinic in Edinburgh, run by NHS Lothian, only accepts patients from the NHS Lothian and NHS Borders areas.

The Sandyford GIDS for children and adolescents is also run by NHS Greater Glasgow and Clyde.

Northern Ireland

The adult GIC in Northern Ireland is the Brackenburn Clinic in Belfast run by the Belfast Health and Social Care Trust. It accepts referrals from throughout Northern Ireland. There is also Knowing Our Identity (KOI) in Belfast, which is the children and adolescents' GIDS for Northern Ireland, which is also run by the Belfast Health and Social Care Trust.

THE ROLE OF PRIVATE CARE

The main focus of this section has been to look at the typical treatment pathways for trans people through the NHS framework. Clients also have the option to seek private treatment and may have created their own pathway through TGNC networks, accessing hormones via the Internet, or seeking gender care abroad. The RCP guidelines acknowledge that issues in NHS gender care can result in some trans people seeking private treatment:

> These factors and the anticipated delay in obtaining treatment on the NHS have led to increasing numbers of people self-medicating. Hormones and hormone-blockers are readily available via the Internet. The medical practitioner or specialist must consider the risks of harm to the patient by not prescribing hormones in these circumstances. The WPATH SOC (World Professional Association for Transgender Health, 2011) suggest the prescribing of a 'bridging' prescription on an interim basis for a few months while the patient is referred to a gender specialist and an endocrinologist. (RCP, 2013, p.21)

If you are working with a trans person who is self-medicating with hormones purchased on the Internet, you may want to explore how they could get access to sufficient medical supervision to ensure that the risk of complications is minimised.

10

DIAGNOSIS AND TRANSITION

The relationship between the medical model and gender variance is complex and has particular, distinct meanings for people exploring and ultimately pursuing transition. The fact that Western understandings of gender variance, including our own system in the UK, require a diagnosis before gender care can be accessed means that the transition experience for many comes preloaded with a sense of illness based on the medicalisation of variance and distress. This chapter considers diagnosis from theoretical and historical perspectives before exploring it as part of the lived experience for trans and gender variant people. In the second half of the chapter, we look at ideas and concepts of transition, contrasting the idea of a single, linear journey with the more varied experience of many trans people.

UNPACKING DIAGNOSIS

As we've seen in the previous chapter, when looking at the RCP (2013) guidelines, engagement with diagnostic categories is part of the idea that gender care is a multidisciplinary process. There have been significant efforts made by professional bodies to depathologise gender variance in recent years and to put the patient at the heart of an informed consent model in regards to their own care and treatment. Nevertheless, trans people need to engage with medical professionals in order to gain access to care. And receiving a diagnosis under the APA's DSM-V (2013) or the World Health Organization's *International Classification of Diseases* (WHO, ICD-10, 2015) is part of that engagement.

As counselling psychologists, we take a somewhat detached stance in relation to diagnosis and diagnostic categories. We work with fellow professionals who are guided by them as a helpful tool, and use them practically in assisting our clients on their journeys, but also do not accept that, by attracting a diagnosis, a person is suffering from a mental illness or that illness located in that person in an individualistic, positivist view of the world. Indeed, all the major psychiatric and psychological bodies, including our own body, the BPS, now assert that gender dysphoria is not a mental illness. It is living in a heteronormative, cisgender world that is likely to increase a trans person's feelings of distress and isolation, given that their variance is often negatively construed by the society in which they live.

There is a considerable literature on the field of diagnosis and its relationship with counselling and psychotherapy, and there is clearly scope for more in-depth reading if you'd like to explore the debates around diagnosis and gender variance. But this chapter gives an overview of key themes and the content and process issues most likely to arise in the counselling space as a result. It's also important to recognise that therapists will generally not be required to diagnose gender dysphoria or to participate in a process of arriving at a diagnosis, if they are providing psychotherapy rather than being linked with diagnostic assessment and medical treatment services. This is important for two reasons:

- It tends to position the therapist as outside the medical field, not part of that power/knowledge structure.

- It can allow the therapist to take a neutral stance, alongside the client, making sense of that diagnosis without, as it were, having 'skin in the game'.

To that end, this chapter is not about equipping the reader with the skills required to make a diagnosis, but rather to see diagnosis and engagement with the medical model more widely in context as part of the lived experience for trans clients.

A CRITIQUE OF PSYCHIATRIC DIAGNOSIS

Different practitioners take different stances in relation to assessment, diagnosis, and formulation. Sue and Sue would argue that 'accurate assessment, diagnosis, and conceptualization are essential prerequisites for providing appropriate treatment' (2008, p.53); whereas Parker attacks this view and suggests that 'diagnosis transforms the varieties of ways in which we might achieve and enjoy mental health into a bewildering range of categories of dysfunction and mental illness…[that] brings with it dehumanization, labelling, the pathologization of many human activities and iatrogenesis' (1999, p.104).

Those like Sue and Sue, who argue for evidence-based practice in the mental health field, favour collecting a range of data from the client at the intake interview and comparing it against statistical models drawn from the experience of experts in that field. This approach, which is strongly supported in the literature, is in contrast to clinical judgement or heuristics where decisions about interventions are made based on the therapist's own orientation and beliefs. In the view of evidence-based practitioners, 'these judgements or inferential errors constitute deviations from the scientific model of gathering information and using a self-correcting model of hypothesis testing' (Sue and Sue, 2008, p.55).

The continuing proliferation of diagnoses in the *Diagnostic and Statistical Manual* (DSM) produced by the American Psychiatric Association (APA) perhaps evidences the impossibility of gathering all forms of human experiencing into a set of universal categories. When the DSM was first published in 1952, it ran to 130 pages and listed 106 mental disorders. Today the DSM-5 has nearly 1000 pages, covering 22 separate categories, each with multiple disorders. Some authors (Cosgrove *et al.*, 2006; Healy, 2006) have linked this proliferation of diagnoses in the last half century to the rise in the power of large pharmaceutical corporations. They argue that the increasing medicalisation of distress directly profits the companies whose drugs have been developed to treat the conditions. They further point to potential conflicts of interests since, in some cases, 100 per cent of DSM panel members (e.g. for schizophrenia and mood disorders) have financial ties with the pharmaceutical industry. Furthermore, Gary Greenberg, a psychotherapist and author, writing in the *New York Times* in January 2012, pointed out that the APA had already earned itself over $100m at that time on sales of the then current edition of the DSM (*New York Times*, 2012).

Quite apart from the critiques on a commercial, capitalist front, a significant attack on assessment and diagnosis as a technique of psychiatry comes from a postmodern, social constructionist approach. One of its more vociferous detractors, Ian Parker, suggests that 'this century has seen a relentless psychologization of society and the proliferation of diagnoses of forms of unhappiness' (1999, p.104). He argues that the mental health field itself is suffering from some kind of psychopathology, which House (2003) terms 'Pervasive Labelling Disorder'.

The social constructionist critique of psychiatry, and with it the practices of assessment and diagnosis, calls into question the modernist notion of a self that is 'construed as a naturally unique and discrete entity, the boundaries of the body enclosing, as if by definition, an inner life of the psyche in which are inscribed the experiences of an individual biography' (Rose, 1996, p.103). By extension, then, the autonomous, bounded self becomes the site of psychopathology, responsibility for which rests with that individual.

In this context, the practice of diagnosis can be seen as a 'technology of the self', something that 'permits individuals to effect by their own means or with the help of others a certain number of operations on their own bodies and souls, thoughts, conduct, and way of being, so as to transform themselves in order to attain a certain state of happiness, purity, wisdom, perfection, or immortality' (Foucault, 1988, p.18). It can be seen as something outside of the self that can instrumentally be applied, in an agreed form as a technology, to a human encounter in order to transform it. For Foucault, this internalisation is part of the Christian dictum 'know thyself' – an exhortation that replaces the earlier Graeco-Roman tradition of 'taking care' of the self as the primary goal out of which self-knowledge was previously achieved. The kinds of selves that people – particularly gender non-conforming people – understand themselves to be comes in part from the interiorisation of the various disciplinary gazes with which gender orthodoxy is produced and enforced in social relations.

The transformative effect of diagnosis, coming as it does from a powerful discursive position in medicine, is that it produces a truth about the individual, 'a process in which certain forms of thinking and acting come to appear to be solutions to the problems and decisions confronting actors in a variety of settings' (Rose, 1996, p.110). Yet, these truths are not arrived at without cost: 'truth is always enthroned by acts of violence. It entails a social process of exclusion in which arguments, evidence, theories and beliefs are thrust to the margins, not allowed to enter the true' (Rose, 1996, p.109). Webb, Schirato, and Danaher explore Bourdieu's concept of 'misrecognition and symbolic violence' to understand how it is that subjects appear to consent to being subject to such violence, particularly with regard to gender politics:

> Misrecognition is the key to what Bourdieu calls the function of 'symbolic violence', which he defines as 'the violence which is exercised upon a social agent with his or her complicity' (1992, p.167). In other words, agents are subjected to forms of violence (treated as inferior, denied resources, limited in their social mobility and aspirations), but they do not perceive it that way; rather, their situation seems to them to be 'the natural order of things'. One of the more obvious examples of the relation between misrecognition and symbolic violence can be seen

in the way gender relations have, historically, been defined in terms of male domination. (Webb *et al.*, 2002, p.25)

This sense that the diagnosis is for the benefit and good of the client, rather than in the interests of the institution which diagnoses, is taken up by Nikolas Rose and is worth quoting in full here since it sums up the complex interrelationships between power and diagnosis:

> ...one can see how psychology, in 'rationalising' their practice, simplifies their diverse tasks by rendering them as all concerned with the personhood of the client or patient. Psychology not only offers these authorities a plethora of new devices and techniques...it also accords these mundane and heterogeneous activities a coherence and a rationale, locating them within a single field of explanation and deliberation: they are no longer ad hoc, but purport to be grounded in a positive notion of the person. And, in the process, the very notion of authority, and of the power invested in the one who exercises it, is transformed. (1996, pp.115–116)

In engaging with diagnostic criteria in gender care, we should be aware that these diagnoses might also 'serve as a form of control, often to control our own anxiety about being in the presence of distress' (Parker, 1999, p.112). Perhaps one of the advantages of the therapeutic stance is that it invites us practitioners to wear the cloak of theoretical knowledge lightly and not to get too invested in a particular theory or way of working that might result in us losing sight both of the client and of ourselves in the process. As Winnicott observed, we are constantly fighting against our own desire to know and to solve and to stay in humility with the unknown:

> It appals me to think how much deep change I have prevented or delayed in patients...by my personal need to interpret. If only we can wait, the patient arrives at understanding creatively and with immense joy, and I now enjoy this joy more than I used to enjoy the sense of having been clever. (1969, p.711)

HISTORICAL CONTEXT AND CURRENT DIAGNOSTIC CATEGORIES

Despite taking a somewhat anti-essentialist stance in our critique of the practice of diagnosis and the creation of diagnostic categories, it is also true to say that the development of a diagnostic category for what was then termed 'transsexualism' was arguably one of the ways in which gender variance and dysphoria came to be recognised as worthy of attention and care. Prior to that, gender variance was largely seen as a 'lifestyle choice', and the surgical interventions that were developed were seen more as cosmetic, elective surgeries than as legitimate treatments.

Interestingly, the development of a diagnostic category for gender variance entered the DSM more or less at the same time as homosexuality left it in 1973. In 1980, transsexualism was included as a separate category but then later assimilated into a larger category dealing with sexual and gender identity disorders. In the DSM-III, transsexuality was defined as:

> A sense of discomfort and inappropriateness about one's anatomic sex;... continuous (not limited to periods of stress) for at least two years;... the absence of physical or genital abnormality, [and] not due to another mental disorder, such as Schizophrenia. (APA, 1980, pp.263–264)

In the DSM-IV, transsexualism became reclassified as Gender Identity Disorder (GID), with different criteria for diagnosis in children, adolescents, and adults. Somewhat bizarrely, the 'Specifiers' for diagnosis included the following paragraph:

> For sexually mature individuals, the following specifiers may be noted based on the individual's sexual orientation: *Sexually Attracted to Males, Sexually Attracted to Females, Sexually Attracted to Both,* and *Sexually Attracted to Neither.* Males with Gender Identity Disorder include substantial proportions with all four specifiers. Virtually all females with Gender Identity Disorder will receive the same specifier – Sexually Attracted to Females – although there are exceptional cases involving females who are sexually attracted to males. (APA, 1994, p.534)

As we have seen earlier, the conflation of sexual orientation with gender identity is part of the heteronormative framework underpinning orthodox ideas of gender performance, rooted in the primacy of heterosexuality. The breathtakingly dismissive tone in which male sexuality is seen as complex and female as simple and reductive speaks to the extraordinary sexism that continues to pervade both professional and layperson understanding of gender difference.

In 2013, the APA published the DSM-5, and with it the diagnosis of GID was replaced with the new category of Gender Dysphoria. The diagnostic category was no longer part of a section of sexual and gender identity disorders and the link between sexual orientation and gender variance was removed. Gender Dysphoria now has its own diagnostic category, with sections dealing with diagnosis in children, adolescents, and adults.

The changes between the DSM-IV and DSM-5 represent a move away from the more essentialist, biological idea of 'sex' in previous editions:

> *Gender dysphoria* refers to the distress that may accompany one's experienced or expressed gender and one's assigned gender. Although not all individuals will experience distress as a result of such incongruence, many are distressed if the desired physical interventions by means of hormones and/or surgery are not available. The current term is more descriptive than the previous DSM-IV term *gender identity disorder* and focuses on dysphoria as the clinical problem, not identity per se. (APA, 2013, p.451)

Although the way in which the psychiatric community understands variances of gender identity has changed in recent decades, in no small part due to trans activism and the growing body of research evidence to support those arguments, trans clients still inevitably need to engage with diagnostic categories.

Some may welcome a diagnosis and see it as a way of accessing gender care, while others may see it as stigmatising and shameful. Part of our job as practitioners working with trans clients is to help them navigate between the polarities of 'silver bullet' and 'shameful disgrace'. In working with clients to make sense of diagnosis, it can be useful to bear in mind the argument put forward by Hausman (1995) that part of the trans person's journey is to move from a position of helplessness to one of agency. He argues that, while gay activists sought to remove diagnostic categories, trans activists have fought to take control of their own diagnoses; to manage them and direct their application and resources. One of our roles, therefore, is to help our clients get a sense of ownership around diagnosis and to bring inside and under their control something that might hitherto have felt outside or 'other'.

EXPLORING TRANSITION

Diagnosis is the key that opens the door to medically supported transition in the UK. As Arlene I. Lev points out, 'the medical model is built on client "dysphoria", although professionals working with this population know that many arrive in treatment having found a solution to their distress, i.e. transition' (2004, p.179). It's also important to realise that transition means different things to different people. For many, transition represents a journey from inauthentic to authentic, with a defined goal in mind. For others, the journey is less clearly defined and linear and is a lifelong process of becoming. In their meta-analysis of 31 qualitative studies exploring the lived experience of over 1000 trans people across the world (but with a Western focus), Moolchaem *et al.* (2015) found that transition issues were one of the most common experiences for trans people. Participants in most of the studies reported facing a range of challenges during the process of transition:

> …such as losing relationships with family and friends, experiencing a lack of support from relevant organizations such as workplaces, educational institutions, health care settings, and social welfare agencies, and being discriminated against by peers and colleagues at work, often resulting in the loss of employment. (Moolchaem *et al.*, 2015, p.160)

In this section, we explore the process of transition and the role of mental health practitioners in being alongside their clients, helping them to make sense of and integrate that experience. As Lev points out, 'the goal of therapy is to assist the client in greater self-knowledge so he or she can make informed decisions about his or her gender expression, self-identity, body configuration, and ultimate direction of his or her life' (2004, p.186). She goes on later to affirm therapy's role in helping clients beyond a simple process of transition, to become more authentic selves:

> Psychotherapy is about an internal process of transformation. Gender therapy is not simply about surgery or hormones or even transition. It is not really about 'becoming' something as much as it is about allowing the false parts of the self to recede so that an authentic self can emerge. (Lev, 2004, p.207)

In being alongside clients in their transition, it is also important for therapists not to be invested in one particular outcome for the client – for example, in defining 'full' transition, including surgeries, as 'success'. It can be hard not to be pulled into the normative, binary model that says that a 'proper' transition is to move from a full-time male role to a full-time female role or vice versa. That in order to be happy and fulfilled, your client needs to be a 'proper' woman or man. Not only can this be a trap for the practitioner, but it can also be a trap for your clients.

 Exercise

–   How important is it for you that people are either male or female in their gender identity, that they 'pick a side'?

- Does the idea of not settling on a fixed identity cause you anxiety?

- Do you automatically assume that a person in transition must move from one socially accepted gender role to another in order to be happy?

- To what extent do our assumptions about gender get in the way of being with clients as they are?

The processes by which people begin to change their gender identity and performance are many and varied. They might change their name and/or gender pronoun, change important legal documents, make changes to the way in which they dress and speak, and they may start hormone therapy and make surgical changes to their physical appearance. The reasons for these changes and the goals that trans people have for their own transitions are personal and unique. Although many lay people may equate transition with what they see in high-profile celebrity cases such as Caitlyn Jenner or Chelsea Manning, practitioners should not make assumptions about the way in which their clients may or may not transition. The lived experience of trans people is as varied and complicated as any other person, and practitioners should be wary of rushing to 'programme' transition and help clients to move along from one stage to the next.

For some, these linear pathways help to give structure to their experience; for others it's an oppressive and essentialist tyranny. Nevertheless, typically, a person with gender dysphoria will transition in order to make some kind of physical change to their appearance so that it aligns more closely to their felt sense of gendered self. Feelings of dysphoria often begin to lessen for trans people as they transition, although for some people they may never go away completely.

In 1997, Katherine Rachlin identified six stages in the typical transition process as a way of highlighting the importance of the client–therapist relationship in negotiating through these stages. Although arguably still quite linear in its conception, it can be a useful heuristic, as shown below.

Distress and confusion

In this early stage, the client may not be fully aware of why they feel the way they do. They are becoming aware that dissatisfaction with their gender identity may be part of the problem. They are likely to be frightened about what facing up to and accepting a trans identity might mean for them and their existing relationships and family structures.

They may have a history of wearing clothing of a gender different to that assigned at birth or of having fantasies going back many years, and some may have tried intensively to deny or repress these feelings through strong and overt gender performance in the opposite direction. For example, natal males with feelings of gender dysphoria may have entered traditionally orthodox masculine professions such as the army or undertaken intensive body-building regimes as a means of 'making the feelings go away'.

Although there is greater visibility for trans identities now in Western societies like the UK's, many clients will have struggled in silence for years before presenting for help. They may have moved back and forth over the years, experimenting with alternative gender presentations before abandoning them. They may have built up a wardrobe of clothes with which to experiment, only to get rid of them all in a moment of disgust over their own behaviour, so-called 'cyclical purging'.

Often, this ambivalence and struggle is part of the experience of many trans people, and working with clients in this stage of transition may involve working through intensely conflicting thoughts and emotions. As Lev suggests, 'the force of gender-variance awareness can rise up like a tidal wave, threatening the entire foundation of one's life and identity' (2004, p.236).

Implications for therapy

Think about how you can work sensitively with intense feelings that may have been suppressed for many years:

- *Normalising* – One way you can work affirmatively is to normalise questions around gender identity. As your client tells their story, you can reassure them that experience of variance in gender identity and accompanying distress is part of human experience and not evidence that they are disordered or mentally ill.

- *Shame and stigma* – There's more about this in Chapter 13 as well as in another book in this series, *Counselling Skills for Working with Shame* (Sanderson, 2015), but working sensitively with feelings of shame, internalised transphobia, and anger will be a vital part of your work.

- *Containment* – Providing a safe and containing environment is, of course, part of any effective therapeutic encounter. However, the importance of safety and confidentiality for trans clients who may have not talked openly about their feelings and experiences before cannot be overstated.

- *Take it slowly* – Don't rush to completeness and solutions. Allow yourself to sit alongside your client in their confusion and focus on the importance of presence and modelling a way of being that is comfortable with ambivalence. Whatever you do, don't rush your client along the path to transition – now is not the time to make any decisions at all but is instead the time to be with any possible pain and confusion until a narrative starts to emerge.

- *Help them to construct a narrative* – Part of your client's distress may come from the fear of letting go of a gendered self that has been central to their identity so far. For example, if they are no longer female, then how can they be a wife, a mother, a girlfriend, a grandmother? What happens to that self? It is important to help your client to make sense of their experience and for another, different narrative to emerge that more closely reflects who they feel themselves to be.

Self-definition

Part of the process of making sense of the intense feelings at the early stages of transition is to help your client arrive at a more stable and affirmative sense of self. The conflict and distress that comes with navigating the gap between an idealised self whom they feel they should be and the self whom they ultimately find themselves to be should lessen as they begin to construct a coherent narrative.

Self-defining as trans can allow clients to identify with other TGNC people and to reach out for support in the community. This might take the form of reading literature, joining online forums, going to events, or joining a support group. The TGNC support movement has flourished in recent years and, certainly for those trans people living in large towns and cities, there is greater access to support and community than ever before.

By becoming connected through self-definition, trans clients can access familiar stories and share their own stories with others who have had similar experiences. As they do so, some of the feelings of isolation and 'otherness' can recede. Prosser (1998) writes about the vital importance of accessing and creating gender identity narratives for trans people. Given the importance of accessing information – often found online – in the creation of an integrated self, clients can often arrive at therapy far more authoritative and informed than their therapist. If this is the case, then it's vital to allow a safe and respectful space for your client to talk through the process issues that arise from having accessed all of this information.

It may be that they have misunderstood something that they have read, or been misinformed. It may be that they are frightened and anxious – frightened about being refused treatment, or about the treatment being unsuccessful. They may want to talk about new relationships they have formed with others both online and in the real world as they engage with trans networks. They may be in an excited rush to 'get on with it' and push forward with transition without having thought all of the implications through. You can be a vital support to your client at this stage, helping them to look at their decisions, their fantasies about outcomes, and helping to explore alternatives. Helping clients to resist the desire to act impulsively at this stage can make for an easier and more positive transition.

 Remember

Don't feel like you have to be the 'expert' in the room. Remember the person-centred dictum that the client is the expert on their own life.

You do not need to enter a competition with your client about who is the most knowledgeable in order to feel like you can help them. Instead, explore what it is that your client wants or needs from you. Are you simply someone with whom they can explore their knowledge, unpack it, and make sense of it in a safe and non-judgemental space?

Identifying options

In helping clients to take things slowly, you can work with them in order to identify the options that they may have. Your client may or may not have started presenting full time in the gender identity they're seeking transition towards. This full-time social gender role transition has been described as the 'real-life experience' (RLE), which, as the subsection below suggests, continues to be controversial.

Your client may want to explore options around coming out to friends and family members. Often, trans people can feel that they don't have permission to come out in their own families until their children are adults or their parents have died. There can be a sense that certain milestones need to be passed before they are 'allowed' to pursue their own transition. It can therefore be helpful for your clients for you to work through ideas that they may have developed around 'permission' and milestoning with them. Issues around coming out are explored in more detail in Chapter 12.

This may also be when they are engaging with medical services for the first time – for example, speaking to their GP about getting a referral for gender care. A recent report in the USA by the National Gay and Lesbian Taskforce and the National Center for Transgender Equality suggested that '50% of the sample reported having to teach their medical providers about transgender care' (Grant *et al.*, 2010, p.6). Although this describes an American experience, it is likely that many trans people will still encounter well-meaning ignorance in their first contact with the medical profession in primary care. In your work with trans clients, it might be helpful for them to work through and effectively harness the anger that they might feel as a result of being misunderstood and misheard.

What is the 'real-life experience'?

The 'real-life experience' (RLE) describes a requirement that has historically been part of the WPATH SOC.

It describes a length of time in which a person needs to live in their desired gender before becoming eligible for certain treatments. Typically, trans people had to provide proof of the RLE for three months before receiving a prescription for hormones and up to two years before being referred for surgical treatment. The rationale for the RLE was to ensure that nobody would undergo irreversible treatment that they might later regret.

Although earlier versions of WPATH's SOC, such as the sixth version published in 2001, listed a number of criteria that a trans person must fulfil to meet RLE requirements; these criteria have now been removed. The seventh and latest version of the SOC, published in 2011, no longer lists any specific parameters for the RLE. In an apparent effort to move gender care away from a gatekeeping role to a more informed consent model, WPATH emphasise that the SOC are merely clinical guidelines, and are intended to be both flexible and modifiable in order to meet the circumstances of the patient and the preferences and judgement of the clinician.

Acting to make changes

At this stage of transition, your client is likely to be engaging with gender care. Typical treatment pathways for the UK are explored in Chapter 9, and it's likely that, unless your client is seeking completely private treatment, they will be under the care of one of the UK GICs. Not all clients will choose to make body modifications through electrolysis, hormone therapy, or surgeries (the various forms of non-psychological interventions in gender care are explored in full in Chapter 11), but most will want to explore the possibility. At times, trans people can feel that the strong desire for body modification is a necessary part of attracting a diagnosis that will give them access to gender care. It is important that you give your clients space at this time to choose what kinds of interventions are right for them and the pace at which they might want to engage with them.

Increasingly, some trans people are happier in a non-binary gender role. For them, 'successful' body modification is not about taking, for example, a male body and feminising it so that it is 'fully' female. They may be happier to partially feminise some aspects of their male body so as to deliver a more mixed-gender presentation that more accurately reflects their identity. In the past, clinicians have been more reluctant to offer hormonal and surgical interventions unless their patient indicated a willingness to 'go all the way'. With a more flexible framework around gender dysphoria identification and diagnosis, and an informed consent model of patient care, clinicians are now more open to considering a range of ways in which trans people may choose to live.

Once again, in therapeutic work with non-binary clients, it's important to avoid a rush to judgement and conclusions. Part of that process will involve an exercise for you and your supervisor in exploring your own preconceptions around gender and any unconscious processes that you might be bringing to the work. Your clients need to be allowed the space to make sense of their identity without having to fit one of the binary identities that their family, friends, and wider society might prefer for them.

 Exercise

Between 2 June 2010 and 29 November 2012, Juliet Jacques wrote a regular series of blog posts for *The Guardian* newspaper about her journey of transition under the care of the team at the Charing Cross GIC in London:[1]

1	The full series of posts is available at: www.theguardian.com/lifeandstyle/series/ transgender-journey, accessed 06 December 2017.

– What comes up for you as you read these posts?

– Does it help you to get a perspective on an individual's experience of the journey of transition, its ambivalence, and its complications? Although not representative of everyone's experience and, at the time of writing, up to seven years old, there are many points along her journey that might resonate with your own clients.

Coping with the consequences of transition

Although your client may have had a strong and persistent desire to live in a different gender to the one they were assigned at birth, it does not mean that they are prepared for all the consequences of life in that gender role.

One of the big questions that can come up at this stage of transition is what to do about the life that preceded transition. Clients' families may be unsure about what to do with family photos or how to refer to your client pre- and post-transition. Clients themselves may be ambivalent about the options available to them. Some may wish to ritually burn everything that was part of their identity pre-transition, to get rid of any evidence or markers that they were at some time in their lives different from the person whom they now find themselves to be. In Lewins' (1995) stage model of trans identity, for example, the final stage of 'becoming a woman' is 'invisibility'. The argument here is that 'successful' transition is marked by seamless integration within a particular gendered group – what has been referred to colloquially as '**stealth**'.

As with so many aspects of transition, there is no right answer here. The important thing is to help your clients explore what is behind their strong desires. If, for example, they do want to make a clean break with the past, you could help them by exploring what the likely consequences of this move would be for their sense of self, for their family, and for intimate relationships. You might also want to explore ideas of perfectionism and the desire for the transition to be 'perfect' and 'successful'. In doing so, you can work with your client to understand what life would be like for them if the transition were not 'perfect', if, at some point, they were misgendered – what effect would that have on their sense of self and how able would they be to let that experience go, or challenge it in a way that was constructive for them?

An alternative option post-transition is for your client to integrate their pre- and post-transition selves; to acknowledge that there was a time in their lives when they struggled to be authentic. In doing so, they can recognise how far they have come and what they have overcome in that process of transition. Although their past selves do not have to be foregrounded, they can be acknowledged as foundational.

Moving on with a life in which gender identity is not a central issue

This is the last part of Rachlin's (1997) model, and this may be the case for many of your clients. Having engaged with gender care, perhaps over a number of years, they may be happy to let that experience go and to engage with day-to-day life. To live their lives as most other people do, seeking out and maintaining intimate relationships, doing the weekly supermarket shop, socialising with friends, planning holidays, and worrying about paying the bills.

For some people, however, it may be harder to let go of a life in which gender identity is not a central issue. Many clients struggle with having placed a great deal of emphasis on transition. They might have seen the conclusion of transition as the end of any and all problems; that, having transitioned, they would no longer be plagued by doubt, anxiety, or depression. Although transition itself may have significantly reduced or eliminated their feelings of dysphoria, they are just as likely, as we all are, to have periods of low mood, depression, or anxiety. By normalising the idea that people, both trans and cisgender, experience problems in day-to-day living, you can help your clients realise that, although they have reduced their gender dysphoria, this is not some kind of magical solution to all of life's challenges and problems.

Having come to the end of a medical transition, clients can also suffer from a kind of structure hunger and feel that there is still more that they can do. People who struggle in this stage may opt for more elective surgeries in the hope of extending their transition and improving their physical appearance. Working through issues of perfectionism as well as helping clients to manage endings will be important here. Indeed, having spent many years under the care of professionals in gender care, some may find it hard to manage the ending of their time with a GIC. Supporting clients in appropriately moving on from the ending of that relationship and identity as a 'person in transition' will be important in helping them to find a way forward to a life where gender identity is not a central issue. As they do so, some clients may wish to leave the process of transition behind them and move on with day-to-day living. However, others may choose to become part of transgender rights and support groups as a way of using their experiences to help and support others.

WHAT ABOUT DE-TRANSITION?

The process explored above is a helpful way of making sense of a typical transition journey. However, as has been said before, transition journeys are not typically linear and they are likely to be highly idiosyncratic. Although not common, some clients may choose to 'de-transition'. This is more likely to occur early in the process as clients work through feelings of ambivalence and working through the consequences in terms of its impact on their relationships with friends and family and at work.

As explored earlier in this chapter, one of the most important things in working with TGNC clients is to avoid the temptation to rush to closure. Being able to sit with 'not knowing' and to help the client to begin to tolerate greater levels of ambivalence can be the key to working with movements towards and away from social transition and different forms of treatment. It can sometimes take clients a considerable amount of time to make decisions about identity and, for some, it may be a lifelong journey. This is part of the rationale behind the RLE, in that it arguably gives trans people sufficient time to experiment with life in their preferred gender role before making irreversible body modifications.

Sometimes, clients may seek therapeutic support in their desire to de-transition after years of hormone therapies and/or surgeries. Due to the standards of care and the way in which trans people are supported through treatment pathways in the UK, this is likely to be rare, and practitioners working with this population should seek specialist supervision in order to be able to work effectively. Nevertheless, working with feelings of loss, anger, and disillusionment will be important here. It may be that transition did not deliver the 'silver bullet' that they had hoped it might at the outset. Working with those feelings of disappointment and normalising a certain level of distress around day-to-day living (including the loss of relationships and opportunities that they may have had pre-transition) may help these clients to settle more happily in their new identity and to let go of their desire to de-transition and reverse what may have been years of treatments.

11

NON-PSYCHOLOGICAL TREATMENTS AND INTERVENTIONS

The focus of this book is on working therapeutically with issues in gender identity. Nevertheless, in the context of trans identities, it is often the case that a part, if not a significant part, of trans experience will be engagement with non-psychological treatments and interventions, including **gender surgeries**. From a therapeutic point of view, it's about working with the client's relationship with their body – their body now and how they might want their body to be in the future. A great deal of the distress that a TGNC person might feel can come from a sense that their physical self does not properly match their internal sense of self.

There are many forms of non-psychological treatments and interventions that a trans person might consider as part of their transition, but we focus here on four key areas:

- Endocrinology

- Gender surgeries

- Hair removal or augmentation

- Speech and language therapy.

As before, we start this chapter with a caveat or two. Not only do we wish to avoid the assumption of 'born in the wrong body' that reduces trans identities simply to external signifiers such as genitalia, but we also want to assert that all of us have a relationship with our bodies and a desire to change them in different ways and at different times. In that way, we want to be clear that we see issues that trans people face with respect to their bodies as part of a common human condition of body dissatisfaction and not as something 'other' and outside the experience of cisgender people.

Finally, as with most specialist areas of knowledge and practice covered in this book, we do not set out to provide an exhaustive exposition of the areas under consideration. In part, this is because these areas are specialist and complex (as in the case of endocrinology), and, in part, because there are already a number of texts available if the reader wants to get deeper into the subject. As we have said before, therapists and counsellors need to have a 'good enough' working knowledge of the main processes in order to allow them to work knowledgeably and affirmatively with their TGNC clients.

MULTIDISCIPLINARY WORKING

The professional field of gender dysphoria is a multidisciplinary one, ideally with various disciplines working on-site together as in a Gender Identity Clinic, or liaising through a network to provide joined-up care for trans clients. Those professionals who work in isolation can end up leaving clients out on a limb, seeking the care they need themselves to move forward on their treatment pathways. Multidisciplinary ways of working are all the more vital for patient care when you consider the sheer number of professionals who might be involved. Key practitioners working together in providing and endorsing medical interventions for gender reassignment might include endocrinologists, surgeons, psychologists and psychiatrists, speech and language therapists, electrologists and laser hair removal practitioners, psychotherapists and counsellors, social workers, and nurses and GPs.

TREATMENT AS A MEANS OF STRIVING FOR AUTHENTICITY

Gender-related treatments and interventions can all be thought of in the context of facilitating clients in becoming more authentic in the world. This is an aim that is integral to counselling and psychotherapy, and working with TGNC clients is no different in this regard. In fact, striving towards authenticity is central to the process of expressing gender. In the case of trans clients, authenticity means challenging the simple, binary, cisgender, heteronormative assumptions of birth. All of the other disciplines involved in the care of a trans client should be working towards the same aim: helping clients become who they are in the world; not creating someone new, but facilitating *what is* to emerge in the external world outside the self.

Authenticity has been defined as 'the unobstructed operation of one's true, or core, self in one's daily enterprise' (Kernis and Goldman, 2006, p.294). Breaking it down, *action authenticity* refers to the 'feeling that one's outward expression of identity matches one's internal identity', and *relational authenticity* to having our identity recognised by others, reflecting our sense of self (Martinez *et al.*, 2016). *Action authenticity* means that one's actions are a reflection of one's inner self, rather than more a reflection of what others expect of you. *Relational authenticity* relates to the degree to which one's social self is congruent with one's self-concept – how people react to and validate who you think you are. As identity is formed through relationships with others, even at a distance, for example through social media and televised or printed media, rather than in a vacuum, others are central to the formation of a secure self and social identity.

In the context of gender dysphoria, *action authenticity* involves the performance of gender-relevant behaviours consistent with one's inner conceptualisation of gender (West and Zimmerman, 2009). How authentic we want to be varies across individuals, but trans people can often find themselves, at least at some stage in their lives, being authentic in one or more domains and 'performing gender' in a way that's so inauthentic in others that it inhibits their ability to really feel connected to others.

If authentic living includes *relational authenticity*, *action authenticity*, and *dispositional authenticity* – the consistency of authentic traits across contexts (Wood *et al.*, 2008) – then reflect for a few minutes on how challenging being authentic is when one is not supported by cisgender heteronormative privilege and discourse. The price of not being authentic can be increased self-alienation, and it's not surprising that there may be confusion or ambivalence initially for some trans clients around the psychological and non-psychological interventions that they do or do not desire and how these may affect their sense of who they are and want to be in the world.

 Remember

Both yourself and your client may have assumptions about the 'rightness' of different treatments and interventions. It can be helpful for you both to take a pause in your work and consider any planned or discussed treatment through the lens of how it might help the client to increase relational, action, or dispositional authenticity in their everyday lives.

ENDOCRINOLOGY

Hormone therapies for changing the sex characteristics are prescribed by a medical practitioner, generally in shared care with a gender specialist (if they are not already one themselves), or with the involvement of a specialist endocrinologist or specialist prescribing practitioner. The involvement of particular specialist clinicians can depend on the complexity of the client's medical, psychological, and social history.

Simplifying the process for the sake of clarity of understanding, there are broadly two kinds of hormones that might be prescribed:

- *Hormone blockers* – These are drugs that act to suppress the hormones that are currently being expressed. For example, in a natal male, a hormone blocker will act to suppress the production and expression of testosterone.

- *Cross-sex hormones* – These are the hormones of the gender to which the person wishes to transition. For example, in a natal female who wishes to transition to a male gender identity or to masculinise some aspects of their presentation (such as facial hair) as part of a non-binary or other identity, testosterone may be prescribed in addition to hormone blockers.

It is important for the therapist to be aware of the differences between these two kinds of hormone treatment, since different meanings are likely to be made of the treatments by your client. In the case of hormone blockers, clients might describe their experience as one that silences or eradicates a part of the self previously felt to be problematic. For example, a trans woman might talk about the pleasure that she feels at finally not being able to feel the pernicious masculinising effects of testosterone. In contrast, she might welcome oestrogen as a somewhat beneficent treatment that is helping her to become more authentic and finally allowing her to feel and appear more feminine.

The initiation of hormone therapies to treat gender dysphoria would be expected to have specialist psychological endorsement as to its likely benefit or potential harm for the client, following detailed assessment and discussion with the client as part of the consenting process. It is not appropriate in this book to give a detailed explanation of the endocrine system, specific prescriptions, or the risks and detailed effects of hormone therapy for masculinisation or feminisation. Psychologists who carry out specialist assessments for psychological endorsement of these hormone therapies would, however, be expected to be at a sufficiently senior grade, know these, and have trained through observation and in supervised consultations to reach a level of skills and experience in order to conduct such assessments.

Clearly, one of the principal goals of hormone therapy is to change the body of the person away from their birth gender towards the gender that which more accurately matches their internal, felt sense of gender identity. For a trans person, this might mean, for example, moving fully away from a male body towards as fully feminine a body as possible. For a non-binary person, the goal may be less clear and may be more about decreasing some of the more obviously masculine body traits without needing to make the body clearly feminine. Although we do not intend to explore all the effects of hormone therapies here, there are several significant ones that are worth exploring since they are likely to form part of the content of therapy with a trans person, especially if they are starting on hormones for the first time.

Case vignette: Ali

Ali is a non-binary individual who was natally assigned female. They have established themselves well in a non-binary social gender role at home with friends and family and at work. They are distressed, though, because, socially, outside the people whom they know, they keep being misgendered as female. Ali is now considering starting testosterone therapy but wants to explore whether this would be the right decision. They know a lot about the effects of testosterone, including those that are irreversible, and it worries them that they may end up being misgendered as male instead. They don't know exactly how they might feel about that, but think that it has to be better than being perceived as female.

 ### Reflection

The initial response for a non-specialist therapist to this might be that they don't know enough about the medical side so as to be able to help Ali. However, many trans people have found it beneficial to talk about gender and gender reassignment treatments in their non-specialist counselling in order to clarify for themselves what they would like and the implications of the different options available to them.

By suppressing birth sex attributes and potentially introducing cross-sex hormones, there is a clear effect on the sexual functioning of the person and, by extension, their ability to procreate. As such, reproductive issues and the fertility implications of treatment should always be discussed before starting hormone therapy. It is likely that this will be thoroughly covered by the prescribing practitioner, but it is worth checking out with your client what they feel about the possible effects on reproduction and working through the potential loss of that functioning as part of their transition.

In addition to impacts on reproductive capacity, hormone suppressants and cross-sex hormones can have a range of physical effects for your client. Although these effects may be obvious and welcomed by your client, it's important to explore the meanings that the trans person makes of these changes, how they feel in themselves, and what kinds of messages they get back from others about how their identity is being read and interpreted in social situations and in intimate relationships.

The effects of testosterone therapy for masculinisation can include, but not exclusively, the voice deepening, increased muscle mass, facial hair growth, increased body hair, redistribution of body fat, clitoral enlargement, increased libido, androgenic hair loss, and irritability. Feminising hormone therapy (oestrogen treatment), again not exclusively, can result in the redistribution of body fat to create a more feminine shape, refinement of facial skin, breast development, reduced muscle mass, reduced libido, suppression of erectile function, and shrinkage of genital material. If your client is having testosterone suppressed with a hormone blocker as well, then these effects are likely to be more pronounced.

 Remember

If your client is buying hormones on the Internet and using them without adequate medical supervision, then they are putting their health at risk. You may want to explore ways in which they might receive hormones under supervision so that any possible side effects can be measured, monitored, and dealt with by a qualified professional.

The emotional impact of hormone therapies

Clients will generally reflect at length on how endocrine treatment might affect them physically, their sense of self, their psychological and physical well-being, their relationships and families, their careers, work, and much more, in fact their whole lives, before committing to this significant and life-changing stage of gender reassignment treatment. They need to make sure that they have realistic expectations of the effects of treatment and the timescale for these and not overestimate how much endocrine treatment will facilitate a gender role transition.

Not everyone is dysphoric around the same parts of the body, and this needs to be factored in, rather than making automatic assumptions about what trans people might want. For example, anecdotal evidence from clinical practice would suggest that an increasing number of trans women are happy to use their penis for sexual relations without feeling uncomfortably 'masculine' about doing so, whereas many others wouldn't dream of it. The former group may not want their erectile function suppressed or intend genital reconstructive surgery, and their hormone treatment will need to take this into account. A more personalised regime may not include suppression of testosterone through hormone blockers in order that erectile function and sexual enjoyment of the penis is not compromised as much as it would otherwise be with an optimal female range level of testosterone, even if the feminisation effects are reduced as a consequence.

The impact of hormone therapy on expressions of sexuality are often particularly relevant for more in-depth discussion when clients are in existing valued intimate relationships that may be adversely affected by their gender treatment. The therapist can then usefully help clients and their significant others to negotiate with each other through the challenges of gender reassignment, where the parties concerned want to retain the relationship. In working in this informed and affirmative way, we become ever more aware that there is no such thing as a single pathway through transition, and different clients will have different needs and expectations of effects of interventions such as hormone treatment. Indeed, as it is their own body, they are likely to come to the therapeutic encounter with far more detailed information than the practitioner will possess. What is important here is not to be an expert on hormone treatment per se, but to be the one person who is willing to collaboratively and non-judgementally unpack the emotional impacts of the choices that the trans person might be wrestling with around treatment.

Case vignette: Alex

Alex, age 40, who was natally assigned male but has a female gender identity, would like to make a social gender role transition to female and go through gender reassignment treatment. She has come for counselling so as to discuss how she can do this without compromising the life that she has built up for herself over many years and that she shares with her girlfriend. Over the course of a year, she chooses to go on low-dosage oestrogen therapy, which gives her some physical feminisation, but she chooses not to increase this to optimal feminising levels for her or to suppress testosterone. If she were single, she says that she probably would elect for an optimised hormone regime for feminisation but she does not want to compromise her active sex life with her girlfriend as it is. She is not distressed by using her genitalia in this way and is not planning genital surgery. Alex completes her gender treatment at this stage, having transitioned fully to a female social gender role.

 Reflection

–   What assumptions and potential judgements might Alex's therapist have to put aside in order to work with Alex towards what she wants?

Possible challenges in prescription and administration

We mentioned earlier that gender care is a multidisciplinary field involving the intersection and cooperation of a number of different healthcare professionals. Although the prescribing professional for hormone treatment will be a specialist endocrinologist or specialist prescribing practitioner, these clinicians typically rely on a local GP for ongoing and shared care. The local GP may be requested to supply repeat prescriptions for patients or, indeed, to administer certain treatments. For example, hormone blockers and testosterone injections might need to be administered at a local surgery.

However, some of the drugs might be being used in a way that is unfamiliar to the GP; for example, a typical GnRH analogue (hormone blocker) is more commonly used as a treatment for prostate cancer. In these circumstances, it is not unusual for GPs to question treatment, delay repeat prescriptions, or refer back to specialist gender care providers such as GICs. The reasons for this are varied and, although often felt by patients to be evidence of transphobic views, may very well be to do with a lack of confidence on behalf of the GP in providing appropriate care. In these circumstances, not only can you support your client in working through their feelings of confusion and anger but you can also help to advocate with them and for them in accessing the care that they need and are entitled to.

GENDER SURGERIES

General public discourse around trans identities, often encouraged by the media, can tend to have an unnecessarily prurient obsession with how trans people might choose to make changes to their bodies through surgery. Most members of the public are not aware of the importance and impacts of hormone treatments and instead can demand to know whether a person is a 'full transsexual' by having gone through surgeries which the cisgender, heteronormative majority might see as the 'natural', teleological end point of a person's transition.

However, just like endocrine treatment and other physical interventions, not all trans people want surgeries and many are content to live as they have been bodied from birth. As with so much of what we have talked about in this book, we encourage practitioners to be aware that each person will have a different relationship to their gender identity and how it is expressed and embodied. Do not automatically assume that all trans people will want to undergo all surgeries or, indeed, that they will want to do so all in one go. For those who do want gender-related surgeries, the following describe the most common.

Trans men

Trans men will often prioritise having testosterone therapy and chest surgery, as these produce effects that are more immediately socially visible and aid day-to-day living in their reassigned gender role. Chest surgery, often called '**top surgery**', is technically referred to as *bilateral mastectomy with male chest reconstruction*. Prior to surgery, a number of clients are likely to have bound their breasts in order to reduce their likelihood of automatically being gendered as female in social spaces. For many natal women with larger breasts that can't simply be hidden by using layers of looser clothing, a binder can help to flatten chests and give them the appearance of a male chest.

Binding, although helpful in the short term, can be extremely uncomfortable, causing difficulty in breathing, back pain, and bruising to the ribs. Although clinicians and surgeons might sensitively talk through the physical aspects and impacts of chest surgery, you may be one of the few people whom your client can talk to in order to unpack the emotional aspects of surgery. Clients may have to wait a considerable amount of time for referral for top surgery and then for a surgical date. Helping them to process feelings of helplessness and anger can be a key part of being with your client through the process of transition.

 Remember

As always, language is important when working with trans clients. It is likely that trans male clients will want to avoid using strongly gendered words when referring to their own bodies. As such, it can be helpful to refer to a client's chest rather than their breasts. It not only involves a more neutral tone but it also uses the language of masculine gender identity, since men typically refer to their 'chest' rather than their 'breasts'.

Many trans men do not go on to have genital surgeries, often referred to as '**lower surgery**', since the surgical outcomes for trans men in this area can be less positive than for trans women. Many prefer to meet their sexual and relational needs in different ways, such as using strap-ons or letting go of the need to have penetrative sex with a partner. Should your client wish to proceed with genital surgeries, there are a number of options that they might consider with a specialist surgical team. As we have said before, you do not need to be a medical expert in order to help your client work through the process issues relating to surgery, but you need to be familiar enough with some of the main procedures. There is literature available should the reader want to find out more about specific procedures and their impacts:

- phalloplasty (creation of a phallus)

- metoidioplasty (creation of a micropenis)

- urethroplasty (creation of the urethra)

- scrotoplasty (creation of a scrotum and placement of testicular prosthesis)

- implantation of penile prosthesis

- vaginectomy (removal of vagina)

- salpingo-oophrectomy (removal of ovaries and fallopian tubes) and hysterectomy (removal of the uterus).

Trans women

As with trans men, trans women may consider a range of surgeries that alters the appearance of their chest to create breasts as well as a range of genital surgeries to change their body so that it more authentically reflects their sense of self. Once again, there is no single right answer here, and different clients will choose different paths in their approach to surgeries.

Clients may not necessarily choose to have genital reconstructive surgery, which includes a neo-vagina. Another option is to have cosmetic vulvoplasty, which involves penectomy, orchidectomy, labioplasty, and clitoroplasty. This can better suit those trans women who don't require the vagina in order to feel identified as a woman and comfortable with their bodies, nor for sexual purposes or where the risk of creating it is not acceptable to the client or the surgeon. It is a very individual choice to make, and specialist clinicians will no doubt explain the procedures and risks to your client from a medical point of view. However, it can be useful for you to offer a separate and safe space in therapy so as to explore the pros and cons of the available options. Surgeries for trans women include:

- **augmentation mammoplasty** (breast augmentation)

- penectomy (removal of penis)

- orchidectomy (removal of testes)

- vaginoplasty (construction of neovagina)

- labioplasty (construction of labia)

- clitoroplasty (creation of clitoris)

- thyroid chondroplasty ('Adam's apple' reduced)

- cricothyroid approximation (vocal cord surgery)

- facial feminising surgery (various surgical procedures as desired, which can include: rhinoplasty, blepharoplasty, genioplasty, brow-contouring, hairline-lowering, brow-lifting, cheek augmentation, and jaw-reshaping).

All of this technical and medical terminology can perhaps appear daunting at first – both for you and for your client. However, it is important to be able to engage in a familiar and comfortable way with the language of surgery in order to be able to provide a containing and professional space for exploration.

Case vignette: Jon

Jon is 20 years old and has been living as a man since leaving school two years ago. He is accepted by friends and family in a social male role and they use his male name, pronouns, and title. He is now at university and his peers and tutors also treat him as male, but he finds it very frustrating that strangers often misgender him as female, which leaves him having to choose not to say anything or challenging the misgendering and risking a conversation and intrusion into his personal affairs that he would rather avoid. He has just started taking testosterone therapy and has sought counselling to support him through the process of change and to help him manage social situations better than he feels he is doing currently.

Reflection

What are the key issues likely to be here for Jon, and how can the therapist best support and facilitate him in negotiating these?

Surgical outcomes

The therapist can play an important role in helping to prepare clients for surgery as they navigate through the choices available and manage the feelings that come up as they move through the clinical process of referral, approval, and the final surgeries themselves. As with all aspects of transition, there is also an important role that mental health professionals play in working with the client over their feelings in relation to surgical outcomes.

Some trans people can invest a great deal of importance in surgeries, seeing it as the final step in confirmation of their identity in an embodied way. However, surgical outcomes for any kind of procedure are not guaranteed, and this can be even more the case with respect to some of the complex genito-urinary procedures undertaken with trans patients. In the event of the outcome not being what was expected, you can play a vital role in helping your client to deal with and process the disappointment and anger that comes with the loss of a body or a self that was imagined and hoped for. Given the uncertainty of many surgical outcomes, helping to prepare your client for a variety of outcomes right from the outset can make processing surgical outcomes easier.

Indeed, some trans clients experience ongoing, chronic pain after surgery and may attempt further surgeries in order to rectify suboptimal outcomes. Just as with any cis person managing chronic pain on a day-to-day basis, mindfulness-based techniques can be helpfully explored. Originally developed by Jon Kabat-Zinn and his colleagues at the MIT-based Stress Reduction and Relaxation Program, mindfulness has proven to be an effective technique for helping not only with pain, but also with self-compassion and self-acceptance (see Hilton *et al.*, 2017).

Remember

Assume nothing and be open to the experience and feelings of the client. It is important to provide a therapeutic space where clients can raise issues without feeling that they will be judged for not making a 'successful' gender role transition by so doing.

Non-binary people

The variance in non-binary presentation and appearance and the motivations for change are discussed in more detail in Chapter 7; however, non-binary individuals may elect for the same surgical interventions as more binary gendered people, or adapted versions, but possibly motivated towards a different personal and social outcome. They may want to appear less male or female in their appearance towards an androgynous ideal, or perhaps to masculinise or feminise it more to reduce being misgendered as their natally assigned gender. For example, some non-binary individuals natally assigned female may identify as non-binary **transmasculine** and may look quite male or androgynous-to-male in their appearance.

It can take longer for non-binary people to access the surgeries they want, as the clinical literature and experience to support these interventions do not exist in the same degree or over the significant length of time as does that for their more binary counterparts. This is likely to change, and, indeed, already is changing, as treatment of non-binary people becomes increasingly mainstream in gender clinics and clinicians' experience in this area grows with seemingly positive treatment outcomes, with hopefully the clinical research to follow. Until more longer-term evaluation of the efficacy of this treatment is available, though, it may still feel more challenging for non-binary people when trying to access treatments quickly. As explored in Chapter 7, modelling an acceptance of 'not knowing' and helping your client to be able to sit with uncertainty can be helpful in working through the issues related to accessing both hormonal and surgical treatments with non-binary clients.

Cisgender people

It's important to acknowledge that the non-psychological treatments and surgeries we have explored above are not just available to trans people, but are also sought by cisgender men and women, and often also for gender-related reasons. They might elect for them to reinforce their social presentations as men and women, reduce personal insecurities, reduce the visible physical effects of ageing, or to better meet a socially constructed ideal representation of what it means to be a man or a woman. This might range from common surgeries to the face, breasts, and chest to cisgender men requesting phalloplasty after losing their genitalia in an accident or military situation and cisgender women electing to have vaginal and labial surgeries for various reasons.

Recognising that all people, regardless of their gender identities, seek plastic surgeries can help to normalise procedures, not only for clients but also in the minds of cisgender practitioners, who may automatically see hormonal and surgical interventions as something outside the norm or something that only TGNC people seek.

 Exercise

Think about your own primary and secondary sex characteristics, whether you identify as cisgender or have a trans identity, and the relation between them and your gender identity:

– How important are your genitalia to your gender identity?

– What role does your chest or do your breasts play in communicating your gender socially, and how important is it in sexual relationships or encounters where they feel or appear to others as discordant with your gender identity, social gender presentation, and role?

HAIR REMOVAL OR AUGMENTATION
Hair holds a significant and very gendered place in most societies, whether it appears facially, on the body, or on the head. Hair on the head is often styled in gendered ways, at different lengths, and has in itself been frequently gendered, with haircuts being described as 'masculine' or 'feminine'. Rarely has a haircut been depicted as truly androgynous, even if it can be worn by any gender. It can seem impossible to escape gender in haircuts, since even if gender is not explicitly referenced, we can be told that the hairstyle 'suits' certain faces rather than others. Moreover, hair salons will generally have books of 'male' and 'female' haircuts, with an assumed association between hair preferences and wanting to fit social gender stereotypes to appear more socially attractive as that gender.

Trans women
Androgenic hair loss (sometimes referred to as 'male-pattern baldness') is seen as an undesirable development for men, but is far more negatively framed for women. This leaves many trans women feeling insecure about their presentations and reliant on wigs and expensive treatments to help fit social expectations in a way that can significantly impair their confidence in being in the world as women.

Similarly, the presence of facial hair, whilst enhancing the social masculinity of a **trans man**, can feel fundamentally undermining of femininity for trans women. Many cis women themselves can have visible facial hair, often influenced by ethnic origin, age, and specific medical conditions such as polycystic ovarian syndrome. Whilst often embarrassed by it, cis women can seek treatments without their social and personal identity as women being challenged in the same way. Facial hair distribution in these cases is generally not the same as for natal males, and even when it is, and quite significantly so, they are likely to still be categorised as women. For trans women, having facial hair can be experienced and even socially perceived as 'falling short', a 'failure' in the performance of womanhood.

Although cis women regularly remove body hair in the West by shaving their legs and armpits and undergoing any number of beauty treatments such as waxing, sugaring, and threading, the removal of facial and body hair is a defining issue for many, if not all, trans women. Even when their testosterone is suppressed within the female range as part of hormonal therapies, trans women can still have a density and distribution of facial and body hair that causes great distress.

Once again, helping your client to work through the feelings that accompany not only their relationship to their own body hair distribution but also the challenges that come with its removal can be an important part of the therapeutic work.

Trans men

Trans men may want facial hair as an expression of their masculinity, but, as discussed earlier, many individuals are on a gender spectrum and some prefer a smooth face and a more androgynous or non-binary appearance. Therapists should never assume their client's preferences, but instead should acquire a good understanding of the individual's gender identity (without making initial binary assumptions based on appearance) and preferred social gender role and presentation. Trans men and those on the more masculine end of the gender spectrum may embrace body hair developing, especially with the prescription of testosterone therapy as a sign of the body becoming more masculine and of them moving more towards becoming and being seen as male bodied.

Exercise

Consider a range of different external markers of your own gender identity:

- How easy is it for you to deconstruct social representations of men as having a deep voice and beard and of women having smooth, hairless skin?

- How do you think it would feel to have a change in the pitch and resonance of your voice such that you were frequently incorrectly gendered?

- How are we all subject to messages (both subtle and overt) towards normative gender presentation?

- How does gender affect our experience of hair on our faces, bodies, and genitalia and the social meaning in the societies within which we live?

SPEECH AND LANGUAGE THERAPY

The way in which we speak and the sound of our voice is an integral part of our interaction with others and how we present to the world. It cues others into our gender, age, class, and so on. In general, as with many other aspects of external signifiers of gender – the voice is often given little conscious thought for those who are cisgender. For trans individuals, though, the voice can miscommunicate who they are and cue people into hearing and seeing an incorrect gender, it can be a liability. Yet, nevertheless, the voice, for most people, has to be employed on a daily basis. The voice therefore raises issues around authenticity as well as concerns that changing it may fundamentally alter who we are and how we are known, to something unknown and other.

Speech and language therapy can be effective in helping a trans person to alter their voice such that it becomes more congruent with their expressed gender identity. The therapy relies on considerable motivation, practice, and commitment on the client's part and is not always easy to maintain, particularly for those individuals who may be avoiding talking around others who are less known to them in order to avoid questioning or feared ridicule.

Moreover, there is not really a social understanding of what constitutes a 'trans voice'. Built on binary, cisgender norms, the general expectation of the public is that it is or will be closer to that expected of the other gender than to the presenting one. Trans men are assumed to be aiming towards a 'male voice' and trans women towards a 'female voice', with often a limited understanding of what constitutes each, except that we tend to attribute gender, age, class, and other characteristics when we hear a voice, without giving it much thought.

Often, visual cues can help a trans person to avoid being misgendered as part of a social interaction. Many trans people will say that they tend not to get misgendered if someone is looking at them but that it can be more likely on the phone. This would suggest that visual cues are more dominant than the auditory cues in the way in which we attribute a gender to a person in social interactions. For someone who is non-binary, voice presentation might again be part of moving away from an immediately identifiable pitch or tone that can be attributed to one or other of the gender binaries.

 Exercise

Consider how gendered your expectations of voices might be:

- What do you think men and women should sound like and have you questioned your assumptions in this area?

- In thinking about a non-binary individual, can you conceptualise a 'non-binary voice' or is it only possible to think in terms of masculinity and femininity such that those who are outside the gender binary are positioned in a space of ambiguity at best?

Clients can be referred to speech and language therapy in the UK through their GP or a gender identity clinic in-house, or they can self-refer privately. The majority of speech and language therapists will not have been trained in trans voice therapy, but there are specialist practitioners who, as well as providing this service themselves, supervise and train their speech and language therapy colleagues in also working effectively with trans clients. Most people tend to think of pitch and frequency when wanting to modify their voice in order to be more congruent with who they are genderwise, but other areas amenable to intervention include resonance, articulation, rate, volume, language use, and non-verbal communication (Azul, 2015).

It can be helpful for you to affirm with your clients that their voice can, indeed, be authentically masculinised, feminised, and neutralised through professional exercises to change pitch, resonance, and intonation.

Mills and Stoneham (2017) provide a helpful and practical text for understanding and addressing the problems that transgender people encounter with their voices.

12

COMING OUT, ACCEPTANCE, AND CISGENDER PRIVILEGE

Coming out is often seen in popular culture as a simple, linear process, a movement from keeping an aspect of identity hidden to making it publicly known. However, as we have seen with transition in Chapter 10, we should be wary of jumping too quickly to the conclusion that coming out is always and automatically a stepping away from being inauthentic and closeted to being authentic and well adjusted.

We identified in Chapter 10 that 'knowing' the self is part of a confessional-inspired truth-telling about identity, rooted in the Christian dictums that have so strongly influenced Western culture and society. With heterosexuality and cisgender identity constructed as clear, stable identities, the appeal to minorities is to 'come out' and so occupy a complementary opposite identity. In doing so, the normative, orthodox discourse not only produces a binary 'thing-ness' (Sedgwick, 1990) out of difference – heterosexuality vs homosexuality, cisgender vs transgender – but it also continues to support the unexamined 'truth' about itself that it is, indeed, immutable, strong, and stable.

If instead we agree with the Butlerian assertion (Butler, 2006) that gender identity is something contingent and performative, then we can question ideas of fixity and stability and trouble the notion that coming out is always the teleological end point of an experience of greater and greater enlightenment and clarity about identity. The enlightenment ideals within staged models of identity development (and transition for that matter) can often get us tied up in yet another binary notion that somehow being 'in' is always bad and that being 'out' is always desirable, good, and healthy.

As we explore questions of coming out, acceptance, and cisgender privilege in this chapter and outline typical processes and implications, we encourage the reader to, yet again, be wary of rushing to judgement about coming out and making automatic assumptions about its benefits everywhere and for all people. As Rasmussen points out when exploring the process of coming out in the context of sexuality:

> ...people's ability to continuously negotiate their identity is necessarily mediated by varying circulations of power relating to age, family background, economic position, and race. The dominance of coming out discourses...belies the idea that coming out is not necessarily an option, or a desired objective, of all people who are non-heterosexual identified. (2004, p.147)

WHAT IS COMING OUT?

At its most basic and obvious, coming out is about revealing a previously hidden aspect of one's identity either to oneself, or more commonly to others. It is part of a process by which people with non-conforming identities bring them into public discourse and, as such, it's something that cisgender, heterosexual people don't tend to have to do. They are never asked the question 'When did you first realise you were straight?' or 'How do your parents feel about you being cis?'

As Israel and Tarver point out, 'perhaps the most significant mental health and social support issue faced by transgendered individuals revolves around the disclosure of one's transgendered status and needs to others' (1997, p.182). Coming out is a process that's often wrought with fear, primarily the fear of ridicule and rejection – precisely the means by which we have seen that gender conformity is produced and policed in society, from childhood onwards. To act counter-culturally brings with it the threat of isolation and a kind of social annihilation. As Lev (2004, p.248) suggests, 'fear and avoidance are the flip side of anger and resistance' and, more than anything else, coming out, and managing the relational fallout of coming out, is at the heart of much of the therapeutic work with TGNC people.

 Exercise

National Coming Out Day

The Human Rights Campaign (hrc.org) celebrates National Coming Out Day every year in October. They celebrate coming out as lesbian, gay, bisexual, transgender, queer (LGBTQ), or as an ally, and 2016 saw the 28th anniversary of the event.

Go to www.hrc.org/resources/national-coming-out-day (accessed 06 December 2017) and explore some of the resources that they have made available, including videos as well as *The Transgender Visibility Guide: A Guide to Being You*. Although the site and contents speak from an American perspective, similar resources can be found at www.stonewall.org.uk/your-coming-out-stories (accessed 06 December 2017) with a UK voice.

Trans and other non-conforming people can be in a double bind when thinking about coming out. Like all of us, they seek intimacy with others and want to be authentic with the people they love. However, by being authentic, they fear that they may lose the very love and intimacy that they seek. In a Rogerian sense, they're bound by very strongly felt 'conditions of worth' as they struggle to find the courage to express themselves authentically. That's why it is so important to understand the vacillation that accompanies much of trans people's experiences of coming out. This blowing hot and cold on their trans identity should not be seen as evidence supporting an assertion that they are not really trans, but rather an expression of their fear of the loss that coming out might occasion.

There can also be a disconnect in timing. For the trans person, their coming out represents the end of a long process of internal struggle and conflict, seeking support, and resourcing themselves with knowledge. For the person they're coming out to, this may be the very first time that they have considered this reality, and their apparent unwillingness to accept or process the information may well be partly to do with an adjustment lag. Indeed, it is often argued that the very lack of visibility of trans people (and gay people before them) feeds into a narrative that difference is shocking and something that straight/cis people can legitimately demand time to adjust to.

That is why coming out is so often framed as a political act. Harvey Milk, the civil and gay rights campaigner in San Francisco in the 1970s, famously challenged gay people to come out as an act of self-affirmation and also to challenge the straight-cis view that gay people (and others who don't conform) are somehow a tiny and exotic minority rather than part of a panoply of difference that exists in human experience and identity:

Gay brothers and sisters, what are *you* going to do about it? You must come out. Come out to your parents, your relatives. I know that it is hard and that it will hurt them, but think about how they will hurt you in the voting booth! Come out to your friends, if indeed they are your friends. Come out to your neighbors, to your co-workers, to the people who work where you eat and shop. Come out only to the people you know and who know you. Not to anyone else. But once and for all, break down the myths; destroy the lies and distortions for your own sake, for their sake, for the sake of the youngsters who are being terrified by the votes from Dade County to Eugene. If [conservative politician John] Briggs wins he will not stop. They never do. Like all mad people, they are forced to go on, to prove they were right. There will be no safe closet for any Gay person. So break out of yours today; tear the damn thing down once and for all! (Milk, 2013, p.219)

COMING OUT AND BINARIES

There is something about the phenomenon of coming out that is both produced by and helps reinforce binary ways of thinking and the modernist, positivist idea of the bounded self. By constructing identity as either 'in' or 'out', as 'public self' versus 'private self', a black-and-white discourse of polar opposites is produced. It suggests that boundaries are clear and simple and that there is no porosity to those boundaries. Be aware as you work with clients and their idea of themselves and either 'out' or 'not out' that things may be more complex than this binary construction might suggest. They may imagine that they are not out, but, in fact, others may know or suspect, or they might assume that people are aware of their identity and resist the idea that somehow it is their responsibility to tell them or affirm their identity. Indeed, it may be a cis person's sense of their 'right to know' and to be formally told that might be causing conflict and aggravation in relationships.

LANGUAGE AND COMING OUT

Language can be seen as a vital part of how we come to know truths about ourselves and our identities. When we come out, we have to do so by describing ourselves to others, and choosing those words can be an empowering act for many; to choose how to name yourself rather than to be named by others. Klein *et al.* (2015) researched young LGBTQ people's coming out stories and found that language and labelling was an important issue for most of their participants. One of their trans participants, Brianna, highlighted an interesting intersection on coming out and how this also highlights the identity of the person to whom they're coming out:

> I came to a discussion online about the term 'cisgender' a couple of weeks ago, apparently a few members of this online community objected to being labelled as cisgender. And all the trans people in the discussion were sort of smashing their heads in and going 'What's the reason to object to the word cisgender?' I mean, it's a fairly neutral term, what's wrong with it? And in the end, the decision that the community arrived at was that the problem with the word cisgender was that it was labelling people who preferred themselves to be non-labelled. That they considered themselves 'normal'. And that to be labelled as cisgender sort of makes that 'normal' less concrete. *Brianna*. (Klein *et al.*, 2015, p.316)

As we have seen elsewhere in this book, mainstream society often wants to problematise difference and to locate questions of identity and the labels that they attract only in those people who are not mainstream. A core part of mainstream identity can therefore be seen as not having an identity. Straight people do not see themselves as having a sexuality, cis people do not see themselves as having a gender identity, and White people do not see themselves as having a racial identity. Time spent considering our own privilege as members of a majority group is therefore at the heart of effective affirmative practice with TGNC people.

BEING OUTED

So much of coming out is tied up with power relations – the way in which power is exchanged and transacted between people in social interactions. Sedgwick (1990) writes from a feminist perspective about the closet and how power operates through it. The subject is 'inside', having been placed there by discourse that suggests that difference should be hidden in order to be accepted. But, as if in a Kafkaesque drama, they do not know whether they have been successful in keeping their identity hidden or whether those who compel them to hide are aware that they are hiding and gratified by the power they hold to enforce the hiding as well as by the knowledge they have that the subject is hiding. The famous US military policy of 'Don't Ask; Don't Tell', enforced from 1994 to 2011, was based on this dynamic, and once again has become an issue today.

All of this tortuous negotiation of knowledge and power opens up the possibility that a hidden identity may therefore be revealed without the subject's permission. This game of hide-and-seek is at the heart of bullying and is also the implied threat that underlies the policing of orthodox gender performance (see Beattie and Evans, 2011).

Outings of public figures have been a staple of the more salacious tabloid press for generations, and their effects continue to be felt by trans people today. The significant personal and social impact of being outed has been recognised in recent legislation and is behind the protection of confidentiality in trans identities in the Gender Recognition Act 2004 as explored earlier in Chapter 9.

From a therapeutic perspective, using a staged model of identity, outing can mean that individuals are forced into disclosure before having had the chance to work through earlier stages of awareness, acceptance, and accessing resources. Clients who have been outed before they are ready to deal with the implications of living as an out trans person are likely to need support in working through intense feelings of anger, resentment, shame, and powerlessness.

THE EFFECTS OF COMING OUT

For many trans people, an initial coming out is the end point of considerable soul-searching and internal conflict. It can therefore be experienced as a huge relief and release from tension. Even if the initial response from a family member, partner, or friend is not as positive as they might have wished it to be, it is, at least, 'out there'.

As Plummer suggests, coming out stories 'show the speaker moving out of this world of shadows, secrecy and silence – where feelings and pains had to be kept to oneself and where tremendous guilt, shame, and hidden pathology was omnipresent – into a world which is more positive, public and supportive' (1995, p.50). Talking about identity and authoring identity allows a narrative to be created over which the subject has some control. Although they are always drawing from culture for analogies that imperfectly reflect their own experience, their efforts to author their own story can give them a greater sense of ownership over their identity and how it's put out there in the world.

Coming out stories also form a central part of the LGBTQ narrative – both in literature, films, and culture as well as more recently in blogs, YouTube videos, and other forms of social media. In telling their stories, trans people have the opportunity not only to 'try on' identities but also to make connections with others. Bohan and Russell (1999) centralise the importance of narrative and myth-building as a transformative way of organising experience and building identity. Telling stories is a universal experience, but for those whose identities have been erased, marginalised, or invalidated, having a space in which to create them can be transformative. The power of authoring and re-authoring narratives of the self is borne out and explored by the many social constructionist and narrative therapists (see Gergen, 1991; White, 1995; White and Epston, 1990). They challenge the modernist view that problems in living reside within a bounded, agentic self and instead promote the value of externalising, taking the problem outside of the client and seeing it as socially produced and thereby to be socially solved. As Gergen argues, 'in the therapeutic setting and beyond, we find autobiography is anything but autonomous; it is more sociobiography' (1991, p.164). This only serves to highlight the importance of the therapist not merely as some kind of passive, objective observer but instead as an active participant in the co-creation of a new narrative in opposition to an historical 'truth' about the client in which they were the suffering subject.

COMING OUT AS TRANS

Although there are many similarities in the coming out experiences of LGBTQ people, the process for trans people has some specific differences. The act of coming out can be experienced as a profound release of pressure and tension, like taking the lid off a bottle of fizzy water or champagne. Having repressed parts of themselves for so long, trans people can then want to move forward with their transition at far greater speed than their spouses or close family may counsel. As we have seen, this may be in part due to a lag in processing, but may also be (and be experienced by the trans person as) a move by others to slow, stop, or change the mind of their partner or family member.

Coming out and transitioning can sometimes be felt as a kind of adolescence. Emotions are often just as intense as for a typical teenager, with bouts of manic positivity contrasted with periods of depression, low mood, and disengagement. The seesaw between impulsivity and lassitude, between showing off and hiding, can be extremely wearing for the trans person themselves as well as for their close friends and family. This polarisation of emotion and behaviour may, in part, be due to the experience of having repressed identity for so long, but there is also a hormonal element. In a very real sense, hormone treatment with blockers or cross-sex hormones (see Chapter 11) causes the body to go through a kind of delayed puberty and undoubtedly affects mood.

Coming out as trans is also complicated by the controversial phenomenon of '**passing**'. Seen by many trans people as a negative and loaded term, Richards and Barker define passing as 'a negative term for allowing people to assume that you are part of the normative group when you are not (e.g. a gay or bisexual person could "pass" as heterosexual)' and suggest that it should 'never be used' (2013, p.234).

In the past, some saw 'passing' as the goal of an effective transition; that to be a successful trans person, one should not appear to be trans at all. As Stone argued some time ago, 'the highest purpose of the transsexual is to erase him/herself, to fade into the "normal" population as soon as possible' (1991, p.296). This is a kind of binary tyranny, which, although apparently accepting gender variance, also insists that that variance must be efficiently negotiated and erased. Transition becomes about crossing from one side of the binary in order to disappear into the other, thereby arguably not only rescuing the majority from having to deal with their feelings about difference but also to shore up the binary as the only normative, successful, and healthy way to live and be in the world.

The question then arises: How does your trans client come out as trans if the goal is to become invisible once again? There is no clear and correct answer to this dilemma. Many of your clients will assert a strong desire to 'pass' and to minimise the number of times that they might be mis-gendered. Your work together may, at times, focus on their anxiety about the possibility of being read as trans in social spaces and the shame that it might cause. In a very real sense, these events can be an experience, yet again, of that strict gender policing that insists that difference is wrong and should either be forcibly erased or, at the very least, hidden from view.

The way in which clients negotiate coming out and visibility will be highly idiosyncratic. Anecdotal evidence suggests that greater visibility of trans in social spaces and discourse, coupled with a reduction in panic about sexual and gender variance, allows for more freedom around expression for younger trans people. They have access to less binary narratives and may be happier coming out in a whole range of non-binary identities that may not only trouble that binary but also trouble the idea of fixed identity by their very fluidity. They may also come out as non-binary whilst having a binary gender identity in order to reduce the social expectations of how they 'should' present or act and reduce the fear of being seen to 'fail' to meet a binary social standard.

Exercise

Spend some time reading about trans stories, either biographical or fictional.

You might watch *Transamerica* (Bastian and Tucker, 2005), as Bree (Felicity Huffman), a **trans woman**, comes out to her son, Toby (Kevin Zegers). You could also watch *Transparent* (Soloway, 2014), in particular the scene where Maura (born Mort), a retired college professor, finally opens up to her family about always identifying as a woman.

In these two examples, consider how the trans person handles their disclosure and how the family responds:

– Although clearly dramatised for effect in these instances, what meaning do you make of their coming out stories?

– What process issues could similar experiences throw up for you and your clients?

– Do you find yourself siding with one or other of the characters?

– What does this say about your assumptions and potential prejudices around self-disclosure and gender identity?

DEGREES OF OUTNESS

Lev (2004, p.249) argues that 'coming out is a lifelong venture [that] never ends because there are always people who do not yet know'. Clients may choose to come out in certain settings, but not in others. They may be out to friends, but not to certain members of their family. They may be out in their social life, but not in a work setting, where they may choose to be more androgynous. The choice of whether to be out or whether, indeed, a trans person needs to be out to all people at all times is again a very personal one. At a very practical level, does your client *need* to be out all the time? Does the checkout assistant at the supermarket need to know? Does the customer service assistant on the phone from the electricity supplier *need* to know?

Klein *et al.* (2015) explore this question in their research with LGBTQ youth in Canada. They take a position that coming out is not always an option and neither is it always desirable for all trans people in all situations:

Participants in this study challenged the notion that the opposite of *out* is *closeted*; those who were not out to anybody, or who were out only to some people in their lives, were not necessarily living in shame and secrecy but rather living with the understanding that many factors impact their psychological health. The finding reinforces critiques of coming out models that posit being out as better for one's mental health. For example, Eli felt that coming out as trans in his feminist women's community would cause him to lose his social support system; it was ultimately up to him to weigh the relative costs and benefits of this decision and decide what was best for him and his mental health and wellbeing. Furthermore, this decision cannot be understood without a contextual analysis of power and privilege; beyond the challenges associated with finding acceptance in the larger cisgender women's community, even mainstream cis-dominated gay and lesbian communities have yet to develop any real desire to understand, accept, and welcome trans people as equal members of their communities. In this respect, it becomes evident that the traditional notion that coming out is wholly beneficial for one's mental health might actually be counter to the lived experience of many queer and/or trans youth. (Klein *et al.*, 2015, p.319)

GOING BACK IN

If the possibility exists to come out, it also exists to go back in. At times, TGNC people might experience pressure from cis people to go back into the closet and avoid asserting their gender identity for one reason or another. It is not uncommon for trans people to be told by cis people to stop 'going on about it', or to stop 'flaunting it'. As explored elsewhere, they might be encouraged to 'tone things down' for the sake of particular audiences – often young children or old people who are positioned either as 'innocents' or 'too frail' to cope with a non-conforming identity. While this can frequently be about displacement of the negative feelings of the one doing the insisting, it also suggests that some people can still see gender identity as something to be put on and taken off at will to suit the needs of a heteronormative, cisgender majority. Moreover, given that cisgender, heterosexual people are never asked to tone down *their* gender performance, it further implies that normative identities can never be too strongly performed.

COMING OUT AND THERAPIST SELF-DISCLOSURE

Although we do not intend to go into this topic in great detail here, the issue of therapist self-disclosure needs to be touched on. As with many issues and areas raised in this book, there is an extensive literature available on therapist self-disclosure, although much of it is focused on sexuality rather than gender identity (see Kaili, 2014; Kronner and Northcut, 2015; Scaturo, 2005; Sherman, 2005). It may be extremely stressful for your client to come out and you may be the first person to whom that person has disclosed this part of themselves. It is clearly not a given that all TGNC therapists disclose to their TGNC clients, but they should at least be prepared to spend time reflecting and working with supervisors through the impact of disclosure or non-disclosure in the therapeutic relationship.

COMING OUT AND RELATIONSHIPS

In the exercise earlier, we looked at how fictional characters have handled coming out in their families and close relationships. As well as working through issues of identity with clients themselves, a great deal of the content of therapy with trans clients, at least in the early stages of transition, will involve processing the impacts on relationships.

One of the most sensitive of these relationships can be with the spouse or partner of a trans person who has just come out. Therapists should beware of siding with one or the other in the relationship but instead try to maintain a balance in order to help both parties see the issue from the other person's perspective. The trans client may be in apparent haste to transition and seek your support in bringing the partner on board and, conversely, the partner may want your help in getting their partner to rethink or at least slow the process.

Often, partners can make transition about them, focusing on what their spouse's trans identity says about their gender identity and why they chose a trans person as a partner. They can worry unduly about what others will say or think about them as the partner of a person in transition. Clearly, all of these are valid questions for the partner to explore, and you could suggest that your trans client supports their partner in seeking their own therapeutic support through the process. As you do so, however, beware of being 'played off' by your client against their spouse's therapist as a kind of proxy for conflict between the client and their partner.

Case vignettes

The following vignettes represent different challenges that trans people might encounter with their families after coming out:

Cath and Amy have been together for nearly three years and have lived together for the last nine months. Since moving in together, Amy has felt more and more strongly that she would like to transition. She has always had a butch identity and dressed in traditional male attire. She and Cath have discussed her gender identity since early in their relationship and Cath is cautiously supportive of Amy's desire to transition. However, she's confused about what that will mean for their relationship. She has always identified as lesbian, but now that Amy is planning to live as a man and change her name to Andy, does this mean that she's now somehow straight? Moreover, her father was often violent when she was growing up and she feels ambivalent about living with a man once Amy has transitioned.

Debbie has been in transition for some time, having begun the RLE over two years ago. She is now out at work and with all of her friends and family. Debbie and her wife, Susanne, separated part way through transition as Susanne became increasingly distressed by Debbie's gender identity and presentation. They have two young children and Susanne continues to insist that Debbie present as male, or at the least in an androgynous way, when she makes home visits to see them.

Carol has transitioned after having retired and her wife has been supportive. However, her young grandchildren still call her 'Grandpa' and she is unsure as to how to tackle the issue with her daughter, who seems to be ignoring it.

 Reflection

- How do you think that the trans people in these vignettes will be feeling, and what are the different reasons for the actions of the other people involved?

- How might the meanings that the trans people in these scenarios attribute to what has happened affect their feelings?

- How could they help themselves deal with the situations in terms of their feelings, thoughts, and actions?

THE DIFFERENCE BETWEEN ACCEPTANCE AND AFFIRMATION

In a recent article in *The Advocate*, Lucas Grindley explored the assertion by Pope Francis that 'Jesus would not abandon transgender people' (*The Advocate*, 2016). In an attempt to clarify his previous negative comments about 'gender theory', the Pope reportedly walked the tightrope between, on the one hand, accepting that 'life is life', while, on the other hand, telling reporters: 'Please don't say: "The pope will bless transgender people." OK? I want to be clear; it is a moral problem. It is a problem. A human problem. And it must be resolved the best one can – always with the mercy of God, with the truth [and] always with an open heart.'

This attitude speaks to the whole idea of the difference between acceptance and affirmation and how it advances cisgender privilege. In 'accepting' trans people, the Pope is apparently positioning himself (and, by extension, the Catholic Church) as modern, progressive, and enlightened. But, at the same time, the fact that he takes it upon himself (on behalf of God and the Catholic Church) to define what is within and without the bounds of acceptability shows that his words are not as accepting as they may at first appear.

This tendency to 'accept' rather than 'affirm' identity is something that cisgender therapists need to be aware of in their work with trans clients. If the position were reversed, would cisgender therapists (and others) wait to be 'accepted' by their trans clients and be given 'permission' to be cisgender? In a similar vein, on 21 June 1993, *Newsweek* posed the question: 'Lesbians: What are the limits of tolerance?' This cover story was then lampooned by the *San Francisco Bay Times* some ten days later, seeking to unmask the heterosexist privilege assumed in the headline by renaming *Newsweek* 'Dykeweek' and asking the question: 'Heterosexuals: What are the limits of tolerance?' (1993).

Indeed, as we have seen, acceptance over affirmation may form a large part of your trans clients' coming out experiences and narratives where negative feelings felt by a close relative or partner can be projected out onto others. A spouse may profess to being 'fine with it' but insist that the trans person slows down or avoids transition 'for the sake of the kids'. At work, a trans person may encounter an apparently accepting line manager, who, nevertheless, suggests that your client avoids being 'too overt for the sake of some of the older members of staff'. You can help your clients to uncover these possible projections and help them to unmask inauthentic behaviours and narratives that are being promoted in their social networks.

CISGENDER PRIVILEGE

A core part of privilege in identity politics, explored with regard to cisgender in Chapter 8, is the idea that those with privilege have the privilege of not being aware of their privilege. Equally, the reflexivity at the heart of affirmative practice aims to help the practitioner become aware of the different ways in which they may be privileged and how that affects the therapeutic relationship. The Cisgender Questionnaire, adapted from the Heterosexual Questionnaire (Rochlin, 1972), is one tool that cis practitioners can use to explore and examine their own privilege and power.

 Exercise

Cisgender Questionnaire

Based on Martin Rochlin's famous 'Heterosexual Questionnaire' of 1972, Julie Tilsen developed a version exploring gender identity in 2013.[1] It is meant to be read by cisgender people to draw attention to the way in which trans people are often asked to justify their identity:

– As a cisgender person reading this, do any of these questions feel nonsensical or ridiculous? Are you offended by any of them?

– Does it seem more acceptable to ask a trans person to answer questions like these?

– Even if you haven't asked questions like this of your trans clients, are you curious to know the answers?

– How do you think this affects your work?

1   Julie Tilsen's Cisgender Questionnaire can be read online at: www.facebook.com/
JulieTilsenPhD/posts/767832386567036, accessed 08 January 2018.

13

SHAME, STIGMA, AND TRANS PEOPLE

ROBIN DUNDAS

One of the most challenging aspects of working with trans people therapeutically can be addressing the psychosocial and emotional impacts of your client being part of a stigmatised and marginalised minority group. A particular challenge for psychologists and gender specialists can be identifying where gender-related stigma and cultural transphobia come from, what damage they might be causing, and how best to approach this in clinical practice.

In order to achieve this, attempts have been made to develop concepts from within sexual minority psychology, such as 'minority stress' and 'internalised homophobia'. However, what becomes clear on closer exploration of trans people's lives is that what many gender diverse people experience as a result of minority status and stigmatisation might be better understood as the more profound and complex issue of shame, which has only recently received significant attention in mainstream psychology. Following a surge of research and theory, shame has been identified as a key and complex issue for many individuals in Western societies, particularly those from stigmatised minority groups. It is believed to have roots in development and has been strongly linked to a variety of relational and mental health issues across the life course. However, in spite of becoming a significant focus for researchers and theorists, shame has received very little attention in relation to trans people, which is surprising given that trans and gender non-conforming people have been widely accepted as being, until very recently, one of the most stigmatised groups in Western culture.

In order to address the invisibility of trans people within the shame literature, a fact that may in itself be reflective of trans people's historical erasure and exclusion, this chapter sets out to name and uncover the sources and impacts of gender-related stigmatisation and shame. Specifically, it will endeavour to bring about a greater understanding of shame, both as a response to gender-related stigma and also in terms of the potential interactions of gender-based shame with developmental, intersectional, and general life issues for psychological practitioners. Importantly, it will offer suggestions towards working therapeutically to combat shame's toxic, complex, and often devastating effects.

CHANGING ATTITUDES AND THE ROLE OF TRANS ACTIVISM

Before doing so, however, a chapter on shame and stigma in relation to trans people should not begin without first celebrating the seismic positive shifts in social attitudes towards gender diversity that have occurred over the last 30 years. These have happened largely due to the efforts of trans people themselves, particularly through the transgender movement, which began in the early 1990s in response to virulent transphobia and violence, including a series of tragic and brutal murders in the USA. Trans and other gender diverse people came together during this challenging time through academic and community dialogue, creative expression, political protest, and activism, heralding the beginning of a gender revolution in the West. Individually and collectively, they began to articulate a diversity of previously invisible, prohibited gender experiences and identities, which are now becoming part of the lexicon for gender in Western culture (Bornstein, 1998; Feinberg, 1996; Stone, 1991; Stryker, 2006; Whittle, 2006).

The transgender movement not only cleared the way in the West for a diversification of gender identity and expression, which has been emancipating for gender minority and cisgender people alike, but was also instrumental in the fight for trans people's rights. Due to trans activism, the passing in the UK of the Gender Recognition Act in 2004 and changes in 2008 to the Sex Discrimination Act (Equality and Human Rights Commission, 2008) have meant that trans people in Britain now enjoy significant protections in the workplace and greater acceptance in their personal and social lives, and experience less rejection, discrimination, and stigma. In spite of this progress, however, the limited available research and clinical experience, in addition to the current troubling debates surrounding trans people's use of public toilets in the USA, suggests that gender minority people continue to face unique personal, developmental, social, and institutional challenges. Trans and non-conforming people potentially confront psychological distress and/or physical discomfort or gender dysphoria, issues of disclosure or 'passing' within a new social and/or physical gender role, and continue to struggle for public acceptance or legal recognition of their authentic gender under threat of violence, discrimination, social exclusion, unemployment, and restricted access to medical treatment for gender-related issues (Beemyn and Rankin, 2011; Factor and Rothblum, 2007; Gehi and Arkles, 2007; Gehring and Knudson, 2005; Grant *et al.*, 2010; Grossman and D'Augelli, 2007; Hill and Willoughby, 2005; Koken, Bambi, and Parson, 2009; Lombardi *et al.*, 2002; Whittle, Turner, and Al-Alami, 2007).

What is surprising is that, in spite of these psychologically significant and highly specific issues, gender minority issues continue to be conflated with or eclipsed by the issues confronted by sexual minority people in psychology research and practice. This is indicated by the ongoing labelling of 'LGBT' psychological research, which, in spite of its inclusive heading, continues to privilege the experience of White gay men over that of a diversity of lesbian, bi, and trans people. Given the lack of existing research regarding trans experience in psychology, it is necessary to turn to findings in the sexual minority literature in order to point the way to understanding the impacts and sources of gender-related stigma and shame. What this work tells us is that, although significant social progress can take place for a minority group, often as a result of successful activism by a pride movement, the urge to turn away from a painful history of stigma toward acceptance and 'normality' can mean that toxic shame remains buried and its insidious negative effects on following generations persist undetected. With this in mind, and with full appreciation of the current improved sociopolitical situation of trans people in the West, this chapter will focus on unearthing and better understanding stigma and shame in relation to five key areas:

- The phenomenology of shame

- Development, gender, and shame

- Language and shame

- Body shame and gender dysphoria

- Power, shame, and transphobia.

THE PHENOMENOLOGY OF SHAME
What is shame?

Shame is perhaps best described as the experience attached to a person's profound and painful sense that they are in some way fundamentally flawed, or that something is wrong with them in terms of their being. It has been distinguished from its close relative, guilt, as something that relates to who or what somebody *is* as opposed to what they have *done*. Because shame is related to an individual's being, it is thought to be profound and intractable, whereas guilt can be alleviated through action and compensation, which enables the guilty individual to avoid the indelible mark of shame (Lewis, 1971; Taylor, 1996). In spite of these distinctions, the closeness of shame and guilt has been noted, and there appears to be frequent overlap between these emotions, insofar as, for example, chronic guilt may lead to shame, or a shame-bound personality may lead to a constant nagging sense of guilt. It has also been identified that these emotions can be experienced as blends, such as guilty-shame, or as blends of blends with other emotions, for example anxious-guilty-shame (Gilbert, 1998; Tantam, 1998).

As touched upon previously, there has been a huge amount of interest in shame within the field of psychology over the last few decades. Following this, it has come to be known as a painful, hidden emotion, or the 'sleeper in psychopathology' that coerces the shamed to hide (Lewis, 1971; Nathanson, 1992; Tangney and Dearing, 2002). Crucially, it has been identified at the heart of a wealth of developmental and adult psychological issues, such as emotionally unstable personality disorder, aggression, depression, and anxiety, issues related to sexual abuse and eating problems, and as a result of the discrimination and marginalisation suffered by minority groups.

Although shame is frequently described in the literature as a moral or social emotion, there have been a series of debates within the field of shame theory and research as to the extent to which it should be viewed as an embodied, social, or subjective emotion. These have taken up a great deal of space in the existing literature and seem to depend on the epistemological position of the researcher or theorist. In terms of practical utility, particularly for holistic therapeutic work, shame is best understood as occurring at all of these levels, as a 'biopsychosocial' phenomenon. In terms of this chapter, shame will be understood as an embodied, affectively painful, and cognitive experience that plays a fundamental role in people's identities and self-concepts, and that is mediated by social and cultural meanings and values.

The hidden emotion

Having traced a very brief outline of shame, it is important to appreciate that there have been significant difficulties in clinically identifying and working with this emotion and its negative impacts. This is thought to stem from the fact that shame is an aversive, painful experience, and that expressing shame or revealing shameful or stigmatised attributes may draw attention to the things that individuals feel ashamed of, potentially exposing them to ostracism and abuse. Because shame is therefore often hidden by the person experiencing it, and can be so deeply buried that it is hidden from clients themselves, clinicians have noted that it is often only indicated by other emotional responses or behaviours. For example, expressions and behaviours such as anger, anxiety, avoidance, or aggression are thought to serve a protective or defensive function for many people who struggle with shame. It has also been observed that hiding, defence, and shame avoidance strategies can sustain this emotion as a chronic, maladaptive experience, leading to an entrenched 'shame-bound' personality structure that is hard to detect, understand, and treat therapeutically. Given these findings and clinical observations, we can surmise that difficulties are likely to arise in exploring shame as a complex, potentially hidden phenomenon with trans people as a stigmatised minority group who themselves suffer invisibility, both within society and psychological research.

Stigmatisation and shame

As suggested above, shame has been identified in psychology as a negative response to stigmatisation, which has been defined in a variety of ways by shame theorists. Drawing from the seminal work on stigma by Erving Goffman (1963a, 1963b, 1967), Michael Lewis (1995) relates stigmas to public violations. He suggests that, for a person to fear stigmatisation, it must be obvious, either due to an aspect of an individual's physical appearance or their behaviour: it must have a 'social appearance factor', for which an individual feels responsible, to the extent that it is perceived as a core part of their self and/or identity (Lewis, 1995, 1998). For example, Lewis theorises that certain characteristics become shaming stigmas when they are attributed to people as an identity, rather than merely as a descriptor; as in the case of a person who is described as 'having disabilities', as opposed to being viewed as 'a disabled person'. The latter instance is problematic, as being disabled is set against a positive norm of being able bodied in society and fundamentally defines who and what an individual *is* in a profound and significant way; it is therefore stigmatising and potentially shaming (Lewis, 1995).

Although stigmas and shame have been widely defined as problematic personal or subjective experiences, sociologist Sally Munt (2007) asserts that it is important to understand them as socially or culturally mediated phenomena. She points out that stigmatisation and shame occur for minority individuals within a broad range of persecuted groups around the world, and that the sources and effects of this can only be fully appreciated and addressed relative to social or cultural context. In keeping with this view, psychologists Dawn Leeming and Mary Boyle (2004) suggest that locating shame and stigmatisation solely within the individual can lead to further shame and problems in working therapeutically with its negative impacts on the self. This is due to the fact that people positioned in this way will potentially feel ashamed in relation to socially determined stigma (as something that originates in them, rather than in society), will feel ashamed of being ashamed, and may also feel responsible for this entire situation, leading to repression, hiding, and self-erasure. Although it is largely omitted from the existing psychological literature, stigmatisation is a central issue for gender minority people, who are frequently punished for visibly violating Western gender norms and failing to conform to conventional male and female gender stereotypes.

 ### Remember

It is important not to automatically assume that a trans client is struggling with the negative impact of having a stigmatised identity. However, since stigmas and shame can often be hidden from view, it may be appropriate to probe more deeply with your client if shame or stigmatisation do not appear to be presenting issues.

Due to the potential issues surrounding shame mentioned above, it is crucial to build a trusting therapeutic relationship before attempting this type of work. Importantly, some clients may genuinely not experience any issues in relation to shame and stigma, and may be offended by your questioning this; some clients may be struggling deeply due to having a stigmatised identity, but might not feel ready to address this in therapy. These clients might feel threatened by your attempts to explore this further and express anger or become avoidant and/or anxious.

In order to address these potential issues, the appropriateness of working with shame with a trans client should be discussed in supervision in order to avoid distress or further shame.

Working therapeutically with shame

Individuals tend to feel responsible for stigmatised attributes and identity, potentially amplifying associated feelings of shame. Re-locating shame and stigma within society or history can be key to uncovering and beginning to work therapeutically with this emotion. Therefore, it may be important to explore whether your client feels that having a stigma is their fault, or to what extent they feel that their stigmatised identity or attributes define them.

It can be helpful to sensitively explore ways of making your client's relationship to stigma more explicit and to reduce a potential sense of responsibility for their stigmatised identity or attributes. To help achieve this, there are some positive ways in which you can reframe your client's stigmatised identity; for example, it may be useful to consider 'de-essentialising' their stigmatised identity as attributes that they *have* rather than something they *are*.

Given that shame is often suppressed and compartmentalised by clients, it can be important to name shame in therapy, particularly if your client is unaware that this is an issue in their lives. However, if your client is resistant to this or finds it overwhelming, it can be therapeutic to approach shame and stigma indirectly, for example by working with a client's lack of self-compassion or their negative self-cognitions.

Working dynamically with these issues can help your client to build more positive self-concepts and scripts and can help to generate warmer, more compassionate, or kinder feelings towards the self. Compassion-focused therapeutic techniques as developed by Paul Gilbert (2011) can be highly effective in working with shame and stigma.

Case vignette: Jeanette

Jeanette is an engaging, upbeat 24-year-old woman. She has approached you as she has been binge-drinking every weekend and recently experienced several 'crazy blackouts' in social situations.

She tells you that she vaguely recalls several fights in the straight bars she socialises in with men who have given her transphobic abuse. This led to a recent caution from the police, following an incident where she physically assaulted a man in a nightclub. She tells you that she has never had a problem like this before and that she is not an angry person; you find this easy to believe as she is very charming and looks stylish and feminine.

As the session progresses, she tells you that she is sure that her anger is not about her being trans as she has had a loving upbringing and was always encouraged to be herself. She feels that she made a very smooth gender transition many years ago and was surrounded by supportive friends and professionals.

 Reflection

- What do you think might be going on for Jeanette and how could you begin to formulate this with her?

- How would you work with her to understand and manage her problematic anger and destructive behaviour?

- Do you feel embarrassed or uncomfortable asking your trans client about stigmatisation or shame?

- Where might these feelings be coming from, and how can you manage them with your client?

- Do you have a stigmatised identity or feel that you have stigmatised attributes, either gender-related or otherwise?

- How do you feel about these?

- Are your own feelings regarding shame and stigma affecting how you feel about your client and the work you are doing together?

DEVELOPMENT, GENDER, AND SHAME
Gender conformity, shame, and 'fitting in'

Gender has been identified as the most meaningful and significant identity that we have in the West, taking precedence over ethnicity, age, or other identifying factors (Kite, 1994; Mass *et al.*, 2003). Therefore, it is unsurprising that Western children have been found to internalise culturally mediated gender norms at a very young age (Bem, 1987) and are commonly punished and shamed throughout development when they violate Western cultural expectations for their natally assigned gender role (Efthim, Kenny, and Mahalik, 2001; Kaufman, 1989; Osherson and Krugman, 1990; Zahn-Waxler, Cole, and Barrett, 1991).

Observations from psychotherapeutic work support these findings; as we have seen earlier in the book, gender-based shame has been identified as the painful humiliation experienced when the 'regulatory arm' of the gender binary metes out emotional and physical penalties to 'sissy boys' and 'unmasculine' or feminine men (Corbett, 2009). Nathanson (1992) also suggests that gender-related shame develops as young people learn to identify and value themselves in terms of the sexual development of their bodies during puberty, in relation to Western cultural and social gender ideals and in direct comparisons to peers. He states that, as adolescents develop increasing awareness of their bodies, they can experience shame regarding attributes such as breast size, weight, body hair, and muscle development if these do not fit the prevalent normative image of masculinity or femininity.

Problematic gender-related shame can persist well into adulthood, and psychological research tells us that deviating from established Western male and female gender roles in adulthood can result not only in social disapproval, but also in self-devaluation (Brown, 1986; Pleck, 1981). Additionally, it has been found that failure to attain gender-related ideals in terms of appearance and behaviour can represent a direct threat to individuals' self-concepts (Bem, 1987). Researchers have also concluded that the more adults tend to evaluate themselves in relation to Western societal masculine or feminine ideals, and fail to meet those standards, the more they may be subject to shame (Efthim *et al.*, 2001).

In spite of the clear identification of gender role presentation as a potential source of shame in psychological theory and research, there is no mention of the effects of the social and cultural enforcement of gender stereotypes on trans children, adolescents, or adults in psychological research. In order to explore this further, it is necessary to turn to work within transgender studies, anecdotal evidence from gender specialists, and sociological research.

Trans academic and activist Jay Prosser states that not belonging to a socially sanctioned gender group in childhood can generate a profound sense of shame for trans children. He asserts that the question 'Are you a boy or a girl?' constitutes 'unreadableness' for trans children in Western societies and can lead to alienation and increased vulnerability to abuse. He also states that, for these individuals, not having a place in a culture that insists on belonging can lead to shame and 'the sexual violence which re-inscribes shame' (Prosser, 1998, p.179). In support of these assertions, gender specialist Randi Ettner, drawing from extensive clinical and therapeutic work, observes that trans children's perceptions of peers and significant others' negative responses to their gender expressions frequently evolves over time into a 'bad me', or a 'shame-ravaged self' (Ettner, 1999, p.104). She suggests that American gender minority adults who have experienced chronic, gender-related shame since childhood can 'rival – if not surpass – other individuals in terms of shame-damage that has affixed itself to the self, defying triumphant living' (Ettner, 1999, p.106).

Adolescence and gender conformity

Trans activist and author Riki Wilchins observes that the pressure to conform to culturally enforced gender norms intensifies during puberty and teenage years, due to the fact that Western society begins to recognise children's developing bodies as sexual objects, or 'potential surfaces for eroticism or procreation' (1997a, p.128). She asserts that puberty is a time that is particularly 'ripe for shame' and observes:

> ...all adolescents are coerced into maintaining a consonance between the cultural meanings of, for example, their newly developing breasts or sprouting beards and their entire expressive language of possible clothing, gesture and stance... [T]he dressage of gender becomes a daily ritual and begins to dictate our lives and our interrelationships. Girls are brought down from the trees, boys from playing with the girls. (Wilchins, 1997a, p.128)

She tells us that puberty can therefore be a particularly painful and isolating time for trans adolescents.

Large-scale empirical evidence from sociological research supports this anecdotal and clinically based literature. Beemyn and Rankin (2011) identified that, out of a sample of 3474 trans people living in the USA, 87 per cent had a sense of being fundamentally different before the age of 12. This figure rose to 97 per cent by the end of puberty, coupled with the awareness that their difference was specifically related to gender. Their experiences of being different were almost exclusively negative, and for some resulted in suicidality, depression, anxiety, and eating issues (Beemyn and Rankin 2011).

Non-gender-related shame: Interactions

Non-gender-based shame has also been identified as a highly significant issue in childhood and adolescence in mainstream psychological literature, indicating that it is also important to explore the potential impact of non-gender-related shame with trans clients. For example, Schore (1994) suggests that if there is insufficient mirroring of a child's emotional world by a primary caregiver, this can lead to them experiencing a shame response that, in a common feature of caregiver–child relationships, will develop into the child's sense of themselves as devalued or unlovable. Similarly, Rosenberg *et al.* (1994) found that Western children identified in their research as shame-prone reported that their primary caregivers were more likely to use person-focused disciplinary messages, such as '*you are* bad', versus 'you have done a bad thing', express disgust, tease, communicate conditional approval, and use love-withdrawal techniques. As a result of this, these children were found to have a more negative self-image or 'damaged self' and demonstrated behavioural problems in relation to this. Andrews (1998, 2002) and Fiering, Taska, and Lewis (2002) also identified that neglect and physical and sexual abuse during development can contribute to damaging and lasting shame experiences in relation to identity and the body.

In response to these findings and anecdotal reports, Dundas (2016) investigated the lifetime shame experiences of nine trans adults across the UK and found that all the participants experienced a degree of gender-related shame in childhood due to deviations from Western cultural ideals regarding masculinity and femininity. This was compounded by prohibitions on gender expressions by parents, peers, and others and was also exacerbated by a lack of language through which participants could express non-normative gender feelings. Shame was reported as a sense of invisibility or alienation in childhood or as a feeling of being fundamentally different due to non-normative gender feelings. These experiences became particularly problematic in adolescence as participants reached puberty, with some reporting shame and confusion at being mistaken by others as gay in adolescence and adulthood, due to their non-normative gender expressions. This led in some cases to the internalisation of gender norms, to the extent that participants themselves mistook their non-normative gender feelings for sexual identity, further contributing to confusion and alienation.

Importantly, the research also suggested that shame at non-normative gender experiences or having a stigmatised identity was amplified and complicated by earlier shaming relationships to significant others. For example, those who had emotionally inconsistent parents or received constant negative feedback from family and/or peers appeared more vulnerable to the effects of shame at their non-normative gender feelings or the negative effects of having a socially stigmatised identity. The findings also indicated that those who experienced shame due to sexual abuse were highly vulnerable to the negative, shaming impacts of having non-normative, stigmatised gender feelings and identities.

 Remember

Both gender- and non-gender-related issues might be impacting negatively on your client's life, relationships, and mental health, constituting a complex presentation. How can you explore any potential relationships between these issues in a compassionate, clear, and containing way?

Working therapeutically with shame

Gender roles are highly significant in development and in adulthood, and non-conformity to Western masculine and feminine norms can be highly shaming. It may be important to explore with your client how they experienced or expressed their gender at different stages in their lives, particularly as they learnt about gender and sexuality in their childhood and teenage years.

For example, did your client feel able to express themselves in terms of gender when growing up, or were they exposed to prohibitions on their gender feelings or expressions in the form of punishment or other forms of negative feedback? You can explore if they were subject to sexuality or gender-related bullying, and whether their gender identity was mistaken for sexual preference. Understanding the potential impacts these experiences had on them emotionally and psychologically can help you both uncover how this might be affecting their adult sense of self.

One approach to addressing earlier experiences of both gender- and non-gender-related shame might be to help your client to experience a more compassionate relationship with the child whom they once were. So-called 'inner child work' might involve encouraging clients to write a compassionate letter to their younger self to help alleviate the effects of shame that have taken root during childhood and adolescence.

 Exercise

Research suggests that *everyone* is potentially subject to the shaming impact of gender-related norms throughout their lives:

- Can you recall times in your life either as a child, teenager, or adult when you felt doubt or shame about your gender or were shamed by others for non-gender typical behaviour?

- How did this make you feel?

- Are you experiencing any feelings of discomfort in relation to your client's gender expressions or identity?

- How might this be affecting your work together?

LANGUAGE AND SHAME
History, language, and gender 'trans'gressions

History and language both play an important role in trans people's experiences of stigmatisation and shame. Therefore, it is important that practitioners working with trans people have an understanding of the significant potential psychological and emotional impact that language can have on gender non-conforming individuals. For example, when thinking about the terms used to identify non-normatively gendered people in the West, it is important to consider that they are never neutral, but are imbued with historical and cultural meanings and values specific to Western understandings of sex and gender. Roscoe (1998) and Whittle (2000), among others, describe how trans people have enjoyed high social status and occupied valued roles at different times in many societies around the world. Ettner, however, argues that, in the Western world today, 'and particularly in America, the transsexual is the equivalent of the Biblical leper... [S]hunned and ostracized, these individuals are the only group that it is still politically correct to mock' (Ettner, 1999, p.9).

As a result of this, trans writers and activists have asserted that 'trans' should also stand as an abbreviation for 'transgressive', insofar as trans people in the West can be defined by their 'transgressions' against 'normal' gender, such as blurring or blending conventional male and female gender roles, presenting as gender ambiguous or neutral, taking on a gender role different to that assigned at birth, or being in any way visibly trans (Bornstein, 1998; Stryker, 2006; Wilchins, 1997a, 1997b).

By way of explanation for this, it has been suggested that the stigmatisation and ostracism of transgender people in the Western world has occurred against a historical and cultural backdrop of heteronormativity, or heterosexism. Recent sociological and psychological work further suggests that the English language is inescapably problematic for sexual and gender minority people due to its emphases on dualisms and polarities such as gay/straight, male/female, and masculine/feminine (Beemyn and Rankin, 2011; Richards and Barker, 2013). The very words we use (or, importantly, do *not* use) to articulate gender and sexual experience can therefore make it extremely 'difficult to think of sex, gender, gender identity and gender expression within a more dynamic framework that is inclusive of transgender people' (Beemyn and Rankin, 2011, p.17).

As touched upon in the last section, Dundas (2016) found in his research that a lack of language through which to express gender experience outside normative male and female concepts was a significant source of shame for participants in his research, both throughout childhood and in adult life. A lack of available language meant that participants were unable to articulate subjective, embodied gender experiences, leading to feelings, of invisibility and shame, repression of actual gender feelings, and attempts to conform to stereotypical male and female, straight or gay social/sexual roles. Repression of gender feelings and conformity constituted cultural erasure and invisibility for participants, which, in turn, were linked to a variety of emotional, psychological, and body issues, including depression, suicidality, anxiety, and, in one case, restricted eating.

Language also played a crucial role for participants in disclosure of their actual gender identities, or 'coming out'. Finding accurate words and labels for repressed gender feelings and identities was crucial in the resolution of both shame and gender dysphoric feelings. Importantly, language continued to be key for participants in forming an identity after coming out, enabling them to claim a diversity of normative and non-normative identities as authentic and accurate in expressing their gender. For example, some participants felt that they were simply men and women and did not identify as trans people; some people found it affirming to identify themselves as queer and/or as trans people or as transsexual; one participant claimed multiple gender identities, relating to their life pre- and post-transition; and another participant preferred not to identify in terms of gender at all.

Working therapeutically with shame

An open and reflexive approach to language in exploring the potential sources and impacts of stigmatisation and shame on trans people's lives is necessary in work with gender diverse people. Finding and using language that fits with clients' experiences of gender may not fit with your own expectations or political view as a therapist; it also may not fit with dominant trends or understandings within either broader society or the trans community. However, whether the terms used by your client to describe gender are socially normative or are radical, queer, or non-normative, specific terms may not only represent authenticity for an individual client, but may also have developed for them as an important resistance to shame and stigma. Acknowledging and respecting this where it arises is key in working affirmatively with trans clients.

As you work with TGNC clients, be aware of how they choose to identify themselves in terms of their gender and the personal meanings that they attach to these words. For example, do the words that they use to identify themselves fit with their gender feelings or the lived experience of their identity? Or are there other, more positive or accurate words that they feel fit better with their sense of who and how they are? Maybe you can help your client to express their gender in other ways outside language, for instance through art, music, or imagery.

 Exercise

– How do you feel about your client's use of language in therapy and what is *your* opinion on how people who make a gender transition should talk about themselves in terms of gender?

– How might your views, your own vocabulary, and your understanding of gender be impacting on your work with your client in terms of shame?

BODY SHAME AND GENDER DYSPHORIA
Shame and gender dysphoria

As explored in Chapter 10, it should be borne in mind when working with a highly diverse trans population that, as with the term 'trans-sexual', gender dysphoria, in addition to being a description of subjective experience, is a medical or psychiatric diagnosis. For some, 'gender dysphoria' does not accurately reflect the nature of their gender identity issues, and may feel pathologising, shaming, or offensive; equally, others may feel validated by receiving professional confirmation of gender issues via diagnosis or identification of gender dysphoria. Reflexivity is required in both cases, in order to address the potential impact that this terminology might have on individual clients and also on your own thinking about the lived, embodied experience of gender-related distress.

With specific regard to gender dysphoria and shame, Prosser suggests that the body constitutes a fundamental aspect of our being and is the 'seat' of identity for trans people. He also theorises that proprioception is 'the fundamental organic mooring of identity – at least of…corporeal identity' (Prosser, 1998, p.80), and that proprioception, body image, and the self may be fundamentally linked. Following this, he concludes that the painful, proprioceptive 'wrongness' experienced by gender dysphoric people will often be experienced simultaneously as a wrong and, by extension, bad self (Prosser, 1998, p.79).

What he suggests in his work is that gender dysphoria might be thought of, in part, as a type of profound body shame, or that shame at being differently gendered can blend with feelings of discomfort and alienation in a person's body in complex and powerful ways:

> ...born of the self watching the self, shame reflects a split in the subject. In the split, gender dysphoric subject shame is felt specifically all over the body; and perhaps body image and shame are generally intimately related. (Prosser, 1998, p.179)

Gender clinician Arlene Lev points to the lack of existing knowledge regarding these important issues, stating that there are few practice guidelines for health professionals with which to assist trans people 'who are struggling with the ramifications of living within a rigidly gendered culture or the internalised shame that manifests as gender dysphoria' (2004, p.239). Therefore, in order to explore this further, we will turn to findings from the mainstream literature relating to body shame and link this to trans people's own accounts of gender-related distress, social stigma, and cultural transphobia.

Body shame

Gilbert was one of the first to explore the phenomenon of body shame in psychology. He argues that shame, in addition to being a social, cognitive, and emotional experience, can penetrate to the most subtle level of our being, including our physiology, via micro intersubjective and macro institutional influences, and that these different domains are interrelated in people's experiences of shame (Gilbert, 2002). He also suggests that bodily shame experiences can operate at an intimate, personal level, in terms of touch and feeling, particularly the contouring and potentially emotionally regulating touches of caregivers. Empirical psychological research has also suggested that body shame may be at the heart of eating disorders such as bulimia and anorexia nervosa, particularly in adolescence (Gilbert and Thompson, 2002; Goss and Gilbert, 2002), and a variety of body image problems across the life course, some connected to actual disfigurement and injury, others to invisible psychological wounds (Gilbert, 2002; McKee and Gott, 2002; Veale, 2002). Elsewhere, it has been identified that body issues and profound self/body hatred may occur in relation to experiences of severe childhood neglect and physical and sexual abuse (Andrews, 2002), potentially contributing to eating disorders (Cole and Putnam, 1992; Wonderlich et al., 1997) and other self-harming behaviours (Herman, 1994).

With direct relevance to gender minority individuals and gender-related body shame, Gilbert theorises on how capitalism and culture may interact as 'evolved algorithms and economic systems', which produce evolutionarily based, gendered body values and standards such as the hip-to-waist ratio in women and muscularity in men. When these ideals function as tokens in social exchange, those who fail to meet agreed-upon standards may feel devalued or stigmatised. He also briefly suggests, although does not explore in any depth, that minority gender identities may become stigmatised as they have 'bodily expressed meanings that oppose pre-existing cultural norms and standards' (2002, p.19).

Whose body is it anyway? Society, heteronormativity, and body shame

Drawing on her own experiences as a queer trans person, Wilchins suggests in her seminal work *Read My Lips* (1997a) that all individuals depend on language to communicate their subjective, embodied experience and therefore rely on other members of their 'speech community' to tell them what their bodies mean and how they ought to appear. She asserts that people do this through comparison and polarities such as old and wrinkly versus young and smooth, fat versus slim, and so on, and that, as a result, the meanings and values that culture and language attribute to bodies can be limiting and painful for many. She states that, in addition to culture and society's role in how people frequently negatively evaluate their bodies, the gender system exacerbates problems with self/body experience and knowledge through its 'monolithic' assertions that 'big breasts must mean one thing and hairy backs another' (Wilchins, 1997a, p.140). In response to this social and cultural enforcement of shaming body norms, she asks, 'Who gets to say which bodies "count", and why? How small a percentage counts as negligible? Whose body counts as the standard for normal and how different can I be before I become pathology?' (Wilchins, 1997a, p.50).

In a similar vein, trans academic and historian Susan Stryker (1994) discusses the impact of Western cultural transphobia and associated shame on experiences of gender dysphoria and medical transition. She asserts that language and the body are fundamentally linked in human experience and identifies that the existing lexicon for the body and gender do not accommodate trans people's bodies at all. She suggests that, as a result, many people who seek gender reassignment surgery in order to resolve gender dysphoric feelings are stigmatised and positioned by society as 'unnatural', 'hybrid', or 'monstrous' in relation to modernist scientific and medical discourses, which inform heteronormative views of 'real' or 'natural' sex and gender (Stryker, 1994, p.179). Similarly, Prosser suggests that, for conventional thought, gender dysphoria and associated treatment can mean 'the brutal mutilation of healthy bodies, and that sex reassignment surgery does not so much effect sex change as it transmogrifies "normal" men and women into unsexed or hermaphroditic monstrous others simply through the excision of their "natural" functioning sex' (1998, p.81).

Wilchins illustrates the potential impact of Western culture's views on gender dysphoria and transition, describing the subjective, lived experience of a combination of gender dysphoria and shame for some trans people:

> ...to have this experience [gender dysphoria] is to feel a unique kind of discomfort and pain. It affords little respite. For it is not just there in the shower, in dating situations, before strangers on the street, when applying for a job, undressing, in the act of making love, and in the eyes of family and friends, but it is also in our heads whenever we think about what constitutes 'me'. (1997a, p.120)

Dundas' (2016) findings supported this anecdotal evidence, by demonstrating that trans participants in his research experienced shame both during pre and post-transition and/or surgery due to the fact that they felt they could not be viewed as 'real' men and women as they lacked male and female reproductive organs and capacities and other 'natural' feminine and masculine physical attributes, in keeping with powerful heteronormative discourses that pervaded their experience and identity throughout their lives. This became a problem in romantic relationships for a transfeminine participant as she experienced shame at not being accepted by cisgender, male heterosexual partners as her actual gender, due to not having a vagina. She described being coerced by one cisgender male partner into accepting a gay male sexual identity, in spite of this being at odds with her own identity as a heterosexual woman, causing shame and distress.

Importantly, the research also found that gender-related body shame and gender dysphoria were exacerbated for some through blending with non-gender-related body issues, such as eating issues or other body-image problems in relation to cultural or social standards. Also, increased vulnerability to body shame as a result of gender non-normativity or gender dysphoria was clearly linked to early abusive or neglectful relationships and non-gender-related social pressure by varying degrees, resulting in complex body/shame binds consisting of a variety of different threads.

Given the significance of the relationship between gender dysphoria, stigma, and shame suggested by the limited literature, it is important to consider that some trans people may be at high risk of experiencing body shame as a dimension of gender dysphoria, and that bodily gender dysphoria may be blended or closely linked with shame as a result of rigid, binary ways of thinking about gender in Western culture. It is also important to consider how to sensitively approach work with gender dysphoria, given that language, social norms, and scientific or diagnostic discourse regarding real, natural, and, by extension, valid sex and gender can create problems for some people who seek surgery and hormonal treatment to relieve gender-related distress.

 Remember

All individuals are likely to experience body shame and related issues of low self-worth if they physically deviate from social and cultural gender norms and ideals. The body is therefore potentially a source of shame for some trans people. Also, body shame may be a particularly difficult problem for trans people during puberty, due to increased peer and societal pressure about gender, particularly if individuals have previously experienced sexual or other forms of abuse.

Working therapeutically with shame

It may be important to explore your trans client's relationship to their body in therapeutic work, in terms of Western masculine and feminine ideals, non-gender-related body issues, and any links between these. This may involve a complex presentation, and might constitute areas of considerable distress or vulnerability for your client; you should therefore discuss working with body-related issues in supervision before attempting to work with them in therapy, particularly if your client has experienced abuse.

If you feel that it is appropriate to begin working with the body with your client, then there is a range of questions that you might sensitively explore. For example, how do they feel about their body? Do they feel that their body is congruent with their gender identity? What do different aspects of your client's body mean to them, and are there any relationships or other influences in their lives that reinforce a negative image of their body? What role might social ideals or media imagery regarding masculinity and femininity be playing in how your client relates to their body? Do their feelings about their bodies impact on their romantic or sexual relationships?

Just as with a cisgender client, you should not automatically assume that all trans clients will have a negative body image. However, for those trans clients who do, as you work through and explore these questions together, you can think about helping your client begin to generate a warmer, kinder felt-sense of their bodies. Paul Gilbert's compassion-focused therapy could again provide some important insights into working in this way.

One possible approach to challenging limiting language in relation to the body can be to explore your client's bodily experiences in a more abstract way. Try to bring your client into the feeling or 'felt-sense' of their gender in their body and ask them to describe this outside of male and female categories, labels, and other conventional language. For example, do their gender feelings have a colour, texture, or even a temperature? Reflect these descriptions back to your client as accurately as you can as they present them.

Before attempting this, always be careful to explain to your client what this exercise involves. You should also explore with them whether they feel ready/able to engage with body-focused work.

Case vignette: Lianna

Lianna is a 32-year-old woman who has come to see you because she is convinced that everyone she meets guesses that she used to live in a male gender role, which has led to social withdrawal and depression. She 'passes' extremely well and looks very feminine. She has been accepted by her friends and family and tells you that she has a good job and a good life. She tells you that she has no reason to be unhappy and that everyone tells her how lucky she is and how good she looks. In spite of this, she feels constantly sad, anxious, and self-conscious and also feels that she has no right to these negative feelings. Even though she is polite and charming during your session, you can't escape the feeling that she might be very angry with you.

She has responded well to hormone treatment and had successful vaginoplasty some years ago but wants to receive further surgery to make her breasts bigger and her nose smaller; she feels that this will improve her situation and make her happy. She also frequently asks you for feedback about how she looks. You reflect to her later in the session that it must have been difficult for her in her life being trans. She looks extremely annoyed, but smiles and laughs, telling you that being trans has been the least of her problems and that it's professionals like you who have made life harder for her.

Reflection

- What do you think might be going on for Lianna?

- How could you respond to her anger and begin to explore her feelings with her?

- Why might Lianna be asking for feedback about her appearance, and how could you respond to this therapeutically?

- How do you feel about discussing your client's body in therapy?

- What are your assumptions regarding the relationship between genitals and gender identity?

- Do you feel that your client is a 'real' man or woman if they don't have a penis or a vagina?

- Do you feel embarrassed or ashamed talking about sex or your client's body?

- If so, why might this be the case?

- What impact might this be having on your work together?

Exercise

- How do you feel about your body?

- Do you feel that you live up to the ideals or expectations of your gender identity, i.e. do **you** 'pass' in your gender role?

- Have you ever felt that your gender or sexual behaviour doesn't measure up to masculine or feminine ideals, or that your body doesn't measure up in other ways?

- How did this make you feel, and how might this impact on your work with your clients?

POWER, SHAME, AND TRANSPHOBIA
Heteronormativity, sexism, and power

Understanding and working with the power dynamics between therapist and client is key in any therapeutic relationship. Existing research, however, suggests that this is a particularly sensitive and crucial part of working with stigmatised, minority individuals. For example, contemporary shame theorists have identified highly significant relationships between stigmatisation, shame, and power, which have psychological implications for gender diverse people as a minority group. Gilbert suggests that shame may have developed as a result of power dynamics within social hierarchies and that shame in humans may be loosely analogous to submission displays within other primate social hierarchies (Gilbert, 1998; Gilbert and McGuire, 1998). Supporting this view, there is evidence from research within both sociology (Madsen, 1995) and psychology (McGuire, 1988; McGuire and Troisi, 1987a, 1987b) that power-stratified relationships and status cues have emotionally, neurophysiological benefits for dominant individuals and negative (potentially shaming) consequences for those in submissive or socially excluded positions (Gilbert, 1998). Expanding on the notion of shame as a function of power, Macdonald describes the social, pervasive, and regulatory function of shame by quoting Scheff (1988, p.387): '[Shame] is the most frequent and possibly the most important of emotions (because of its role in maintaining conformity) even though it is usually invisible' (Macdonald, 1998, p.162).

With relevance to trans people's experiences of stigmatisation and shame in relation to power and social status, trans writer, performer, and activist Kate Bornstein (1994, 1998) describes the sociopolitical position of trans people in the West. She points out that Western societies are both hierarchical and gendered and that 'gender as a system has a "deathgrip" on all of us culturally and socially' (1998, p.35). In a similar way to the theory of hegemonic masculinity explored in Chapter 3, she suggests that a useful heuristic in understanding social hierarchies in the Western world is a view of them as a type of pyramid, with those at the top tending to be cisgender heterosexual White males and those at the bottom being trans and other minority people, particularly those who do not visibly conform to able-bodied, White European, heterosexual, or heteronormative ideals. She suggests that 'moving up or down on this pyramid representation of the gender system is a function of *power*, not of humanity' (1998, p.40), and that 'gender, identity and power are each a function of each other, inextricably woven into the web of our culture beneath an attractive tapestry called the bipolar gender system' (1998, p.42).

In keeping with these observations, Dundas (2016) found that shame can occur for trans people as a psychologically damaging effect of power relations, particularly where individuals are exposed to discrimination and abuse by cisgender others. Specifically, findings from his research highlighted shaming, oppressive dynamics where cisgender privilege was asserted within relationships to uphold existing ideals regarding masculinity and femininity and to affirm the authority of cisgender people in trans participants' lives.

The research concluded that trans people can occupy relatively powerless positions in their relationships, not only to significant others, but also to powerful institutions such as psychology, law, and medicine, due to their non-normative gender feelings and expressions. These relationship dynamics, in addition to the lack of available language mentioned earlier, can lead to shame and repression of an authentic gendered self. Importantly, the research also identified that, even in the most repressed situations, participants exercised power by resisting these power dynamics in a variety of explicit and less obvious ways.

Discrimination and transphobia

Given these findings, it is important to consider how hierarchical relationships in society can have a direct role in discrimination, marginalisation, abuse, and shame for your client. Psychological research specifically on discrimination against trans people in the UK and USA is scarce; however, the research that does exist suggests that physical and verbal abuse, discrimination, and marginalisation continue to be common and are pervasive (Hill and Willoughby, 2005; Tee and Hegarty, 2006; Whittle *et al.*, 2007). Furthermore, these findings suggest that these problems exist not only in the personal, public, and professional domains, but also extend to medical settings and trans-specific healthcare (Raj, 2002; Whittle *et al.*, 2007). In terms of the potential psychological or emotional impact of this on trans people, psychological research from the last decade in the USA suggests associations between trans people's experiences of discrimination and anxiety (Devor, 2004), distress (Rachlin, 2002; Sanchez and Vilain, 2009; Winter and Udomsak, 2002), and depression (Nuttbrock, Rosenblum, and Blumenstein, 2002). Moreover, high levels of depression, anxiety, and suicide reported in other research with gender minority individuals (e.g. Grossman and D'Augelli, 2007) suggests that there is a clear relationship between psychological and emotional distress, self-harm, and living as a trans person in a transphobic social environment.

Working therapeutically with shame

It may be helpful to explore with your client any awareness they have of shaming or abusive power dynamics in their lives, both in the past and the present. For example, what relationships are significant in your client's life and how is power negotiated in these? Is your client able to express themselves fully in these relationships, both in gender- and non-gender-related terms, and are any dynamics shaming for them?

You might also explore your client's relationship to the institutions that affect their lives. Do they depend on you, a gender identity clinic, their GP, or perhaps a psychiatrist or other mental health professional for their gender treatment and/or affirmation of their actual gender identity?

If they feel powerless in relation to an aspect of their gender, it can be helpful for you to explore ways in which they might have exercised power elsewhere in their lives (even under very difficult circumstances) and what the impacts of this have been.

In the context of our exploration of the relationship between shame and power, and as explored later in Chapter 15, your client may have experienced transphobic abuse at work. If so, you can direct them to further information on their rights under the Equalities Act 2010. They may also wish to consider joining a trade union since these organisations actively offer support and protection against discrimination towards trans people at work.

If your client is experiencing threatening and/or transphobic behaviour in public, you should both be aware that transphobic abuse is now considered a hate crime in the UK. Your client should be encouraged to report any transphobic incidents to their local LGBT police representative (every area in the UK has one).

Case vignette: Dan

Dan is a 52-year-old man who has been referred to you because, although he made a successful transition to a male role many years ago and has been living very stably as himself with a loving partner, he has been cutting his arms in the bathroom at work.

He tells you that he comes from a very strict family who never allowed him to express his gender while growing up. His father is a traditional Italian man, who doesn't believe that Dan is male. He would lock Dan up in a cupboard whenever he refused to wear dresses as a child. Dan recalled that he was also bullied by girls at school, which led to him trying to be as feminine as he could in his teens, which was very painful for him.

Dan transitioned to his actual gender role 15 years ago. He tells you that he had a difficult time with the doctors and psychiatrists during his transition, as they put obstacles in his way when he requested treatment with testosterone therapy and surgery.

He tells you that he has no idea why he has started to self-harm, something that he hasn't done since he was 19. He explains that he works as an architect in an overtly masculine, hyper-competitive practice. He has been experiencing a lot of pressure from his strict boss at work, and the company he works for is in financial difficulty.

At the end of the session, he tells you that he has been unable to sleep and eat and feels too embarrassed to talk to anyone about this or his self-harming.

 ## Reflection

- What might be going on here for Dan?

- How might you be able to identify what is triggering his self-harm and work with him to manage this?

- How do you identify yourself in terms of gender, ethnicity, and sexual orientation, and how might this fit within the broader social hierarchy?

- How might this impact on the power dynamics between you and your client?

- Have you ever been subject to discrimination or abuse due to gender, sexuality, or other stigmatising factors?

- How might this be affecting your work with your client?

- What is your professional role in relation to your client, and how does it impact on how you interact with your client?

- Do the power relations between you and your client lead to either of you feeling ashamed?

This chapter has briefly considered shame and its relationship to development, language, and, crucially for many TGNC people, to the body. It has also briefly unpacked ways in which shame is created and maintained through the operation of power relations. In all of these themes, some time has been spent looking at specific implications for therapeutic interventions and highlighted their potential use through case vignettes. Clearly, the literature on shame and ways of working with it therapeutically is rich, and there is a lot more that could have been written about. So, as with all segments of this book, if you are interested and if you are coming up against shame a lot in your work with clients, please use this chapter as a springboard to read and explore more.

14

TRANS SEXUALITIES AND INTIMATE RELATIONSHIPS

We have been using 'trans' as an umbrella term to describe different gender minorities (Lev, 2004) and expressions of gender that perhaps deviate from the cisgender heteronormative expressions assumed by default in many societies.

Sexualities and gender are not synonymous, although they tend to be treated as such, and trans people's experience of both can be erased or rendered invisible where binary, cisgender heteronormativity provides the canvas upon which everything else is written (Lenihan *et al.*, 2015). Types of sexuality other than those considered 'the norm' can be marginalised and struggle to attain validation, even more so when the perceived divergence is magnified through having intersecting, socially transgressive identities. Same-sex relationships have become more mainstream in certain cultures but are still heavily prohibited in others; asexuality, kink, and polyamory are still contentious and, where practised, there can be negative social reinforcement of being 'too open' about it. Furthermore, it can be challenging enough for those who are cisgender to communicate about their sexuality where it diverges from heteronormativity, and is all the more so for those who are trans where the challenge of describing relationships and sexualities in relation to gender identities that fall outside the binary can be considerable.

As therapists, we need to be open to the diversity of sexual practices, not just those that we are familiar with, but also those that go beyond our experience. Our clients will certainly find it even more difficult to disclose and express themselves in an authentic way if they feel treated as somehow 'exotic', 'different', or 'accepted' rather than respected and validated. As we have already seen, language plays an important role here and has the ability to inhibit as well as enable the articulation of sexuality and gender (Lev, 2004). We therefore need to develop and demonstrate a facility with the necessary language to be able to facilitate clients in talking around this area – language that reflects a respectful, validating position. Of course, we are not talking about non-consensual sexual practices, which are illegal and can be addressed in the same way as any other illegal non-consensual activity, with the usual therapeutic boundaries of confidentiality. Nevertheless, understanding the laws around sexuality in the country in which you practise and the wider issues that affect sexual expression and intimate relationships is important.

This can be especially important in working with sexual practices such as bondage, discipline (or domination), sadism, and masochism (BDSM), which is a consensual sexual practice, but around which there can be many misconceptions and fantasies, including what is legal and what is not. Sprott and Berkey (2015) explore how *Fifty Shades of Grey*, both the book (James, 2012) and film, brought BDSM/kink to a wider audience and how the literature in the area often focuses on exploring behaviours over how those behaviours are formative of identities. They cite van Anders' (2015) Sexual Configuration Theory, which looks at different intersections of sexual identity across practices (such as BDSM/kink), partner number (monogamy vs polyamory and many others), as well as gender choice (homosexual, bisexual, heterosexual, and so on). The theory uncovers different forms of stigma and privilege based on different intersections. For example, heterosexual kinky people are argued to have a more privileged sexuality than, say, LGBTQ kinky people who may be marginalised both for their sexuality as well as their sexual interests and behaviours. Understanding how 'these intersections create different kinds of stresses, and different kinds of resources for coping' (Sprott and Berkey, 2015, p.507) is key to working therapeutically with traditionally stigmatised sexualities and identities. The BPS *Guidelines and Literature Review for Psychologists Working Therapeutically with Sexual and Gender Minority Clients* (2012) contains useful information on ways of working with this and other forms of sexualities and sexual identities, including helpful case studies; and *Sexuality and Gender for Mental Health Professionals* by Richards and Barker (2013) is a similarly helpful resource.

Exercise

All of us have our own sexual behaviours, identities, and internal experiences related to sexuality in sexual scripts. Take some time to reflect on your own sexual identity and sexual scripts:

- How aware are you of your own sexual identity and preferred sexual practices?

- What does it feel like for you to feel sexually desirable? What about the times when you have felt more or less so?

- What sexual practices and desires are you aware of not expressing or feeling shame around? How might this affect your client work?

- How associated are gendered and sexed bodies and sexual attraction in your sexuality?

- How easy is it to understand others' sexuality where it is not gender specific in attraction or more gender specific than yours?

EVOLVING SEXUALITY

How trans people experience their sexuality may vary at different points in their lives. Conversely, other people may perceive a trans person's sexuality differently according to what gender they are presenting as and how much of the time. This can place pressure on the trans person to conform to social expectations of normative sexuality so as not to be perceived as being 'sexually motivated' in wearing particular clothing or finding specific ways of presenting to be sexually arousing.

Most of us have an experience of 'feeling sexy' at one time or another, often helped by a particular form of clothing that we feel makes us look more attractive or desirable. However, for trans people, this can often be problematised. The diagnosis of Transvestic Disorder – included as a differential diagnosis under Gender Dysphoria in the DSM-5 (APA, 2013) – may require distress over six months in key areas of functioning and allow additional specifications of 'with fetishism' or 'autogynaephilia' (a paraphilic tendency of a biological male to be sexually aroused by the idea of being female). Singling out specific forms of sexual behaviour, script, or identity in this way can sometimes contribute to a shameful identity (see Chapter 13) for people that want to express themselves in this way, feeling that their forms of desire are 'wrong' or 'disordered'.

More significantly, there can be anxiety amongst trans people that they will not be taken seriously in relation to their gender dysphoria, if it becomes apparent that they have sexual practices and desires which sexualise gender presentation and the imagined body. As we have said, it is not unusual for people generally to find the thought of themselves in erotic wear and certain situations sexually arousing. If their gender identity feels more congruent with a different body than the one they inhabit, it may be an aspect of feeling more comfortable thinking of interacting sexually in that desired body that makes it, in itself, desirable.

The point is that there can be many areas of intersection between sexuality and gender, and in order to fully understand the client's experience, the therapist needs to listen to and explore with the client, resisting the temptation to label and interpret who and what they are or are in the process of becoming. For example, it may be that they found wearing female clothing during sexual relations with others or in masturbation to be sexually arousing early on in their life – especially as it felt taboo – whereas now it might just feel comfortable and familiar. It could be that they have never found wearing clothing of their felt gender sexually arousing or that they did and still do. These are not unusual personal narratives and there are many other possible ones, too, since there are many different intersections in human experience.

 Exercise

- How many different sexual identities and sexual practices are you aware of?

- What additional reading do you need to do around gender and sexualities in order to increase your knowledge of sexual diversity, especially as to how it intersects with gender?

- How might expressions of sexuality change or stay the same at different points of a social gender role transition?

INTIMACY IN RELATIONSHIPS

Negotiating and renegotiating intimacy in existing relationships when one partner, or sometimes both partners, are going through a gender role transition can be tricky and reliant on good, open, honest communication. It can be affected by the life stage of the partners, their age, how long they've been together, and their individual sexual orientation and identities. As therapists, we can never assume the 'best' outcome but instead we can support and facilitate people in moving forward during a time of significant change.

Partners of people going through gender reassignment may also find intimacy difficult, and the trans person themselves might find it increasingly hard to compromise in the way in which they may have been doing before to meet their partner's preferences. Gender and sexuality is strongly associated in most societies, such that when one partner changes their social gender role then that can also change how the other is seen socially in relation to sexual orientation. Moreover, as their partner's body changes, conflicts may be brought up for them around what it means for their own sexual identity. If their partner is moving towards a different gender role, including some form of change to their embodiment, are they even attracted to this newly gendered, physically changing body, and what does continuing intimacy mean about them and their sexuality?

There are many couples who continue to be intimate in the same or in new ways as gender reassignment progresses. It can be an opportunity to become more creative in expressing intimacy – for example, moving beyond simple, penile–vaginal intercourse – or in becoming more aware of what the other person really does like and dislike. Many trans men might prefer their chest not to be touched but may feel freer post-chest surgery regarding intimate touch with this area. It can also be hard for a partner to let go of a sexual practice previously engaged in by the couple, particularly if there are heteronormative norms around the practice, such as penile–vaginal intercourse for previously straight-identified couples. The natal female in the relationship can feel that she is 'right' to continue to insist on this, even when the natal male partner would prefer otherwise or would like a hormone regime that suppresses testosterone, resulting in no or very limited erectile function. Respecting their body and intimate boundaries can be difficult for the trans person to enforce when faced with the power and persuasion of heteronormativity and the unquestioned assumption that being cisgender is 'normal'.

 Exercise

– How can you, as a therapist, facilitate your client in identifying what they want in their sexual relationships, in setting boundaries around physical intimacy, and in challenging the assumptions of heteronormativity?

If trans people can feel under the critical scrutiny of a heteronormative cisgender social lens, even more so arguably can their intimate and sexual partners, whether trans themselves or not. Sexual attraction to gender variance itself is still othered as transgressive and seen as rather socially taboo to openly acknowledge. Trans people, as the rest of the population, can have diverse sexual identities (Moradi *et al.*, 2009), but the rise of asexual and pansexual identities can also help people to move away from the expectations of cisgender, binary models of gender and sexuality.

The partners of trans people also need to negotiate formulating, expressing, and developing their own sexual identities in relation to the trans person, whilst, rather controversially, often having to avoid indicating an attraction to gender diverse people or specific types of gender diversity, unless they themselves are trans, in which case it can be interpreted in a non-threatening way by others. As we have seen in the work of van Anders (2015), sexuality can be defined along a number of intersectional themes of partner choice, partner number, and sexual practice – therefore, choosing not to define sexuality in terms of gender at all is another option (Kuper, Nussbaum, and Mustanski, 2012). In the therapeutic space, room can be given for a diversity of sexual identities and potential expressions to emerge, where not only the trans person is not pathologised or misconstrued, but neither is their partner. Partners may be heterosexual, gay, bisexual, pansexual, asexual, genderqueer, trans, cisgender, and many more identities and ways of being, but the focus therapeutically is usefully on the quality of the relationship and what it means for the client.

Case vignette: Janice

Janice is a trans woman who met her partner Bryan online and they have been communicating for several months but have never met. She has arranged to meet him soon but is now getting anxious as to how it will work out in person. Bryan has always communicated with her as a woman online but she met him through a trans-specific site and her friends have advised her that this may not be a long-term relationship as she is planning to have genital reconstructive surgery. Bryan has always seemed very supportive but Janice cannot help but wonder what he really wants with her.

 Reflection

Reflect on what feelings this brings up for you and how your objectivity working with this client might be affected:

– What meanings do you place around how this couple met and what does it mean for Janice's experience as a sexually desirable being if you work within those meanings?

–   To what extent are you being influenced by cisgender bias, whether cisgender yourself or not?

–   Would it make a difference to your formulation of this case if you found out that Bryan is a trans man?

DISCLOSURE

How trans people disclose their gender history, especially if their appearance and presentation differs from what it might once have been, varies from individual to individual. However, most will have put some thought into this in advance of dating and developing new relationships. Some will date but then end the budding relationship before it becomes physical in a way that will out them, whereas others may disclose their trans identity at the outset but set boundaries around how physical intimacy can be expressed. Yet others may feel less dysphoric around their genitalia specifically and express their sexuality using it and the body they have, simply because they have it, rather than by preference.

Clearly, disclosure of being trans to a new partner can be a source of anxiety, with the attendant fear of rejection and even physical harm. Timing that disclosure is therefore a significant decision; too soon and it might seem overwhelming to a date who was only expecting a coffee and to explore how they got on; too late and the date might feel like they have been deceived or deliberately lied to. Not disclosing at all is something that the trans person may need to reconcile with their fear of how their partner might feel about them if they knew, or, indeed, the fear that they might already know and be waiting for the trans person to disclose in their own time.

Disclosing within a relationship is arguably even more challenging to negotiate than disclosing in new or prospective relationships. The trans person may already be embedded in established relationship and gender norm expectations. The partner may or may not be anticipating any disclosure, they may suspect, or they may have no idea at all. There are many different types of disclosures, as many as there are ways of being trans, but they can all potentially involve risk of loss and feeling vulnerable and exposed.

A non-binary person, natally assigned female, who is already established in a marriage with a male spouse, can be only too aware how the news may impact on their partner and their feelings around their sexuality. The partner may not understand what being non-binary means and attempt to invalidate the identity and experience. The implications of disclosure can therefore feel overwhelming and the trans person may obsessively worry about the impact that their disclosure will have. Will they still be an object of desire for their partner? Will their partner be angry and feel deceived? Will they leave them?

The trans person may experience even more pressure to conform to gender stereotypes associated with their natally assigned gender following disclosure of being trans. These can include being prohibited from cutting their hair, from not removing body hair, from wearing their preferred clothing, or from telling anyone else, and obtaining validation for the newly emerging trans identity. Alternatively, the partner might prove very supportive and the trans person may feel pressure to make decisions faster than they feel ready, or to take actions that they don't yet want to commit to.

It may seem that these examples and concerns are particularly specific to TGNC people and that a therapist might need specialist insights in order to be able to work effectively with issues and anxieties around disclosure. However, in many ways, the process content is similar, if not identical to, the challenges that all people face when worrying about making a decision. As with all decisions there is loss and a cost involved since, in order to choose something, we must often let something else go. It is the desire to move towards and choose the new thing without having to undergo loss or the costs of that change that can leave people feeling stuck. And when they become stuck, worrying can be a pastime that helps them to feel like they're engaging with the problem, while all the while avoiding actually making any changes. Helping clients to acknowledge and accept that both 'change' and 'not-change' involve cost and loss can help and support them in coming to terms and living with the consequences of their decision.

Case vignette: Paul

Paul, aged 40, is in a relationship of ten years with a male partner, whom he married a year ago. His partner is gay and Paul himself has always identified as a feminine gay man. He has been known to wear female clothing in the past when going out, but this has always been seen as 'wearing drag' by the couple. Paul describes the relationship as close, but over the years he has felt increasingly uncomfortable with his body and identifying as male and hasn't felt able to discuss this with his partner.

He has arranged counselling to get some advice on how to move forward, as his dysphoria around his body is increasing such that he no longer feels comfortable sexually with his partner. Paul doesn't as yet know what he wants to do but feels the present situation can't continue as it is. On the other hand, he doesn't want to risk destroying the life that he and his husband have built up together over a not insignificant amount of time. He has felt rather depressed over the last few months and has recently been started on citalopram by his GP.

 Reflection

– How would you work with Paul over the first few sessions?

– What might be the key issues here?

– How can any potential disclosure to the husband best be managed?

TRUST IN THE THERAPEUTIC RELATIONSHIP

Therapists can be as reflective of the diversity of the population as their clients, but how is trust and rapport developed when the therapist may be assumed to come from a position of cisgender, heteronormative privilege? Can this privilege be acknowledged in the therapeutic space and what might be the challenges for a trans therapist?

The rules for self-disclosure apply here as much as in any other area of therapy. The therapist might disclose their own gender or sexual identity if it is considered in the best interests of the client, but self-disclosure is used selectively and sparingly. It may, indeed, be validating and affirming for some clients to know that their therapist has a similar gender identity or sexual orientation or identities to themselves, or it might also feel intrusive or leading (Richards and Barker, 2013). Some reflection is also usefully given to cisgender, heteronormative privilege in being able to perhaps more freely disclose oneself as being cisgender and heterosexual in the therapeutic space.

Providing an affirmative, validating service rather than being 'accepting' or just 'understanding', as we have seen in Chapter 12, is important in communicating respect and equality in approach, whatever the client's gender identity and expression. This means not assuming the sexual identity, sexual expression, or gender variance itself as the problem, whilst also recognising the socially transgressive and challenging nature of some gender and sexual diversities (Milton, Coyle, and Legg, 2002). It is important to be aware that 'acceptance' can not only reinforce cisgender, heteronormative privilege in having or exercising the power to 'accept' (with all of the attendant potential for self-congratulatory feelings in being the kind of liberal person who is 'accepting'), but it can also work to change the focus from the client to the therapist.

Exercise

Reflect on how you, as a therapist, can further develop an awareness of the impact of heteronormativity on your own life choices and working with clients:

– What does it mean to have an affirmative model of practice?

– What does affirmation look like in the therapeutic setting?

SEXUALITY, GENDER REASSIGNMENT, AND THE BODY

The medical interventions available in gender reassignment treatment discussed earlier in this book, such as endocrine treatment and surgeries, can significantly impact on the experience and expression of sexuality. Changes, such as potentially reduced or increased libido and sexual arousal no longer being linked to erectile function where previously assumed by social conditioning, may take some time to adjust to. After genital reconstructive surgery, having dramatically different genitalia can be even more of an adjustment.

Some people seek counselling to help with negotiating issues arising around sexuality and making the transition from being a sexual being who is male or female bodied, to one which has changed in a way that feels positive but also perhaps alien in relation to expressing sexuality and desire. It may be that the body hasn't changed that much from previously or only in some parts; the adjustment may then be in how particular body parts are construed and experienced. A vagina may no longer be perceived as 'female', and a penis may be seen as practically useful because it's there, but not specifically or exclusively as a 'male' organ. Sufficient change may have been made in the social gender role and body to reduce or eliminate the gender dysphoria, but the sexual behaviour itself may remain similar or the same by choice. Alternatively, the options for expressing sexuality in a way congruent with the client's gender identity might feel limited, and creative discussion of what it means to be a 'man' or a 'woman' in sexual contexts might open up the way for new rewarding experiences and intimacy.

Case vignette: Leon

Leon is a 25-year-old trans man who presented for counselling, having struggled with developing intimate relationships because of his feelings around not being 'a real man' since he doesn't have a penis. He doesn't want genital reconstructive surgery, such as phalloplasty, but wants to change how he feels about his body and his identity as a man so that he can feel more able to develop relationships beyond the casual dating stage.

 Reflection

- How might you facilitate Leon in developing intimate relationships through affirmative discussion and deconstruction of what is 'normal' and what it means 'to be a man'?

- What new meanings and ways of construing male sexuality could emerge?

- What might your own prejudices and assumptions be that could be counterproductive in the therapy?

It's clear that there are as many different ways of experiencing and expressing sexual identity for trans people as there are for cis people, and practitioners need to be aware of their own bias, assumptions, and possible prejudices that privilege certain kinds of selves over others. In this shared multiplicity of experience comes the realisation that working with issues of sexual identity and intimacy in relationships is similar across all clients, since most people are seeking the same kinds of things in their relationships. The specific challenges thrown up by making sense of bodies as they change in transition and how those changes are worked through in intimate relationships are ones that can be tackled through sensitive, collaborative exploration, and an openness to a variety of experiences and preferences.

15

TRANS IN THE WORKPLACE AND SOCIAL SPACES

We have seen in Chapter 9 that the Equality Act 2010 provides certain safeguards and protections for trans people and other minorities in the workplace. In this chapter, less attention is given to legislation and more focus is given to the lived experiences of trans people in the workplace. We also look more broadly at the way in which trans people negotiate difference in social spaces in their day-to-day lives. Once again, our focus here is less on theory and more on case vignettes and exercises in order to help the practitioner become more aware of some of the common experiences of their trans clients.

TRANS IN THE WORKPLACE

'Gender reassignment' is a protected characteristic under the Equality Act 2010, alongside age, disability, marriage and civil partnership, pregnancy and maternity, race, religion or belief, and sex and sexual orientation. Moreover, there is no requirement for the person to be under medical supervision – they may simply choose to change the gender role in which they live without ever having had to see a doctor. The Act expanded existing discrimination legislation and now includes protection from discrimination due to association with transgender people or perception as a transgender person, as well as protection from indirect discrimination because of gender reassignment. The purpose of the legislation is to ensure that there are protections for trans people in all the social dimensions of everyday life, including employment.

The *Trans Employee Experiences Survey* is a report published by Total Jobs that surveyed over 400 TGNC people in the UK in early 2016. It explored the lived experience of trans people in employment and sought to understand how effective the Equality Act 2010 had been in improving their lives at work. Many of those surveyed felt that the Act had been a game changer for them: 'employers are keen on staying within the law, so anti-discrimination legislation is very important' (Total Jobs, 2016, p.24).

Although the survey participants were overwhelmingly White (over 90 per cent), the research did capture the experiences of those living in Great Britain (excluding Northern Ireland) across a broad age range and a diverse number of employment settings. Although the report found that most workplaces had some kind of anti-discrimination policies in place, some had no provisions for trans employees – for example, gender-neutral toilet facilities – and many felt that it was up to them to try and guide their employer's actions and policies.

Case vignette: Steve

Steve has worked as a legal assistant at a solicitor's practice in a small town. Although the practice partners are aware of the legislation that protects him, the main partner working with him on managing his transition at work has confessed to being unsure of the best way to handle things. She is completely supportive, but Steve often finds himself having to guide the business and make suggestions. He welcomes their openness and acceptance but at times wishes it wasn't him having to make all the arrangements and decisions.

 Reflection

– What does the partner's delegation of management responsibilities to Steve say about how trans identities are seen by the company?

– How could you help Steve in reframing the experience?

The employer has a role to play in ensuring the continuation of good working relationships with colleagues. Often, one of the most important things that they can do to support trans employees is to work with them in order to handle how they would like their colleagues to be informed. This can be accompanied with training for employees in affirmative ways of working as well as providing them with the chance to ask questions and become clear about any changes. Maintaining supportive work friendships and a positive working environment can be a vital part of the support network for trans employees, particularly as they transition.

Participants in the Total Jobs survey were also asked about how their colleagues reacted to their transition. About 90 per cent said that their colleagues were positive or neutral, and only 10 per cent reported direct hostility. One participant who had experienced negativity said: 'I am ostracised by my colleagues. One said "Please only talk to me about work, I cannot deal with your personal matters. I have had no training and I don't know what to say"' (Total Jobs, 2016, p.12).

We would like to take a moment to unpack this quotation from the Total Jobs research as we feel that it provides an interesting illustration of many of the subtle discriminations that TGNC and other minorities can experience in social spaces. The work colleague says 'I cannot deal with your personal matters' as if there is something specific about the participant's 'personal matters' that is overwhelming for them. In contrast, we might assume that most cis colleagues' 'personal matters' might be perfectly acceptable and can be dealt with.

This idea of what is acceptable to be spoken of, by whom and in what settings, has been explored in research looking at the way in which talk of sexualities and gender identities is policed in school settings. The parallels between this research and the participant experience, above, are striking. Allan *et al.* (2008) explored the discourse of a school as a place of safety and innocence and suggest that the 'desexualisation' of the school environment, whilst argued as being a neutralising force, is, in fact, supportive of default heterosexuality. They uncover discourses suggesting that LGBT people are considered to 'flaunt' and 'promote' their sexuality, and, as such, force their ideas onto other people, 'invading their private thoughts and spaces' (Allan *et al.*, 2008, p.319). There are parallels here for our survey participant whose colleague refused to allow 'personal matters' to be brought into the working environment and would 'only talk...about work' (Total Jobs, 2016, p.12).

Allan *et al.* (2008) further explore the argument that talking about difference is tantamount to being contaminated by it. Using the metaphor of separate bounded spaces within which it is acceptable or unacceptable to discuss sexuality and gender identity, they see the boundaries of the 'closet' as being fluid and encompassing some, but not all, of the spaces within schools. It is what Hubbard (2001, p.56) terms 'the schizophrenic spatial lives that many gays "not out" in public space lead'. In a similar vein, Macgillivray (2008) poses the question 'What is school for?' and uncovers a strong discourse that school is for academic work and learning and that all matters of social policy should be handled within the family. School staff should therefore keep silent in order to remain neutral on the issue of homosexuality.

Using this research as a parallel for trans experiences, once again we see that a refusal to talk or engage can be positioned as neutrality.

Many trans people, like the survey participant, can be manoeuvred into a situation where their ability to live fully in a work environment is restricted by appeal to apparently common-sense arguments that 'work' and 'personal' domains should be kept separate.

Often, it can be hard for trans people to access sufficient support in challenging the transphobic 'work is for work' arguments. On the face of it, a colleague asking to keep discussions to work and away from personal matters may seem like a harmless enough thing. But Allan *et al.* (2008) found a similar parallel process in their research when they promoted inclusion of same-sex stories in primary schools curricula in England. They found an attitude amongst staff suggesting that 'the project needs to stay within the space of the staffroom so that teachers can "get to grips with it first" in order to examine their own "prejudices as staff" before working out ways of moving forwards' (p.319). Although this research was undertaken before the Equality Act 2010 was enacted, perhaps Conoley's assertion that 'homophobic attitudes are among the last utterable prejudices among adults' (2008, p.219) needs to be updated and replaced with 'transphobic' instead?

Finally, in parsing this short quotation from the research, we turn to the phrase 'I've had no training and I don't know what to say'. This is once again a common experience for many trans people. They are often positioned as exotic, unusual, special, and 'other' – so much so, that an ordinary member of the public would not be able to have a conversation with them without adequate training. Although we acknowledge that this book is itself a piece of 'training' for professionals in mental health, we also assert that trans people are not so different from cis people that training is required in order to be able to engage in dialogue. Indeed, a sensitive and reflective practitioner would be able to work perfectly well with a trans client without specialist training. The training itself does not make it possible to engage, it merely provides the practitioner with an opportunity to increase their knowledge base, challenging reflexivity to promote greater empathy. Similarly, in the work environment, although trainings will inevitably help colleagues understand what the trans person is going through, so will simple engagement and dialogue with that person.

Nevertheless, despite the risk of negative reactions from colleagues and managers, over half of respondents said that their workplace performance had improved as a result of coming out. Some cited the relief from being preoccupied with anxiety over how coming out would go down with colleagues as well as a sense of greater freedom to be able to be themselves.

One of the most interesting findings came from these questions that were asked: 'Have you ever felt it necessary or do you now hide your trans status from colleagues at work?' Of the 435 people who answered this question, 52 per cent said 'Yes'. One participant said: 'I will go stealth in my next employment. I do not want special treatment, dispensation or other; I wish to at last be an equal employee who is valued for their skills, attitudes and achievements. My gender shouldn't affect my employment or abilities' (Total Jobs, 2016, p.17).

There is a sense for some that if they can find employment where they do not need to transition while there, then they can just make a fresh start without gender being the main issue. There are parallels here with the stage processes of transition and coming out explored in Chapters 10 and 12, where the end goal can be seen as living a life where gender is no longer the principal concern. The challenge for trans people seeking to escape life always and at all times being about gender is that there are often cis people around them seeking to pull them back to their gender-centric identities. Often, it is not the trans person themselves who 'goes on and on about gender', but instead the colleagues and managers who insist on asking questions and demanding to know intimate details of trans people's lives and identities.

 Remember

Although this book is oriented towards supporting the practitioner with information around problems in living for TGNC people, it may very well be that gender is not the problem that your trans client wants to work through with you. Be careful about automatically problematising gender and wanting to direct your client back to questions of gender identity unnecessarily.

Overall, the Total Jobs research uncovered five consistent themes in the lived experiences of British trans people in response to the question 'In your opinion, what are the biggest challenges facing trans jobseekers in the UK today?':

1. *Lack of understanding and ignorance* – Many feel that ignorance drives fear of difference and failure to 'see the person'. This can often be a problem right throughout the organisation since, at a senior level, trans people can be seen as problematic through fear of potential disciplinary procedures or litigation in the event that they get things wrong.

2. *Discrimination and transphobia* – Trans people sometimes feel that their employers pay lip service to the regulations and legislation. There may be policies in place, but no real action is taken on a day-to-day basis to prevent 'microaggressions' as well as casual transphobic comments and implicit or explicit bias against trans employees.

Case vignette: Jen

Jen is a sales assistant in a high street clothing store and has worked there for the past two years. In the last three months, she has begun presenting as a woman full time at work. Although she follows procedure, Jen's line manager has already said that she doesn't approve of her 'lifestyle'. Last week, a customer came into the store and directly challenged Jen, asking her loudly, 'Are you a proper woman, or are you just a bloke in a dress?' She was stunned and replied, 'I am trans.' The customer shouted a string of obscenities at her and stormed out. Although her line manager witnessed the incident, she took no action, saying that Jen should expect difficulties as a result of her 'choices'.

 Reflection

– Of course, while you can help Jen to work through her feelings as a result of this incident, what role do you believe a therapist can play in helping her affirm her rights and the responsibilities of her employer and managers?

– What do you think has helped to frame your thoughts and beliefs on where a mental health professional's role and responsibilities are with their clients?

3. *Lack of acknowledgement of non-binary people* – The rights of non-binary people are addressed to a lesser degree in the Equality Act 2010, which can make things more problematic for non-binary employees whose employers would prefer them to 'pick a side'.

Case vignette: Jaimie

Jaimie has asked friends, colleagues, and official agencies to use a non-gender-specific pronoun. Nobody seems to understand why this is important or seems to be making any effort to accede to this request. Official agencies have refused outright.

Reflection

- What does Jaimie's experience say about how non-binary identities are managed in the workplace?

- What resources could Jaimie access to support himself in making changes?

- As his therapist, how can you help him to access those resources?

4. *Transitioning* – One of the biggest challenges for TGNC people is applying for jobs while in the process of transition and finding employment when out as trans.

5. *Getting past the interview stage* – At the interview stage it is almost impossible to prove prejudice on the grounds of gender and an offence under the Equality Act 2010. As one survey respondent commented, there is the problem of '*looking weird* in interviews; when your appearance and deportment ticks enough *how strange* boxes in their heads that you don't get a fair hearing' (Total Jobs, 2016, p.22).

Case vignette: Jayne

Jayne recently started living full time as a woman and, having taken a break from work for six months, has begun to apply for jobs in her female identity. After a lack of success, she made some applications as (in her words) 'a fake male' and was employed as a case worker for adolescents experiencing learning difficulties. She hates having to compromise by presenting as male (or at least androgynous) at work and is anxious about how transitioning might affect work with her clients and co-workers. She's considering waiting at least six months before she says anything.

 Reflection

- What are the upsides and downsides of waiting for Jayne?

- How could you support her in coming out at work?

TRANS IN SOCIAL SPACES

In Chapter 12, we touched on the complex and controversial concept of passing. When considering the psychological impacts of trans identities in social spaces, passing inevitably comes up in forums and publications as well as in counselling. Although not directly addressing gender identity, Goffman (1963b) writes extensively about how the stigmatised person manages their identity in social spaces. In language that was acceptable for the time, Goffman talks about 'the stigmatized individual' and 'normals', as well as consistently and only using male pronouns. Nevertheless, what he writes about is pertinent:

> The stigmatized individual may find he feels unsure of how we normal will identify him and receive him… This uncertainty arises not merely from the stigmatized individual's not knowing which of several categories he will be placed in, but also, where the placement is favourable, from his knowing that in their hearts the others may be defining him in terms of his stigma… Thus in the stigmatized arises the sense of not knowing what the others present are 'really' thinking about him. Further, during mixed contacts, the stigmatized individual is likely to feel that he is 'on', having to be self-conscious and calculating about the impression he is making, to a degree and in areas of conduct which he assumes others are not. (Goffman, 1963b, pp.13–14)

The dilemma of how to manage an identity that may be socially stigmatised is at the heart of why passing is such a prevalent and controversial ambition or practice. Chapter 13 covers the phenomenon of shame and stigma in far more depth, but it's clear that a desire to pass is, at least in part, linked to feelings of anxiety and shame. This, in turn, gives rise to a reasonable questioning of why cis should be the standard that everyone should follow; that somehow cis identities are better, more valid, and more real than trans identities.

Encoded in passing is also the suggestion that trans people intending to pass as cis are pretending in some way, 'passing themselves off' and deceiving the public. However, that challenge could be turned on its head by posing the question that, if a trans person is walking down the street simply being themselves – as much as any other cis person is – then aren't we all engaged in some kind of a performance of self to one another? That the trans person is no more making a counterfeit presentation to the world than any cis person also engaged in social presentation, asking the world to accept or affirm a particular aspect of their identity.

More helpfully, a desire to pass could be seen instead as simply not wishing to draw unwanted attention to oneself in a pragmatic way. One example of this might be working on voice pitch on the phone to customer service at your bank in order not to be misgendered. Moreover, trans people are often in very real danger of violence and, for some, passing or 'going stealth' is just about being sensible. Furthermore, if we accept that being misgendered in social spaces is the source of much of the dysphoria felt by trans people, then passing could be reconstructed or reimagined as one of a number of strategies designed to reduce negative affect and to boost self-confidence.

It is clear that misgendering is a key source of distress for trans people in everyday life. The misgendering may, indeed, be intentional and designed to hurt, but it might also be accidental and unthought. The question to be explored in therapy is whether this misgendering, accidental or otherwise, somehow makes that person's gender identity less valid. In other words, does the trans person *automatically* give the cis majority the right to decide whether they're successful, valid, or real? To what extent are they able to let go of negative experiences and not be defined by them?

Case vignettes

The following vignettes represent different challenges that trans people might encounter in social spaces:

> Heather goes to a large high street PC store. She picks up some printer paper, goes to the counter, and pays for her purchase. The cashier, without glancing up, says, 'Thank you, sir.'

> Nick hears two people laughing, whilst doing his weekly shop. He turns around and sees one of them looking at him.

> Mary hears two young children discussing whether she is male or female. They agree that she is female based on her trainers.

 Reflection

- How do you think that the trans people in these vignettes will be feeling, and what are the different reasons for the actions of the other people involved?

- How might the meanings that the trans people in these scenarios attribute to what has happened affect their feelings?

- How could they help themselves deal with the situations in terms of their feelings, thoughts, and actions?

Part of our work as therapists and counsellors can involve affirming the belief that non-passing trans people can be happy, find jobs, be romantically loved, and live successful, fulfilling lives. Although the desire to pass is understandable, passing itself should not be the gold standard by which success in transition can be judged. Although we know that society can be unkind and transphobic, we affirm the fact that there is nothing intrinsically *wrong* in being trans. Calling out and attempting to humiliate people for their difference, with the threat of violence, loss of friends, job, and family, discrimination, and lack of access to proper healthcare, can all make life for trans people intolerable. But it is vital to continue to keep in mind, both for our clients and for ourselves, that there is nothing intrinsic to being trans in these challenges. They are a product of our society.

Working through issues of passing and social identity with your clients, perhaps integrating 'not passing' into ideas of the self, is often an important part of the work. Some of your clients, for whatever reason, will always be 'read' as trans and that might upset them. Situating your practice in compassion-focused therapy (Gilbert, 2013) can help your client to explore integrating their non-passing identity and to let go of the punishing need to try to fit in. You can work with them to find ways of being OK with not fitting in, of realising that most people, in different ways, fail to fit in and worry about being rejected by others.

HELPFUL TECHNIQUES: EXPLORING COMPASSION-FOCUSED THERAPY

Compassion-focused therapy (Gilbert, 2013) grew out of mindfulness-based cognitive therapy (MBCT) as developed by Jon Kabat-Zinn and others (see Kabat-Zinn, 1982, 1990, 1993, 1994). The approach is founded on Buddhist meditation practices, where *mindfulness* is defined as the awareness that emerges as a by-product of cultivating three related skills: (a) intentionally paying attention to moment-by-moment events as they unfold in the internal and external worlds; (b) noticing habitual reactions to such events, often characterised by aversion or attachment (commonly resulting in over-thinking); and (c) cultivating the ability to respond to events, and to reactions to them, with an attitude of open curiosity and compassion.

There is a considerable literature on MBCT and its effectiveness in working with chronic conditions such as pain, stress, and depression, and the reader is invited to explore the approach and techniques further.

In the specific context of working with TGNC people, and as we have seen in Chapter 13, compassion-focused therapy/MBCT can offer a powerful tool to help break down chronic patterns of shame and self-criticism:

> ...shame-based self-criticism and self-attacking are among the most pervasive problems in Western societies and seriously undermine our contentment and well-being. They're the opposite of self-compassion. Rather than feeling support, kindness and enthusiasm for ourselves when things go wrong, we feel anger, disappointment, frustration or even contempt for ourselves. (Gilbert, 2013, p.351)

Gilbert (2013) uses a CBT-based approach to help clients develop more self-compassion through analysing self-critical thoughts and fears through two lenses:

- How I think others feel about me and view me.

- What I feel and think about myself.

He suggests that our 'go-to' place is often to catastrophise and feel that we're not good enough. In an example of all-or-nothing thinking, we often feel that *everyone* views us negatively and that we are *always* a failure. Much of our unhappiness can then be found in the gap between an idealised version of the self (perfect and not attracting any criticism or shaming from others) and the self whom I find myself to be (not perfect and failing to live up to standards I believe others are judging me by and which I am using to judge myself).

In a form of radical acceptance that finds its roots in mindfulness, compassion-focused therapy invites clients to find ways of letting go of these perfectionist, all-or-nothing views of themselves and others by showing how harmful they can be and how they can lead to feelings of 'stuckness' and despair.

As the client begins to let go of polarised thinking patterns and to allow that a Winnicottian 'good enough' self is good enough, the therapist can then help them to distinguish between patterns of thoughts and behaviours that are self-attacking and those that are 'compassionate self-correction'.

There are many examples, exercises, and techniques that are written about in far greater detail than is possible to cover here. For readers interested in building compassion-focused ways of working into their practice, we would recommend reading Gilbert's (2013) *The Compassionate Mind* and exploring the rich literature around MBCT or even attending an eight-week mindfulness course, many of which are available throughout the UK.

The more that people resist the binary rules of heteronormativity and are simply out there in the world, then the more that discourse of normativity is challenged. Although we have to resist the positivist temptation to always see the arc of history as inexorably moving towards greater and greater enlightenment, it's hard to deny that, historically, Britain has been a deeply homophobic and unpleasant environment for LGBTQ people. In contrast, we now have a position where the most recent UK election saw 45 out gay MPs elected, making up 7 per cent of the total, not only the highest level of LGB representation ever in the UK, but also in the world. In contrast, just 7 of the 535 members of the US Congress are openly gay at the time of writing. Moreover, in the summer of 2017, Ireland voted Leo Varadkar, not only the first man of colour, but also the youngest and the first out gay man as Taoiseach. At the same time, in Serbia, not a particular bastion of LGBT rights, the President nominated an out gay woman as Serbia's first female and first openly gay Prime Minister.

If these events say anything about Western society (perhaps the USA excepted for now), then it is that it gradually appears to be becoming more tolerant and open to difference. Affirming difference may not be every LGBTQ person's experience all around the country, but as the campaign says, 'It Does Get Better', and organisations and governments keep fighting for greater protections for minority groups. Our affirmative work as therapists and counsellors is a contribution towards that effort.

 Exercise

As we have seen, the challenges that trans people can face in social spaces can often reduce gender to a specific set of physical traits. The meaning applied to external signifiers of gender by the trans person and others can make a big difference to how they feel about themselves in social spaces. For example, a 6'3" natal male who spent time body-building in his twenties, but who has now transitioned, may find it a lot harder not to be singled out in public because broad shoulders and height are a traditional male attribute.

The exercise in Table 15.1 may be a helpful tool for practitioners to examine their own beliefs and assumptions around physical appearance and gender identity. Take some time to consider your own relationship to the following attributes. Although you don't need to go through these attributes (and others) as an exhaustive list, they are points that you should be aware of in both your own and your client's experience of being in social spaces.

Table 15.1 Helpful tool for practitioners to examine their own beliefs and assumptions	
Typical feminine physical attributes	Typical masculine physical attributes
• Make-up/feminine features • Longer hair • No facial and/or body hair • Feminine shape/fat distribution • Breasts • Higher voice • No 'Adam's apple' • Women's clothing/jewellery/ accessories	• Physical size – tall and broad shouldered • Facial and/or body hair • Muscularity/male fat distribution • No breasts • Deeper voice

– Are they important for your own gender identity?

– How do you perceive and make meaning of them for yourself and for others whom you encounter?

– How do you think you come across with your clients?

– What impact do these gendered markers have on your relationship with clients across the gender spectrum?

– If you're working with a TGNC person, how is your gender identity and expression likely to be understood and experienced by your client?

Therapy and counselling clearly have an important role in helping TGNC people make sense of their experiences in social spaces – of which employment is just one. Moreover, you have an equally important role in being alongside and affirmatively advocating for your clients when they experience prejudice. In part, your work in the psychology of identities helps to affirm that gender is not something discrete and to be problematised at an individual level, but instead is something that is socially produced and mediated. Although you may work one-to-one in the privileged therapeutic space with your clients, you do so as a way of affirming TGNC identities and their right to be experienced, performed, and enjoyed out in the world just as much as any more mainstream and binary identities are.

16

INTERSECTIONALITY AND GENDER

This book has had two main areas of focus: first, how gender identity is made sense of in all of its variance; and, second, how mental health professionals can work affirmatively with questions and issues of gender identity and diversity in the counselling room. Although we have a specific focus on gender, we acknowledge that all of us are not simply defined by one aspect of our identities, but that the many different subjectivities that we hold will work dynamically with one another, affected by both time and context. 'Intersectionality' refers to this interactivity between different social identity structures and, importantly, how interactions are productive of both privilege and oppression. In this chapter, we will look at the history and meaning of intersectionality, its implication for trans identities, and the impact that it has on the counselling process. As always, we start with a caveat that the literature and research on intersectionality, especially as it applies to gender, is considerable. In this chapter, we aim to explore some of the main themes to draw attention to its importance in understanding and working with gender. The reader is once again encouraged to use this as a stepping-off point in order to continue to explore and to become an ever more aware and affirmative practitioner.

A WORD ON LANGUAGE

Before we start, we'd like to foreground this discussion on intersectionality with a recognition that an important debate exists in the literature, academia, and journalism about when and, indeed, whether to capitalise words that refer to racial characteristics: 'black' vs 'Black', 'white' vs 'White', and so on. We recognise that, at different times and in different contexts, writers have chosen to capitalise one or other of the words in order to communicate a certain prejudice. For example, a number of White supremacist websites will capitalise the word 'White' but not 'black', potentially to give greater prominence to their racial identity than the one they seek to denigrate. Moreover, writers have pointed to the way in which Asian, Hispanic, Arab, or other racial, cultural, and ethnic identities are capitalised in the written work as an argument for capitalising all such descriptors.

As we have seen in our exploration of the language that we use to describe gender identity, language can reflect and foster bias and even invite violence, and so the choice to capitalise or not is not a trivial one. Whilst we acknowledge that the terms 'Black' and 'White' are not themselves representative of the heterogeneity of those markers, our decision, mindful of the debate in the literature, and in a deliberate attempt to avoid bias, is to capitalise all such descriptors in the text in this book.

UNPACKING INTERSECTIONALITY
What is intersectionality?

A critical legal studies scholar, and one of the founders of critical race theory, Kimberle Crenshaw coined the term *intersectionality* to show how the separation of different areas of identity in public policy, for example gender identity and race, worked to render the experience of Black women invisible. She argued that movements for racial equality were sexist as they were ostensibly led by Black men who pursued the goal of equality with White men. Moreover, she argued that the women's movement was racist since it was led by White women who equally prioritised the goal of equality with White men. For Crenshaw, this meant that Black women needed to develop their own ways of conceptualising identity structures that recognised the unique intersections of their Black and female subjectivities:

> Black women sometimes experience discrimination in ways similar to White women's experiences; sometimes they share very similar experiences with Black men. Yet often they experience double-discrimination – the combined effects of practices which discriminate on the basis of race, and on the basis of sex. And sometimes, they experience discrimination as Black women – not the sum of race and sex discrimination, but as Black women... Yet, the continued insistence that Black women's demands and needs be filtered through categorical analyses that completely obscure

their experiences guarantees that their needs will seldom be addressed.
(Crenshaw, 1989, p.149)

In articulating intersectionality, Crenshaw was building on the work
of (mostly Black) feminist writers and activists in the USA for over a
century, from the famous words of Sojourner Truth at a women's rights
convention in Akron, Ohio, in 1851: 'Ain't I a Woman?' She was also
making explicit the idea that identity categories are not simply additive
– you cannot measure oppression by simply adding together different
minority subjectivities, for example identifying as a Black, lesbian woman
(Bowleg, 2008). Furthermore, she argued for a systemic, rather than
individualistic, focus, resisting the temptation to see subjectivity as resting
within a modernist idea of the bounded self, but instead realising that it is
constantly being negotiated in social structures and relationships. As such,
intersectional researchers and practitioners are invited to use their insight
to drive advocacy, activism, and movements for social change (Robbins
and McGowan, 2016).

Intersectionality is not simply another way of describing a focus on
diversity and difference: it's a way of exploring how different subjectivities
are productive of power and privilege as well as oppression. Writing about
the researcher Patricia Hill Collins' (2000) work on intersectionality as a
'structural matrix of domination', Bonnie Moradi suggests that

multiple forces of oppression are mutually dependent in shaping people's
experiences and are situated within various cultural and historical matrices
of domination. For example, constructions of sexuality involve the mutual
dependence of heterosexism, neocolonialism, racism, sexism, and other
forms of oppression intersecting to construct different groups of people
(e.g., men from developed countries, trans and gender nonconforming
people, White women, women of color) as agents, consumers, objects,
and commodities in relation to one another within current U.S. and
global matrices of domination. (2017, p.108)

Although its roots are in the exploration of the intersection of race
and gender identity by feminist scholars, intersectionality has since
been expanded to explore a whole range of identity categories and
their interrelationships. In considering the operation of privilege and
oppression through intersecting identities, we might now explore gender,
race, ethnicity, class, economic status and wealth, (dis)ability, religion,
sexual orientation, parental status, education level, body shape (including

weight, height, etc.), relative athletic prowess, hair colour, political beliefs and affiliations, and many more.

 Exercise

- When you reflect on this introduction to intersectionality, what kind of person do you immediately imagine? Write down as many aspects as you can of that imaginary person.

- Which aspects of identity does this imaginary person share with you and how many are different?

- What does this pen-portrait tell you about the dimensions of intersectionality that you're likely to focus on in your work?

- With what kinds of clients would you consider intersectionality and whom would you overlook?

- Do you tend to consider intersectionality as being intrinsic (within you and people like you) or extrinsic (located in others and in people different from you)?

- What can you do to promote an intersectional way of thinking and working with all of your client base – even those whom you wouldn't consider in your immediate pen-portrait exercise?

What does intersectionality mean in practice?

As its most basic level, intersectionality means that 'every person in society is positioned at the intersection of multiple social identity structures and is thus subject to multiple social advantages and disadvantages' (Gopaldas, 2013, p.91). As we have seen, those advantages and disadvantages are not fixed – instead they are fluid and contingent not only on context but also age and a whole host of other factors. For example, a young Black man might experience his masculinity in one way in his role as a waiter in an upmarket London restaurant, and in yet another in his role as a postgraduate student of International Relations. A middle-aged Asian woman working in a city bank as a derivatives analyst might experience her feminine gender identity in one way in a predominantly all-male environment at work, and in yet another with her girlfriend in the evenings. In a similar way, a man who has spent his career building the respect of his colleagues may experience a profound loss of that male privilege following retirement.

All of us are subject to the ways in which our relative privilege is shaped by structural inequities in the societies in which we find ourselves. One interesting thing that an intersectional view of the world can give us, therefore, is what Collins refers to as a 'heuristic device' (1998, p.205) or tool for thinking about how these inequities are produced, maintained, defended, and reproduced. And, further, how the different identity categories are not discrete but mutually interdependent and productive.

 Exercise

Consider your current client list:

- Are you aware of the intersectional dynamics that might be at play in the work?

- Are you aware of any clients whom you might focus on group differences and culture as explanatory factors for their presenting problems?

- To what extent is there any empirical evidence in the literature for your assumptions?

- Do you take the same attitude to both privilege and oppression when considering the operation of power in the life of your clients?

The challenge, then, if we cannot escape structural inequities and the power relations they produce, is to ask ourselves what we can do about it. Foucault wrote extensively about the phenomenology of power, its relationship with knowledge, and its role in the production of identity. He suggested that the appropriate response to an experience of subjectification is resistance:

> I would like to suggest another way to go toward a new economy of power relations, a way that is more empirical, more directly related to our present situation, and one that implies more relations between theory and practice. It consists in taking the forms of resistance against different forms of power as a starting point. To use another metaphor, it consists in using this resistance as a chemical catalyst so as to bring to light power relations, locate their position, find out their point of application and the methods used. (Foucault, 2000b, p.329)

For Foucault, the right response to an experience of privilege or oppression is to resist it so as to uncover its means of operation and reproduction.

From a practical perspective in counselling and psychotherapy, this brings us back to the idea of the reflexive and affirmative practitioner. Intersectionality challenges us to work as hard as we can to look at our own privilege and oppression and how that operates both intrapsychically within our clients and ourselves as well as intersubjectively between us.

And a good place to start is to hold in awareness the fundamental power imbalance apparent in all therapy that flows from the difference between the trained, 'expert' therapist and a client who is distressed and seeking help. Moreover, for some mental health professionals, like the authors of this book, there may be the added dimension of having the title of 'Dr' with all that it can connote in terms of implied privilege as well as client and practitioner fantasy.

Perhaps one of the most difficult aspects of intersectionality then is that it directly challenges all of us to own our own privilege and the ways in which it can work to oppress others. White feminists surely did not and do not see themselves as agents of oppression – quite the reverse. Yet, the interlocking experiences of oppression experienced by women of colour that gave birth to intersectionality directly challenged privileged White feminists to recognise and then work against the racism, classism, and heterosexism of their own feminism (Cheshire, 2013).

Cheshire goes on to explore the seminal work of McIntosh (1989) on White, heterosexual privilege – especially as it relates to thoughtless privilege. She gives the following example:

> A White lesbian woman, for example, will likely find the card industry heterosexist because when she goes to her local card store to purchase a romantic card for her lover she cannot find one that is appropriate. The lesbian woman knows that the card industry is heterosexist, but she further understands that it is also heteronormative because her straight friends do not even notice that in their local stores they have the privilege of accessing cards that reflect their lived experiences. The lesbian woman knows she is outside of society's assumptions about romantic relationships because she must plan ahead and order her cards over the Internet. The straight woman's sexuality is celebrated and affirmed in all spaces. (Cheshire, 2013, p.10)

Although it's arguably exhaustive to devote a whole paragraph to the ways in which people buy greetings cards, Cheshire's example is illustrative of the small and everyday ways in which different intersections of identity categories are experienced. And it is often activism towards highlighting those everyday privileges that gets certain sections of the tabloid press bulging at the eyes over 'political correctness gone mad'. In these protestations, we can arguably see the cry of a privileged group that is unwilling to work towards a similar privilege for any other group. It's almost as if privilege is a precious and limited resource and that its transaction is a zero-sum game. The more privilege I give you, the less I'll have for myself. Moreover, at the moment, my privilege makes me feel good about myself and I may lose that sense of self-satisfaction of being better than you if I allow you privilege as well.

Dr Martin Luther King Jr. famously spoke of similar processes in his speech at the end of the third civil rights march from Selma to Montgomery in Alabama on 25 March 1965. He spoke of how those with power, the so-called 'southern aristocracy', worked to keep poor White and poor Black people apart so that they would not recognise their shared subjectivities and organise to overthrow a corrupt and unjust system of government that was oppressing them both:

> If it may be said of the slavery era that the White man took the world and gave the Negro Jesus, then it may be said of the Reconstruction era that the southern aristocracy took the world and gave the poor White man Jim Crow. He gave him Jim Crow. And when his wrinkled stomach cried out for the food that his empty pockets could not provide, he ate Jim Crow, a psychological bird that told him that no matter how bad off he was, at least he was a White man, better than the Black man. And he ate Jim Crow. And when his undernourished children cried out for the necessities that his low wages could not provide, he showed them the Jim Crow signs on the buses and in the stores, on the streets and in the public buildings. And his children, too, learned to feed upon Jim Crow, their last outpost of psychological oblivion. *Dr Martin Luther King Jr.* (Carson and Shepard, 2001, p.140)

Although not explicitly articulated as intersectionality in this speech, King references the ways in which privilege and oppression intersect. In this case, although the poor White man is oppressed due to his lower class and lower economic power, he can at least access the privilege that American society affords White people over people of colour.

Finally, before moving on to look at the specific relationship of intersectionality to gender identity and how this might manifest in the therapeutic relationship, we want to point out the relationship between power and privilege and the 'natural' and 'divine'. Whenever we see power relations in societies, we see the hand of the institutions that produce, legitimise, and reproduce that power. More often than not, these institutions – whether legal, religious, medical, or otherwise – have an appeal to a divine, natural order. In other words, White people are superior to Black people because, variously, the Bible tells us so, or physiology and 'science' both 'prove' objectively that this is the case. Discrimination and oppression cannot be seen by those who oppress to simply be a matter of caprice and personal choice, but instead as a way of ensuring God's 'natural' order is maintained. The transphobic person does not see herself as individually biased or hate-filled – she is simply communicating and living out what her god has assured her is the right, just, and 'natural' order of things. Thus, what is in the interest of those with privilege becomes legitimised by recourse to a God-given right for that to be so. As Dyer has pointed out, 'power in contemporary society habitually passes itself off as embodied in the normal as opposed to the superior… [T]his is common to all forms of power' (1988, p.45).

 Exercise

Take some time to write down all the aspects of your own identity and subjectivity and write as many as you can possibly think of. Now, go back and look at that list and consider the intersections of all of those different aspects of your identity, not just the additive effects of the privilege on one side vs the oppression on the other:

– How do they interact?

– Does an exploration of the list and a reflection on its intersectionality bring up anything new for you in terms of how you see privilege and oppression working in your own identity and between that of yourself and your clients?

INTERSECTIONALITY AND GENDER IDENTITY

The Black feminist movement created, researched, and developed the concept of intersectionality from the starting place of gender and race, and therefore gender identity is at the heart of intersectionality's epistemology. Although our book has a focus on trans and other non-conforming gender identities, it is fundamental to our approach that all practitioners work with all of their clients in a way that is aware of intersectionality.

It's clear that power and privilege operate in the production, policing, and reproduction of normative gender identities; a large part of this book is devoted to uncovering and exploring its effects for all of us. Men hold considerable power and privilege over women and shame non-normative masculine behaviours as unnatural in order to retain the power of patriarchy. This is true even to the extent that subordinated men – such as those from non-White backgrounds, with lower socioeconomic status or with sexual minority or non-normative gender identities – still reap the 'patriarchy dividend'. Despite legislation to the contrary, subordinated men and women are often still positioned in their day-to-day lives and experiences as 'less than' cisgender, heterosexual, White men. Yet, these subordinated identities may still continue to police aspects of gender performance in a normative way amongst themselves, one such example being the privileging of 'straight-acting' hyper-masculinity in gay culture.

For women, there can be an overwhelming and oppressive requirement to find 'real' femininity in normative notions of female beauty, organised around ideals based on norms of White, heterosexual women. South Korea has now become the plastic surgery capital of the world, with many parents paying for their children to have double-eyelid surgery to have more 'Western-looking' eyes before they start college. In a similar way, skin-lightening has become a trend in Asia, with women looking to boost their social status through whiter skins. And the trend for conforming to Western standards of beauty looks to be spreading to men, too. Roger Pe, writing for the *Business Inquirer* in October 2016, quotes industry statistics that the global market for skin-lighteners is 'projected to reach $19.8 billion by 2018, driven by the growing desire for light-coloured skin among both men and women primarily from the Asian, African and Middle East regions' (Pe, 2016). In a similar vein, Chris Rock sent up African American women's obsession with hair in his comic documentary *Good Hair* in 2009. In particular, he commented on the various techniques designed to straighten hair or to incorporate weaves made from South Asian women's hair, donated to temples in India, that are intended to give African American women the characteristics of European (or 'White') hair.

Cole and Zucker explore the intersection of femininity and race and suggest that there is a structural inequality related to how African American women are stereotypically portrayed as 'unattractive, aggressive, sexually promiscuous, and bad mothers' (Cole and Zucker, 2007, p.2). Once again, 'real' femininity is conflated with appearance, passivity, chastity, and motherhood, and Black women's ability to access the full power of normative femininity is blocked by their being positioned as outside these characteristics due to their Blackness.

Case vignette: Gemma

Following a serious car accident in which she received severe burns, Gemma has been referred for therapy to help her to make sense of and adjust to her new appearance. A young single woman, she now has significant scarring on one side of her face and fears that she may no longer be attractive enough to ever find a partner. Her therapist is of a similar age, married with one young child, is traditionally attractive, and likes to take considerable time on her appearance in terms of personal grooming and fashion.

 Reflection

– How do you think that Gemma's counsellor might be able to sensitively explore what is present in the room in terms of the different intersections of gender identity and normative expectations of feminine beauty and attractiveness?

– How might both the client and the therapist resist and avoid making these dynamics explicit?

All of these normative interdictions apply to an even greater extent for TGNC people since from the start they are disciplined for troubling or transgressing the binary. When they do come out, they are also often required to be as normatively appropriate in their post-transition gender identity as possible. For many trans people, this can be troubling and confusing. A person assigned male at birth who transitions to a female gender identity can often find that the specific privileges that they had in a male gender identity have now gone. They can find themselves required to possess normative attributes such as feminine beauty, passivity, chastity, and motherhood, and that, moreover, they are now subject to a male gaze when out and about in their daily lives. At times, it can seem to them that they are being singled out for appraisal, whereas often they may simply be experiencing the fact that women are looked at a great deal more in our society than men. Similarly, transmaculine people may find that they have access to some areas of male privilege post transition, but that their access is contingent upon their apparent normativity as well as other intersectional categories such as class, race, age, and physical size.

There are obviously many more different intersections between gender and other identity categories than is possible to explore here in full. Recent research has begun to explore a variety of different intersections, including ethnicity and religiosity among trans people (Collier *et al.*, 2013), TGNC people's experience as parents (Haines, Ajayi, and Boyd, 2014), and trans women of colour's experience of healthcare (Sevelius, 2013), among others. Although the majority of this research speaks from a US-centric experience, nevertheless, some examples from the literature help to highlight some of the themes that we have been exploring so far.

Gender identity and race

Schug *et al.* (2015) used gendered race theory to look at how Asian men and Black women were portrayed in the popular media in the USA. Given that Asian men are prototypically positioned as feminine and Black women (as we have seen elsewhere) as masculine, they were interested to see whether these biases were reflected in popular media. They looked at 8672 individuals across five issues of six popular magazines and found that both groups were relatively invisible. Where Asians were represented they were far more likely to be women, and where Black people were represented they were far more likely to be men. Their findings were consistent with the predictions of gender race theory, which argues that 'stereotypes about race are gendered, with Asians stereotyped as more feminine and Blacks as more masculine' (Schug *et al.*, 2015, p.229).

Exercise

Consider how your Black and Asian trans clients might experience specific operations of privilege and oppression depending on their transition:

–   Are Asian trans women, and Black trans men likely to be able to access greater visibility or privilege as a result of their transition than, say, Asian trans men or Black trans women might do?

–   How do you think that your clients' experience of (in)visibility in the past might affect their expectations as they transition?

Gender identity and sexuality

A great deal has been written about the specific intersection of sexuality and gender identity. Indeed, the relationship between the two is highly productive of assumptions in the general public and attendant homophobia and transphobia. Some researchers have suggested that it is non-normative gender performance that gives rise to homophobia rather than the sexual orientation itself; that gay women and men who otherwise present in a normatively gendered way have less prejudice shown towards them than gay men and women who are more transgressive. As one participant in Mizock and Hopwood's research into the conflation of gender and sexuality in trans people commented:

> I still maintain that the violence that people have against gay people is really gender-based, because gay people – and lesbian and bisexual – are all going against society's definition of what it is to be a man or a woman and how that looks. And so if you are slightly effeminate and gay, you're going to get beaten up. If you're butch and female – lesbian – you're going to be beaten up. And it's really based on gender expression. (Mizock and Hopwood, 2016, p.97)

Trans people challenge binary norms in gender that are also often strongly policed in the LGBTQ community and they may be on the receiving end of prejudice and exclusion for the way in which their sexuality intersects with their gender identity. A previously heterosexual person in a male role who transitions may find herself marginalised as a lesbian woman, and a previously lesbian woman may lose the support of a significant community in his life if he is excluded on the basis of his acquired heterosexual male gender identity (see Bockting, Benner, and Coleman, 2009). This so-called 'privilege exchange' (Mizock and Hopwood, 2016, p.99) is productive of a variety of privileges and oppressions for trans people as they negotiate the changing intersections of gender identity and sexuality.

As we have already seen in Chapter 14, it's a mistake to conflate sexuality and gender identity. Recent research by Katz-Wise *et al.* (2016) suggests that as many as 58 per cent of their sample of TGNC people have reported changes in sexual attraction over their lifetime, with 64 per cent reporting change in attraction post-transition. Their research supports an earlier influential article by Diamond and Butterworth (2008) that reflected dynamic identity construction amongst TGNC people. They suggested that changes in attraction amongst the previously lesbian and bisexual identified natal women in their sample towards men post-transition was less about an attraction to masculine traits and more of a reflection of the shift in interpersonal power dynamics. As men they experienced a more equal power relationship with men and became more open to sexual relationships with them as a result. As Moradi writes, this research fundamentally troubles our taken-for-granted assumptions that sexualities are based on attraction of gendered traits and may in fact (also) be related to power relations:

Both analyses reveal the dynamic process of identity construction across time and place and how recognizing this dynamism could yield fundamentally new ways of thinking about human experience – for example, viewing interpersonal power as central to sexual orientation. In clinical practice, this shift can be subtle but powerful: Instead of asking how clients' gender, ethnicity–race, and sexual orientation influence their presenting concerns, one might ask: How do my clients construct themselves in various interpersonal, structural, historical, and other power dynamics; how do these dynamics shape my clients; and how do these patterns of co-construction shape clients' presenting concerns? (2017, p.117)

Gender identity and disability

Dispenza, Varney, and Golubovic (2016) explored the lived experiences of sexual and gender minority people living with chronic illnesses or disabilities (CID). They drew on research that suggests sexual and gender minority people suffer greater prevalence of CIDs than the general population and wanted to find out what specific needs this population had from their mental health professionals. Their research highlighted four key themes:

- *Competence in intersectionality* – The importance of having an understanding of how different identities intersect to deliver experiences of discrimination and prejudice; at its most basic level, to understand that 'institutional power impacts one's health when power is not allotted to someone who is LGBT and living with a disability' (p.139).

- *Affirmative consciousness* – Affirmative practice means being aware of and resisting one's own prejudices, including 'being open, accepting, compassionate, respectful, non-judgmental, strengths-based, and supportive toward sexual and gender minority persons living with CID' (p.140).

- *Social justice and practice* – Having an orientation towards action and advocacy on behalf of clients logically flows from an affirmative model of practice. In practical terms this might involve recognising the unique needs of sexual and gender minority clients when it comes to referring to appropriately affirmative support groups.

- *Ethical values* – We have seen that there are codes of practice for working with sexual and gender minority clients from bodies such as the BPS; it is important for clients who also experience a chronic illness or disability that practitioners evidence those values in terms of building trust in a commitment to confidentiality and a high standard of professional care.

Gender identity and economic status

Ahir Gopaldas writes from the perspective of intersectionality as it affects economics, public policy, and marketing, and suggests that there are similar dynamic processes at play that affect individuals' experience of economic privilege and oppression. He cites research by Henry (2005, p.769), which reveals that

> young men in working class (professional-class) families are socialized to perceive themselves as impotent reactors (potent actors). In turn, these self-perceptions encourage security-oriented (growth-oriented) investment strategies. The study illuminates how a set of psycho-cultural mechanisms helps keep the poor poor and the rich rich. Insights from this study can inform the educational programs in vocational schools. Young working-class men could be made aware of their own class socialization (e.g., as 'chill,' 'easygoing' men) and familiarized with the socialization of professional-class men (e.g., as 'ambitious,' 'focused' men) to help close the rich–poor gap. (Gopaldas, 2013, p.93)

Case vignette: Casey

Casey is a middle-aged, White trans man from a working-class background in Bolton. He works part time in a small manufacturing business just outside town and comes from a family who worked for several generations in the coal-mining and textile industries there. They have been supportive throughout his transition and continue to be very close. He has come for counselling following the breakdown of his seven-year relationship with his partner and his recent retreat into binge-drinking and occasional acts of violence and other public order offences when drunk.

Casey's therapist, Claire, is a White, middle-class professional in her early 30s. She was born and brought up in Worcestershire; her parents divorced just after she was born. Her stepfather is a senior manager for a global IT firm and her mother has not worked since her children were born. Her stepfather occasionally drinks to excess and was violent towards Claire, her mother, and younger brother at times when she was young. Claire was privately educated and recently completed a PsychD in Counselling Psychology. She is married and she and her husband plan to start a family soon.

 Reflection

- What comes up for you in reading these biographical backgrounds of client and therapist here?

- What different intersections of identity are there for both people and how do you think that these would manifest in the room – in terms of accents, mode, style of dress, life experience, expectations, and assumptions?

INTERSECTIONALITY IN COUNSELLING PRACTICE

Cheshire argues that 'there appears to be a shift taking place in the field of counselling and psychotherapy that is calling for counsellors to adopt more complex models of social identities in their work' (2013, p.8). She cites work by Watts-Jones (2010), who applies intersectionality theory directly in her counselling practice in family therapy.

Watts-Jones talks about a technique called *location of self* that a reflexive, affirmative practitioner can use in her work with clients, bringing intersectionality explicitly into the room. In this approach, the therapist would, for example, specifically locate herself as a middle-class, heterosexual, cisgender, British Asian mother, and mental health professional, and invite the client to do the same and to use what comes up in that context to uncover conscious and unconscious workings of power, privilege, and prejudice. The argument here is that intersectionality cannot simply be thought of as a theoretical and academic construct but instead as something that has immanent effects on and in the therapeutic relationship and process. Although this is a potentially challenging way to work for many practitioners, particularly because of its requirement to make explicit aspects of identity that may be assumed to be hidden, Watts-Jones and others, such as Ecklund (2012), would argue that, because intersectional identities are universal (present for both the therapist and client) as well as always connected to social constructs of privilege and oppression, they are present in the relationship anyway and can be more effectively worked through if they are made explicit.

Moreover, intersectionality has implications for counselling and therapy trainings where there may be an absence of focus on the dynamic interplay of identity categories. Typically (and in the authors' own experience), trainings integrate questions of gender, sexuality, race, and class into a singular module entitled something like 'Working with Difference'. Not only can this help to conflate identity categories as simple 'difference', potentially overlooking complex intersections of power and privilege, but it also tends to position and reinforce Whiteness, heterosexuality, and cisgender identities as the benchmark for measuring difference while simultaneously avoiding studying each of those identity categories. For training institutions to give the same space and attention to studies of Whiteness, heterosexuality, and cisgender identity may seem nonsensical to some, but it could help to uncover the conscious and unconscious privileges that go with these identity categories – including, as we have seen, the privilege of not being aware of that privilege.

INTERSECTIONALITY AND RESILIENCE

As Foucault suggested, wherever there is the operation of power there exists the possibility for resistance and resilience. Bowleg (2013) asked Black sexual minority men about the benefits of their intersecting identities and found that they prized the opportunity it gave them for *psychological growth* through introspection as well as the *freedom* that it gave them to explore new ways of being free from the constraints of normative sexual and gender performance. These benefits gave them resilience in the face of intersecting identities that worked to reduce their access to cultural privilege.

Another process that has been linked to resistance and resilience for trans and sexual minority people has been the membership of communities and groups that help to promote those senses of growth and freedom, referred to in Bowleg's (2013) research. Singh (2013) researched TGNC youth of colour and found that they actively sought connection in like-minded communities, through social media and self-advocacy, as a way of resisting discrimination and oppression.

Moreover, recognition of the psychological growth that comes through facing adversity, exploration of freedom to be outside the traditional societal norms, and the discovery of networks of support can lead to greater moves towards political activism. Pride as a form of political activism can help to reduce internalised shame around minority identity status – for example, internalised racism, transphobia, or homophobia.

Research by Velez, Moradi, and DeBlaere (2015) found that lower rates of internalised racism and heterosexism worked to improve individuals' resilience when it came to discrimination experienced by Latina/o sexual minority people. As Moradi points out, 'resisting internalization of one form of oppression may protect self-esteem when faced with high levels of another form of oppression' (2017, p.116).

 Exercise

- What can you do to actively support your TGNC clients in resisting discrimination and oppression and to build resilience?

- What part could you play in both signposting towards as well as supporting community groups?

- What is your attitude to political activism as a professional – both in the field of gender identity as well as mental health more generally?

It is clear that all of us have a variety of intersecting identities that act to privilege and oppress us and that these intersections are contingent on many factors, including context and time. Although we have only been able to briefly introduce some of the main themes in intersectionality theory here, in particular as they apply to questions of gender identity, the process of engagement with intersectionality challenges us to question taken-for-granted assumptions for both our clients and ourselves. We are invited to consider not only our own privilege, but also how that privilege might be contributing to discrimination against another group. The trans model Munroe Bergdorf was publicly dropped from a lucrative contract with L'Oréal in August 2017, following comments that she made about White supremacist ideology and racism following the violent clashes between demonstrators in Charlottesville, Virginia, on 11 and 12 August 2017. Channel 4 News in the UK interviewed her on 2 September 2017 and in her interview she succinctly highlighted the relationship between White privilege and racism. She had specifically been criticized for saying that 'all White people' were racist and responded by trying to explain and unpack what she called 'structural racism'. She argued that all White people, whether actively racist or not, benefit from the structures in society which privilege White people over people of colour. In her view, unless a White person is actively doing something to dismantle racism then they are complicit in racism, even if they do not actively espouse or profess racist views. Given the outcry over her comments and views, it was clear that this was the first time that many White people who did not consider themselves racist were actively challenged to consider how their own intersecting identities acted not only to confer privilege upon them but also to perpetuate systems and structures that produce oppression for others.

Part III

PRACTITIONER SELF-CARE

17

SUPERVISION AND SELF-CARE

In this chapter, we will be looking at how the professional divide between the 'therapist' and 'client' relies on very specific social roles, at the importance of reflexivity, supervision, and self-care, and addressing the challenges and pitfalls this presents. In engaging with this chapter, the reader is invited to bring to bear all the preceding chapters and how they relate to the therapeutic relationship and the therapist within it. In working with issues of gender identity, the therapy room can be a microcosm where all the issues discussed so far are played out. It's a unique space where we have the opportunity to consciously examine, deconstruct, and acknowledge the impact of privilege where it lies in both the therapist and the client.

New psychology trainees at the London GIC often agreed that the placement interview there was the hardest that they had had to attend in their training. The interview process is both selective and competitive as there are limited placement slots, so it is preferable to allocate them to those most likely to want to develop a specialism in gender. The work itself can be demanding for trainees as a certain level of maturity, previous experience, grounding in self and ego strength, and ability to deal with challenging situations is necessary. We always include questions around use of supervision and self-care.

WHY IS SUPERVISION IMPORTANT?

We would hope that anyone reading this book already has an answer to this question and is in agreement that supervision is important. It is always worth revisiting this periodically, though, as, with many things that we take for granted over time, we can lose sight of the meaning behind the words. Once the excitement and newness of training disappears into the increasing distance, perhaps supervision can seem no longer as necessary or beneficial as it once was. After all, now we know what we are doing and the more specialist our work is, the more specialist knowledge we appear to have relative to other practitioners. But, despite this, we make no apology for re-treading old ground with this in a book on working with gender-related issues. We have discussed in depth how much gender is a part of all of our lives and how it influences self-experience, self-expression, and beliefs that we have about what we can or are allowed to achieve. All of that complex process is brought into therapy and magnified when working around gender and often, in direct relation to it, sexuality.

Supervision has been described as evaluative and gatekeeping (Bernard and Goodyear, 1992), a relationship between senior and junior professional members (Watkins, 1997), a learning alliance (Fleming and Benedek, 1983), and a form of teaching (Linehan, 1980). The assumptive world of the supervisor described by Bernard and Goodyear (1992) and discussed in Watkins (1997) fits particularly well here, where much of what we have explored has been around therapist assumptions and the wider social discourses. The assumptive world is created from the professional and the personal, reflecting our assumptions, values, and life perspectives, our place in the world, and the society within which we live (Watkins, 1997). The therapeutic orientation underlying supervision will vary across supervisor–supervisee relationships and there is evidence that greater compatibility can facilitate more effective supervision. The assumptive world of each individual, however, extends far beyond his or her therapeutic orientation, even if this is influenced by it. In entering into effective supervision, both parties are contracting to having their assumptive worlds questioned when appropriate, particularly the supervisee who may not initially be aware when discussing client issues how much this is affecting their work around gender. Hopefully, we have already conveyed in this book how important increasing self-awareness and reviewing assumptions is for therapists working with gender-related issues, and the potential negative implications of operating from a default, heteronormative, cisgender take on the world.

Later models and definitions of supervision further emphasise the supportive nature of it, the protection of the client outside the role of gatekeeping new members joining the profession, the well-being of the practitioner, and raised self-awareness. A supervisor has been referred to as someone who can bring a detached, yet concerned and compassionate, perspective to counselling practice, identifying material and processes that lie at the periphery of the supervisee's awareness (Woskett, Page, and Page, 2002). Here, the supervisor acts rather like the therapist who brings something just over the border of client awareness into conscious processing. Woskett *et al.* (2002) raise a cautionary note regarding the proliferation of complex models of supervision, linked to specific and increasingly newer theories of counselling. They suggest that, somewhere in the attempt to apply complex theoretical ideas, the humanity of the relationship may get lost. The energy and creativity of the connection between that supervisor and supervisee may be disrupted as both try to apply theoretical learning at the expense of 'tacit knowing', the product of integrated learning, experience, different client encounters, personal development, and the bringing of the self.

Murdoch (2013) reminds us of the joy and engagement that also usefully comprises part of supervision and an effective learning partnership. She explores the transformative nature of this professional dialogue facilitating the supervised therapist in working more skilfully and utilising the self in an appropriate way, emphasising the association between who we are and what we do in relation to therapy either as supervisor or therapist.

In more analytic styles of therapy, the supervisee is expected to be able to engage with depth psychological supervision, along with a recognition of the limitations of knowledge of the client in relation to the fantasies of the supervisor and supervisee around that person. They further need to take into account the countertransference and spend time differentiating between the complexities residing in the client, supervisee, and supervisor (Kugler, 2012). The interdependence of the client, therapist, supervisor, their supervisor, and so on seems particularly apparent when considering more psychodynamic supervision and therapist self-care, one image coming to mind of everyone holding lifelines interconnecting them so that all can stay afloat and move forward, whilst negotiating the peaks and troughs, fluctuating emotions, powerful dynamics, and messy complexities of the therapeutic journey.

Although there are different frameworks for conceptualising and understanding supervision, it is clear that, when working with TGNC clients, it is important to have a supervisor who is at least as reflexive, aware, and comfortable in processing questions of gender diversity and identity as the therapist. All experienced supervisors, as well as peer supervision networks, will be able to offer process guidance and insight, but often practitioners will need to have access to supervisors with extensive, specific experience in gender identity in order to have questions unpacked that they might not be aware need to be asked.

USE OF SELF

The importance of how we bring ourselves to the therapeutic encounter and the meanings made of it have been emphasised again and again throughout this book. Sometimes it might feel that the self we bring is often framed as a 'barrier' rather than also one of our unique assets. Woskett (1999) explores how the self can be acknowledged and integrated into counselling, including anxieties around moving into unchartered territory which isn't written by someone else, using who one is as a culmination of experience, knowledge, feelings, and 'knowing'. The fantasy, particularly for trainees and newly qualified therapists, can be that the client has somehow got the 'short end of the stick' in getting them. There's 'obviously' more experienced, more knowledgeable, more charismatic, well simply just *better* therapists out there that they could have been seeing. This sense can be particularly acute when working with TGNC clients where the counsellor might feel that they are not *specialist enough* to give their client a good enough therapeutic experience.

The reality, of course, is that that therapist is who the client *did* get and what they bring to the therapeutic encounter could indeed be exactly what the client needs. Both may grow out of the therapeutic encounter and it will be unique in that the outcome can only be produced by those two people. When therapy becomes something so structured in its formulation that it's the same, whoever does it, then the humanity of it will have been lost and artificial intelligence may well be the logical replacement for our therapeutic disciplines. Even when clients present with chaotic narratives and lives, with problems that seem overwhelming to the therapist, we can always ground ourselves in the recognition that we simply face another human being in the room, not a diagnosis or a label, not all the various identities that we have explored in gender and intersectionality, just another self. The question then arises: How can we best be of service to that other person? Particularly when the presenting problem is gender-related, it can be hard to just forget about all the theorising, mentally constructing the formulation or report, or wondering how we can get through this challenging session. But, sometimes, the secret to truly connecting with the person in front of us is to let go and bring our self along with the professional persona to the therapeutic encounter.

Research has long emphasised the importance of the therapist–client relationship in therapeutic change over the specific therapeutic modality (see Clarkson, 2003). The so-called 'Dodo Bird Verdict', first coined by Saul Rosenzweig in 1936 and borrowed from Lewis Carroll's *Alice in*

Wonderland, refers to the idea that all therapies are by and large equally effective; it's the common factors (such as the strength of the therapeutic alliance) that are more important than the specific technical differences that separate them. When it comes to working with different gender identities, although we would like to think that what you have read here might inform and improve your therapeutic practice, equally we don't want to be another voice telling you 'how it should be done' at the expense of your direct experience of the therapeutic encounter itself.

It may sound obvious, but, nevertheless, our observance of the effect of 'rote-learned' practice in using questionnaires and applying theory causes us to feel that it's worth repeating: It is important always to be mindful that the ultimate aim of therapy is to help the client. We can explore and affirm their gender identities, their social gender roles, and their positioning outside the binary gender model, avoid being heteronormative and biased by a cisgender-dominant discourse, challenge hegemonic masculinity, and do all the other things that will make us feel like 'good', affirmative, critical gender-aware therapists, but ultimately what matters is the quality of that encounter with that client.

 Exercise

Consider the following questions for self-reflection and discussion in supervision:

– How might your background in gender and sexuality affect and inform relationships with your clients? In what way can a similar background be affirmative for clients but also create barriers to hearing their particular experiences and solutions?

– How comfortable might you feel reflecting with the client on how you both interact in a gendered way in the therapeutic setting and the implications of this in therapy and the world outside?

– How easy is it for you to get beyond the filters of 'man', 'woman', 'non-binary', 'trans', 'gay', 'lesbian', 'bisexual', 'pansexual', 'young', 'old', etc. and connect with the client sitting in front of you? What do you need to do to facilitate personal and professional growth in this area?

– How much time do you spend on personal development of the self that you bring to your professional work?

SELF-CARE

We have looked at the importance of supervision for a range of reasons, of which practitioner self-care is one. But how can we conceptualise self-care beyond professional supervision? Is it simply a question of choosing the right kind of face cream or bubble bath because 'we are worth it'? In therapeutic work, especially in core areas of self-identity such as gender, it may take arguably a little more than that, particularly as it means shifting from the role of helper to seeing oneself as needing of care and support. As therapists, it is easy to overlook how much we witness human suffering and trauma. In the process, we are inevitably confronted with our own fears and challenges, ideally stimulating professional and personal growth, but also undoubtedly psychologically draining and physically exhausting ourselves to maintain therapeutic attention, concentration, and presence to a greater extent than we sometimes acknowledge.

The therapist has been likened to a musician where the instrument is ourselves. We need to take care of our 'instrument', especially since there are additional ethical issues to be considered when our 'instrument' is allowed to deteriorate, in that it can be reflected in the service we provide to our clients, potentially causing harm (Bush, 2015). Bush distinguishes between *macro-self-care* (larger things such as holidays, exercise, socialising, interests and hobbies, supervision, good personal care) and *micro-self-care* (more simple, small self-care actions such as mindful activities) and puts forward a range of self-care options that can be integrated into the therapist's day. The solid foundations for these are also the basics of good diet, exercise, and sufficient sleep. Some possible *micro-self-care* activities include brief meditations, short walks, sitting outside, a massage, rewarding cooking, listening to music, caring for a pet or garden, or having a coffee with a colleague talking about something other than work. The list is endless but is also highly idiosyncratic – what is enjoyable for one individual might be another's idea of hell – so, focusing on what relaxes, calms, and grounds that person is what matters. Moreover, it's important to have the kind of supervisory relationship that makes it easy for a practitioner to highlight when they feel overwhelmed, when stress is building up, and potential burnout and compassion fatigue are on the horizon.

In the same way, when we identify support resources and networks with our clients, we need to be mindful of these for ourselves as practitioners. Supervision has been placed here at the heart of good practice for the necessary support to work as an effective professional and to continue to improve as a therapist. It is also beneficial to be a member of not only the appropriate professional body but also in networks relating to specialisms so that the therapist does not feel alone in their particular work with clients. In gender care, the BPS Psychology of Sexualities Section, the British Association of Gender Identity Specialists (BAGIS), and the World Professional Association for Transgender Health (WPATH) all offer useful forums and events to link up with other professionals in the field, but practitioners can also create their own professional discussion groups in their workplaces and training institutions. Arguably, what is 'other' becomes more mainstream through assimilation by the mainstream, and sharing knowledge, good practice, and experience facilitates good practitioner self-care.

GLOSSARY

This glossary contains terms used in the book as well as some that you may come across in your work with TGNC people. It is not intended to be an exhaustive list, and the reader is directed to any number of trans support websites as well as glossaries found in books dedicated to working with TGNC people for further terms and definitions. The glossary words that are found in the text appear in **bold** where they are first mentioned.

Acquired gender
Specifically in relation to the Gender Recognition Act 2004, acquired gender refers to the gender to which a TGNC person has transitioned. For example, for a person assigned male at birth who transitions to a female gender identity, their acquired gender would be female.

Affirmative practice
A therapeutic approach that embraces a positive view of lesbian, gay, bisexual, transgender, and queer (LGBTQ) identities and relationships and addresses the negative influences that homophobia, transphobia, and heterosexism have on the lives of LGBTQ clients.

Agender
An identity term used to describe a person with no (or very little) connection to the traditional system of gender and no personal alignment with the concepts of either man or woman. It is a term that can also refer to people who see themselves as existing without gender. Other terms for the same identity include 'gender neutrois', 'gender neutral', or 'genderless'.

Androgynous
Having an identity and/or presentation that is neither specifically masculine nor feminine, but instead includes aspects of both.

Androsexual/androphilic

Describes someone who is primarily sexually, romantically, and/or emotionally attracted to some men, males, and/or masculinity.

Asexual

An asexual person is a person who does not experience sexual attraction. Although an asexual person might typically abstain from sexual intimacy, they can, and often do, experience romantic attraction and may still date and have intimate relationships.

Assigned gender

Assigned gender is the gender that a person is assigned at birth, usually conflated with birth sex and based on the appearance of a person's birth genitalia.

Augmentation mammoplasty

This refers to breast augmentation surgery, generally for trans women to increase the size of their breasts.

Bigender

An identity term to describe a person who identifies as both male *and* female and who may fluctuate between traditional 'female' and 'male' gender-based behaviour and identities.

Binding

An activity designed to compress the breasts, using a wrapping or tight piece of clothing in order to create a more masculine or androgynous chest shape. Binding is performed by many people who experience chest dysphoria due to the presence of breasts, as well as by people who experience **gynaecomastia** and are uncomfortable with the presence of breasts. People who bind regularly may desire top surgery in order to permanently remove the breasts.

Historically, binding was done using strips of cloth such as bandages. However, this method can dangerously compress the lungs, which affects breathing, and can permanently damage the breast tissue. People who wish to bind are now recommended to use specialist binding tops, or homemade equivalents such as sports bras and tightly fitting shirts.

Cisgender or cis
Someone whose gender identity and biological sex assigned at birth are aligned (e.g. man and assigned male at birth). From the Latin prefix 'cis', meaning 'on the same side [as]' or 'on this side [of]'.

Cisnormativity
The assumption, in individuals or in institutions, that everyone is cisgender, and that cisgender identity is superior to TGNC identities or people. Like all forms of normativity, cisnormativity acts to make non-cisgender identities invisible.

Cissexism
Refers to behaviour that grants preferential treatment to cisgender people, reinforcing the idea that being cisgender is somehow better than other forms of gender identity.

Deadnaming
When someone is called by their birth name after they have changed their name. This term is often associated with trans people who have changed their name as part of their transition.

Demigender
Describes a partial, but not full, connection to a particular gender identity or just to the concept of gender. Demigender people often identify as non-binary.

Female-to-male (FtM)
A term often used in clinical settings and literature (although this is changing) to refer to individuals assigned a female sex at birth who have changed, are changing, or wish to change their body and/or gender identity to a more masculine body or gender identity. Can be a problematic term as some trans men do not feel that they ever had a female identity to begin with (despite being assigned one). See 'transgender man', 'trans man', and 'transman' as alternative terms.

Gender
Often expressed in terms of masculinity and femininity, gender is largely culturally determined and is assumed from the sex assigned at birth.

Gender binary

The idea that there are only two genders and that every person is one of those two.

Gender dysphoria

Clinically significant distress caused when there is a mismatch between a person's sex assigned at birth and their gender identity. According to the American Psychiatric Association's *Diagnostic and Statistical Manual of Mental Disorders*, 'Gender dysphoria refers to the distress that may accompany the incongruence between one's experienced or expressed gender and one's assigned gender. Although not all individuals will experience distress as a result of such incongruence, many are distressed if the desired physical interventions by means of hormones and/or surgery are not available' (APA, DSM-5, 2013, p.451). See Chapters 8 and 10 for a more thorough exploration.

Gender expression

The way in which a person chooses to outwardly express their gender – most commonly through behaviour, clothing, haircut, or voice – and which may or may not conform to socially defined behaviours and characteristics typically associated with being either masculine or feminine. Sometimes referred to as 'gender presentation'.

Gender-fluid

A gender-fluid person may at any time identify as male, female, neutrois, or any other non-binary identity, or some combination of identities. Their gender can also vary at random or vary in response to different circumstances. Gender-fluid people may also identify as multigender, non-binary, and/or transgender. Gender-fluid people who feel that the strength of their gender(s) change(s) over time, or that they are sometimes agender, may identify as 'genderflux'.

Gender identity

A person's innate sense of their own gender, and how they label themselves, based on how much they align or don't align with what they understand their options to be for gender. Common identity labels include 'man', 'woman', 'genderqueer', 'trans', and more. Often confused with biological sex or sex assigned at birth.

Gender non-conforming

A broad term referring to people who do not behave in a way that conforms to the traditional expectations of their gender, or whose gender expression does not fit neatly into a category.

Genderqueer

Genderqueer people typically reject notions of static categories of gender and embrace a fluidity of gender identity and, often, although not always, sexual orientation. People who identify as genderqueer may see themselves as being both male and female, neither male nor female, or as falling completely outside these categories.

Gender reassignment

This is a more medicalised term that can be used as another way of describing a person's transition, specifically in the context of medical interventions, but can also refer to the wider social gender role transition. Try to use the terminology that the TGNC person is comfortable with.

Gender Recognition Certificate (GRC)

Under the Gender Recognition Act 2004, a Gender Recognition Certificate (GRC) enables trans people to be legally recognised in their affirmed gender and to be issued with a congruent copy of the birth certificate. Not all trans people will apply for a GRC and you currently have to be over 18 to apply. You do not need a GRC to change your gender markers at work or to legally change your gender on other documents such as your passport. For more details see Chapter 9.

Gender surgery(ies)

Sometimes also called 'sexual reassignment surgery' or 'gender confirmation surgery' (although these are debatable terms), this term can refer to any surgical procedure performed on a transgender person in order to change their sex characteristics so as to reflect their gender identity and presentation. Surgical procedures are usually preceded by hormone replacement therapy (HRT) and might include surgery to alter the genitalia (genital reconstruction surgery), chest, and breast tissue as well as facial reconstructive surgery to alter the appearance of the face.

Gender variant

Someone who either by nature or by choice does not conform to gender-based expectations of society (e.g. transgender, transsexual, intersex, genderqueer, cross-dresser, and so on).

Gynaecomastia

Gynaecomastia (sometimes referred to as 'man boobs') is a common condition that causes boys' and men's breasts to swell and become larger than normal. It is most common in teenage boys and older men and usually caused by hormonal changes either as a result of hormone therapy for trans women or as a result of obesity, since being significantly overweight can increase levels of oestrogen, which can cause breast tissue to grow.

Gynesexual/gynephilic

Describes someone who is primarily sexually, romantically, and/or emotionally attracted to some women, females, and/or femininity.

Heteronormativity

The assumption, in individuals or in institutions, that everyone is hetero-sexual (e.g. asking a woman if she has a boyfriend) and that heterosex-uality is superior to all other sexualities. Heteronormativity also leads us to assume that only masculine men and feminine women are straight.

Heterosexism

Describes behaviour that grants preferential treatment to heterosexual people and reinforces the idea that heterosexuality is somehow better or more 'right' than other sexual identities. It further has the effect of making other sexualities invisible.

Intergender

Intergender is a gender identity sometimes used by intersex people to link their sense of embodied selves and their gender identities. Intergender can be considered to be between male and female, or to be a combination of the two. Intergender people may also identify as non-binary, genderqueer, and/or transgender. However, some intergender people consider themselves cisgender, as their gender is reflective of their sex characteristics at birth.

Intersex

A more medicalised term for a combination of chromosomes, gonads, hormones, internal sex organs, and genitals that differs from the two expected patterns of male or female. Formerly known as 'hermaphrodite' or 'hermaphroditic', these terms are now considered to be outdated and derogatory.

Lower surgery

Lower surgery refers to any form of genital reconstruction surgery that may be part of a medical transition and that affects the genitalia and reproductive organs. Sometimes also referred to as 'bottom surgery'.

Male-to-female (MtF)

A term often used in clinical settings and literature (although this is changing) to refer to individuals assigned a male sex at birth who have changed, are changing, or wish to change their body and/or gender identity to a more feminine body or gender identity. Can be a problematic term as some trans women do not feel that they ever had a male identity to begin with (despite being assigned one). See 'transgender woman', 'trans woman', and 'transwoman' as alternative terms.

Non-binary

Non-binary gender (see also 'genderqueer') describes any gender identity that does not fit the male and female binary. Those with non-binary genders can feel that they have an androgynous gender identity; have an identity between male and female, such as 'intergender'; have a neutral or unrecognised gender identity, such as 'agender'; have multiple gender identities, such as 'bigender' or 'pangender'; have a gender identity that varies over time, known as 'gender-fluid'; or have a weak or partial connection to a gender identity, known as '**demigender**'. They may also define as 'intersex', or have a culturally specific gender identity that exists only within their own culture or that of their ancestor. See Chapter 7 for a more thorough exploration.

Passing

A contentious term that describes how TGNC people might be accepted as, or able to 'pass for', a member of their self-identified gender identity (regardless of sex assigned at birth) without being identified as trans. It's a controversial term because it tends to locate power in the (heteronormative, cisgender) observer rather than giving agency to the individual.

Stealth
A way of describing a trans person who is not out as trans and who is perceived by others as cisgender. It can be considered to be similarly problematic as 'passing' for the same reasons.

Top surgery
Generally refers to bilateral mastectomy and surgical chest reconstruction. Top surgery may be a part of medical transition and typically involves creating a more masculine or gender-neutral chest structure and appearance.

Trans (or trans*)
An umbrella term covering a range of identities that transgress socially defined gender norms. Trans with an asterisk (trans*) is often used in written forms (not spoken) to indicate that you are referring to the larger group nature of the term, and specifically including non-binary identities, as well as transgender men (transmen) and transgender women (transwomen).

Transfeminine
Individuals assigned male at birth who may have a more feminine identity and identify as transfeminine. They may or may not identify as non-binary.

Transgender
Descriptive of a person who identifies or has a gender expression as a member of a gender other than that assigned at birth based on anatomical sex.

Transgender and gender non-conforming (TGNC)
An umbrella term developed in the USA by the American Psychological Association Task Force on Gender Identity and Gender Variance's *Guidelines for Psychological Practice with Transgender and Gender Nonconforming People* (2015) in order to describe people who have a gender identity that is not fully aligned with their sex at birth. Intended to be as inclusive of identity categories as possible, it tends to be used in written (and more academic) texts rather than in everyday language, where 'trans' is more commonly used.

Transgender man, trans man, or transman

An identity label sometimes adopted by female-to-male transgender people in order to signify that they are men, while still affirming their history as assigned female sex at birth. Not all trans people will use these terms and may simply use 'man/boy' instead.

Transgender woman, trans woman, or transwoman

An identity label sometimes adopted by male-to-female transgender people in order to signify that they are women, while still affirming their history as assigned male sex at birth. Not all trans people will use these terms and may simply use 'woman/girl' instead.

Transition

A process that some trans people progress through when they shift towards a gender role that differs from the one associated with their sex assigned at birth. Although people may transition in ways other than across the gender binary, trans people may proceed through social transition (e.g. changes in gender expression, gender role, name, pronoun, and so on) and/or medical transition (e.g. hormone therapy, surgery, and other interventions). See Chapter 10 for a more thorough exploration.

Transmasculine

Individuals assigned female at birth who may have a more masculine identity and identify as transmasculine. They may or may not identify as non-binary.

Transphobia

This is a non-clinical term to describe a negative attitude toward people on the basis of their being trans or in some way not conforming to conventional gender roles. This negativity may also be internalised by trans people themselves after being socialised within transphobic societies, structures, and families.

Transsexual

A more medicalised term, it is best to avoid using it as a noun ('transsexualism' is used as a medical diagnosis in the World Health Organization's *International Classification of Diseases*, Version 10: 2015, ICD-10, 2015), and has been a commonly used term in the past to describe people wanting to go through medical gender treatment. 'Transsexual' predates the term 'transgender' but has since fallen into less usage among the trans community as it may imply that sex characteristics are more important than gender identity. In some cases, the term 'transsexual' is still used to refer to a subset of the transgender community who medically transition through surgery, or plan to do so, by changing their sex characteristics. Alternatively, it sometimes refers only to transgender people within the gender binary, i.e. trans men and trans women, or only to those who experience dysphoria. Although it is no longer widely used as an umbrella term, individuals sometimes use transsexual as an identity label as a matter of personal preference.

Transvestite

Individuals referred to or who identify as transvestite may generally wear clothes either in private and or in public that are associated with a different gender identity to their own but are usually not wanting to make a social gender role transition or have gender-related treatment. This typically means someone who was natally assigned male who dresses in feminine clothes, or someone who was natally assigned female (less common usage) who dresses in masculine clothes. The concept of 'transvestitism' pre-dates widespread use of the term 'transgender', so, in the past, wearing clothing of the 'opposite gender' (particularly drag) was one way for transgender people to express their identities, but, interestingly, it is an identity that could arguably be both transgender and cisgender. Since transvestitism is not necessarily linked to gender identity, a trans woman, for example, may choose to wear male drag just as much as a cis woman. They may each do so for their own reasons, without necessarily using it as a way of expessing their gender identity.

Two-spirit

An umbrella term traditionally used by Native American people to recognise individuals who possess qualities or fulfil roles of both genders.

REFERENCES

Addis, M.E., Reigeluth, C.S., and Schwab, J.R. (2016) 'Social Norms, Social Construction, and the Psychology of Men and Masculinity.' In Y.J. Wong and S.R. Wester (eds) *APA Handbook of Men and Masculinities*. Washington, DC: American Psychological Association.

The Advocate (2016) 'Pope Francis says Jesus would not abandon transgender people.' 10 March. Retrieved from: www.advocate.com/religion/2016/10/03/pope-francis-says-jesus-would-not-abandon-transgender-people (accessed 06 December 2017).

Allan, A., Atkinson, E., Brace, E., DePalma, R., and Hemingway, J. (2008) 'Speaking the unspeakable in forbidden places: Addressing lesbian, gay, bisexual and transgender equality in the primary school.' *Sex Education 8*, 3, 315–328.

American Psychiatric Association (APA) (1980) *Diagnostic and Statistical Manual of Mental Disorders*, DSM-III (Third edition). Washington, DC: APA.

APA (1994) *Diagnostic and Statistical Manual of Mental Disorders*, DSM-IV (Fourth edition). Washington, DC: APA.

APA (2013) *Diagnostic and Statistical Manual of Mental Disorders*, DSM-5 (Fifth edition). Washington, DC: APA.

American Psychological Association (2015) 'Guidelines for Psychological Practice with Transgender and Gender Nonconforming People.' *American Psychologist 70*, 9, 832–864.

Anderson, E. (2012) *Inclusive Masculinity: The Changing Nature of Masculinities*. Abingdon: Routledge.

Andrews, B. (1998) 'Shame and Childhood Abuse.' In P. Gilbert and B. Andrews (eds) *Shame: Interpersonal Behavior, Psychopathology and Culture*. New York: Oxford University Press.

Andrews, B. (2002) 'Body Shame and Abuse in Childhood.' In P. Gilbert and J. Miles (eds) *Body Shame: Conceptualisation, Research and Treatment*. Hove: Routledge.

Andrews, G., Issakidis, C., and Carter, G. (2001) 'Shortfall in mental health service utilisation.' *British Journal of Psychiatry 179*, 417–425.

Austin, A. and Craig, S.L. (2015) 'Transgender affirmative cognitive behavioural therapy: Clinical considerations and applications.' *Professional Psychology: Research and Practice 46*, 1, 21–29.

Azul, D. (2015) 'Transmasculine people's vocal situations: A critical review of gender-related discourses and empirical data.' *International Journal of Language and Communication Disorders 50*, 1, 31–47.

Bastian, R. (Producer), and Tucker, D. (Director) (2005) Transamerica [Motion Picture]. United States: The Weinstein Company and IFC Films.

BBC News (2017, 4 May) 'How a row over one word sank an LGBT petition in Australia.' Retrieved from: www.bbc.co.uk/news/world-australia-39801244 (accessed 06 December 2017).

BBC Two (2012) *Ian Hislop's Stiff Upper Lip: An Emotional History of Britain.* Series 1–3, 22 and 29 November, 6 December.

BBC Two (2017) *No More Boys and Girls: Can Our Kids Go Gender Free?* Series 1–2, 12 and 20 September.

Beattie, M. and Evans, T. (2011) 'Holding Breath: An analysis of gay men's schooldays memories.' *Psychology of Sexualities Review 2*, 1, 10–24.

Bedi, R.P. and Richards, M. (2011) 'What a man wants: The male perspective on therapeutic alliance formation.' *Psychotherapy 48*, 4, 381–390.

Beemyn, G. and Rankin, S. (2011) *The Lives of Transgender People.* New York: Columbia University Press.

Bem, S.L. (1987) 'Gender Schema Theory and Its Implications for Child Development: Raising Gender-Aschematic Children in a Gender-Schematic Society.' In M.R. Walsh (ed.) *The Psychology of Women.* New Haven, CT: Yale University Press.

Berger, J.L., Addis, M.E., Green, J.D., Mackowiak, C., and Goldberg, V. (2013) 'Men's reactions to mental health labels, forms of help-seeking, and sources of help-seeking advice.' *Psychology of Men and Masculinity 14*, 4, 433–443.

Berlant, L. and Warner, M. (1998) 'Sex in public.' *Critical Enquiry 24*, 547–566.

Bernard, J.M. and Goodyear, R.K. (1992) *Fundamentals of Clinical Supervision.* Boston, MA: Alleyn and Bacon.

Bettelheim, B. (1965) 'The Commitment Required of a Woman Entering a Scientific Profession in Present-Day American Society.' In U.S. Mattfield and C.G. Van Aken (eds) *Women and the Scientific Professions* (MIT Symposium on American Women in Science and Engineering). Cambridge, MA: MIT Press.

Betz, N.E. and Fitzgerald, L.F. (1993) 'Individuality and diversity: Theory and research in counseling psychology.' *Annual Review of Psychology 44*, 343–381.

Biddle, L., Gunnell, D., Sharp, D., and Donovan, J.L. (2004) 'Factors influencing help seeking in mentally distressed young adults: A cross-sectional survey.' *British Journal of General Practice 54*, 248–253.

Biggs, W.S. and Chagaboyana, S. (2015) 'Sexuality in Family Medicine.' In R.E. Rakel and D. Rakel (eds) *Textbook of Family Medicine* (Ninth edition). Philadelphia, PA: WB Saunders.

Bilge, S. (2009) 'Smuggling intersectionality into the study of masculinity: Some methodological challenges.' Paper presented at Feminist Research Methods: An International Conference, University of Stockholm, 4–9 February 2009.

Bindell, J. and Fae, J. (2017) *Trans Women Real Women?* Blighty TV. Retrieved from: www.youtube.com/watch?v=Lyj0iowVZOI (accessed 06 December 2017).

Bion, W.R. (1967) 'Notes on memory and desire.' *Psychoanalytic Forum 2*, 271–280.

Blum, A. (2008) 'Shame and guilt, misconceptions and controversies: A critical review of the literature.' *Traumatology 14*, 91–102.

Bockting, W., Benner, A., and Coleman, E. (2009) 'Gay and bisexual identity development among female-to-male transsexuals in North America: Emergence of a transgender sexuality.' *Archives of Sexual Behavior 38*, 688–701.

Bohan, J.S. and Russell, G.M. (1999) 'Implications for Psychological Research and Theory Building.' In J.S. Bohan and G.M. Russell (eds) *Conversations about Psychology and Sexual Orientation.* New York: New York University Press.

Bornstein, K. (1994) *Gender Outlaws: On Men, Women, and the Rest of Us.* New York: Routledge.

Bornstein, K. (1998) *My Gender Workbook.* New York: Routledge.

Bourdieu, P. (1992) 'Thinking about limits.' *Theory, Culture and Society 9*, 1, 37-49.

Bowleg, L. (2008) 'When black + woman + lesbian ≠ black lesbian woman: The methodological challenges of qualitative and quantitative intersectionality research.' *Sex Roles 59*, 5–6, 312–325.

Bowleg, L. (2013) '"Once you've blended the cake, you can't take the parts back to the main ingredients": Black gay and bisexual men's descriptions and experiences of intersectionality.' *Sex Roles 68*, 754–767.

Brannon, R. (1976) 'The Male Sex Role and What It's Done for Us Lately.' In R. Brannon and D. David (eds) *The Forty-Nine Percent Majority.* Reading, MA: Addison-Wesley.

Brescoll, V. and Uhlmann, E. (2008) 'Can an angry woman get ahead? Status conferral, expression of gender and emotions in the workplace.' *Psychological Science 19*, 3, 268–275.

British Psychological Society (BPS) (2012) *Guidelines and Literature Review for Psychologists Working Therapeutically with Sexual and Gender Minority Clients.* Retrieved from: www.bps.org.uk/sites/default/files/images/rep_92.pdf (accessed 06 December 2017).

Brown, L.S. (1986) 'Gender-role analysis: A neglected component of psychological assessment.' *Psychotherapy 23*, 243–248.

Bula, J.F. (2000) 'Use of the Multicultural Self for Effective Practice.' In M. Baldwin (ed.) *The Use of Self in Therapy.* New York: Haworth Press.

Bunton, R. and Crawshaw, P. (2002) 'Risk, Ritual and Ambivalence in Men's Lifestyle Magazines.' In E.S. Henderson and A. Petersen (eds) *The Commodification of Healthcare.* London: Routledge.

Burman, E. (2008) 'Review of S. Wheeler, *Difference and Diversity in Counselling: Contemporary Psychodynamic Approaches.' Psychodynamic Practice: Individuals, Groups and Organisations 4*, 1, 125–127.

Bush, A. (2015) *Simple Self-Care for Therapists: Restorative Practices to Weave through Your Workday.* New York: W.W. Norton.

Butler, J. (2006) *Gender Trouble: Feminism and the Subversion of Identity*. Abingdon: Routledge.

Cancien, F. and Gordon, S. (1988) 'Changing emotional norms in marriage: Love and anger in U.S. women's magazines since 1900.' *Gender and Society 2*, 3, 308–342.

Carson, C. and Shepard, K. (eds) (2001) *A Call to Conscience: The Landmark Speeches of Dr Martin Luther King, Jr.* New York: Hachette Book Group.

Chang, S.C. and Singh, A.A. (2016) 'Affirming psychological practice with transgender and gender nonconforming people of color.' *Psychology of Sexual Orientation and Gender Diversity 3*, 2, 140–147.

Cheshire, L.C. (2013) 'Reconsidering sexual identities: Intersectionality theory and the implications for educating counsellors.' *Canadian Journal of Counselling and Psychotherapy 47*, 1, 4–13.

Chrisler, J.C. (2013) 'Womanhood is not as easy as it seems: Femininity requires both achievement and restraint.' *Psychology of Men and Masculinity 14*, 2, 117–120.

Chrisler, J.C. and Johnston-Robledo, I. (2000) 'Motherhood and Reproductive Issues.' In M. Biaggio and M. Herson (eds) *Issues in the Psychology of Women*. New York: Plenum Press.

Clarkson, P. (2003) *The Therapeutic Relationship* (Second edition). London: Whurr.

Clucas, R. (2015) 'Religion.' In C. Richards and M.J. Barker (eds) *The Palgrave Handbook of Psychology of Gender and Sexuality*. Basingstoke: Palgrave Macmillan.

Cochrane, K. (2013) *All the Rebel Women: The Rise of the Fourth Wave of Feminism (Guardian Shorts)*. London: Guardian Books.

Cohn, A. and Zeichner, A. (2006) 'Effects of masculine identity and gender role stress on aggression in men.' *Psychology of Men and Masculinity 7*, 4, 179–190.

Cohn, A.M., Seibert, A., and Zeichner, A. (2009) 'The role of restrictive emotionality, trait anger, and masculinity threat in men's perpetration of physical aggression.' *Psychology of Men and Masculinity 10*, 3, 218–224.

Cole, E.R. (2009) 'Intersectionality and research in psychology.' *American Psychologist 64*, 3, 170–180.

Cole, E.R. and Zucker, A.N. (2007) 'Black and White women's perspectives on femininity.' *Cultural Diversity and Ethnic Minority Psychology 13*, 1–9.

Cole, P.M. and Putnam, F.W. (1992) 'Effect of incest on self and social functioning: A developmental psychopathology perspective.' *Journal of Consulting and Clinical Psychology 60*, 174–184.

Collier, K.L., Bos, H.M.W., Merry, M.S., and Sandfort, T.G.M. (2013) 'Gender, ethnicity, religiosity, and same-sex sexual attraction and the acceptance of same-sex sexuality and gender non-conformity.' *Sex Roles 68*, 11–12, 724–737.

Collins, P.H. (1998) *Fighting Words: Black Women and the Search for Justice*. Minneapolis, MN: University of Minnesota Press.

Collins, P.H. (2000) *Black Feminist Thought: Knowledge, Consciousness, and the Politics of Empowerment*. New York: Routledge.

Connell, R.W. (1995) *Masculinities*. Berkeley, CA: University of California Press.

Conoley, J.C. (2008) 'Sticks and stones can break my bones and words can really hurt me.' *School Psychology Review 37*, 2, 217–220.

Corbett, K. (1993) 'The mystery of homosexuality.' *Psychoanalytic Psychology 10*, 3, 345–357.

Corbett, K. (1999) 'Homosexual Boyhood: Notes on Girlyboys.' In M. Rottnek (ed.) *Sissies and Tomboys: Gender Nonconformity and Homosexual Childhood*. New York: New York University Press.

Corbett, K. (2009) 'Boyhood femininity, gender identity disorder, masculine resuppositions, and the anxiety of regulation.' *Psychoanalytic Dialogues 19*, 353–370.

Cosgrove, L., Krimsky, S., Vijayaraghavan, M., and Schneider, L. (2006) 'Financial ties between DSM-IV Panel Members and the pharmaceutical industry.' *Psychotherapy and Psychosomatics 75*, 154–160.

Coston, B.M. and Kimmel, M. (2012) 'Seeing privilege where it isn't: Marginalized masculinities and the intersectionality of privilege.' *Journal of Social Issues 68*, 1, 97–111.

Courtenay, W.H. (2000) 'Constructions of masculinity and their influence on men's wellbeing: A theory of gender and health.' *Social Science and Medicine 50*, 1385–1401.

Crenshaw, K. (1989) 'Demarginalizing the intersection of race and sex: A Black feminist critique of antidiscrimination doctrine, feminist theory and antiracist politics.' *University of Chicago Legal Forum, 1989*, 139–167.

de Beauvoir, S. (1949) *The Second Sex* (Trans. by H.M. Parshley). London: Penguin.

Deutscher, P. (2005) *How to Read Derrida*. London: Granta.

Devor, A.H. (2004) 'Witnessing and Mirroring: A Fourteen Stage Model of Transsexual Identity Formation Transsexualism.' In J. Drescher and U. Leli (eds) *Transgender Subjectivities: A Clinician's Guide*. New York: Haworth Press.

Diamond, L.M. and Butterworth, M. (2008) 'Questioning gender and sexual identity: Dynamic links over time.' *Sex Roles 59*, 5–6, 365–376.

dickey, l.m. and Singh, A.A. (2016) 'Training tomorrow's affirmative psychologists: Serving transgender and gender nonconforming people.' *Psychology of Sexual Orientation and Gender Diversity 3*, 2, 137–139.

Dispenza, F., Varney, M., and Golubovic, N. (2016) 'Counseling and psychological practices with sexual and gender minority persons living with chronic illnesses/disabilities (CID).' *Psychology of Sexual Orientation and Gender Diversity 4*, 1, 137–142.

Dodd, J. (2015) '"THE NAME GAME": Feminist protests of the DSM and diagnostic labels in the 1980s.' *History of Psychology 18*, 3, 312–323.

Dow, B. and Wood, J. (2012) *The Sage Handbook of Gender and Communication*. Thousand Oaks, CA: Sage.

Dozier, R. (2005) 'Beards, breasts and bodies: Doing gender in a gendered world.' *Gender and Society 19*, 3, 297–316.

Dundas, R. (2016) 'Stigmatisation, Shame and Trans People.' Unpublished doctoral dissertation, Regent's University, London.

Dworkin, A. (1974) *Woman Hating.* New York: Dutton.

Dyer, R. (1988) 'White.' *Screen 29*, 4, 44–64.

Eagly, A. (1987) *Sex Differences in Social Behavior: A Social-Role Interpretation.* Hillsdale, NJ: Erlbaum.

Eagly, A.H. and Wood, W. (1999) 'The origins of sex differences in human behavior.' *American Psychologist 54*, 408–423.

Eagly, A.H., Eaton, A., Rose, S.M., Riger, S., and McHugh, M.C. (2012) 'Feminism and psychology: Analysis of a half-century of research on women and gender.' *American Psychologist 67*, 3, 211–230.

Ecklund, K. (2012) 'Intersectionality of identity in children: A case study.' *Professional Psychology: Research and Practice 43*, 3, 256–264.

Edwards-Leeper, L., Leibowitz, S., and Sangganjanavanich, V.F. (2016) 'Affirmative practice with transgender and gender nonconforming youth: Expanding the model.' *Psychology of Sexual Orientation and Gender Diversity 3*, 2, 165–172.

Efthim, P.W., Kenny, M.E., and Mahalik, J.R. (2001) 'Gender role stress in relation to shame, guilt, and externalisation.' *Journal of Counseling and Development 79*, 430–438.

Englar-Carlson, M. and Stevens, M.A. (eds) (2006) *In the Room with Men: A Casebook of Therapeutic Change.* Washington, DC: American Psychological Association.

Equality and Human Rights Commission (2008) Sex Discrimination (Amendment of Legislation) Regulations 2008. Retrieved from: www.equality humanrights.com/en/gwaith-achos-cyfreithiol/legal-cases/legal-updates-2007-2012/sex-discrimination-amendment (accessed 08 January 2018).

Ettner, R. (1999) *Gender Loving Care: A Guide to Counseling Gender-Variant Clients.* New York: Norton.

Evans, T. (2010) *The Bridge to Manhood: How the Masculine Self is Shaped by the Father–Son Relationship.* Saarbrucken: Lambert Academic.

Evans, T. (2015) *Counselling Skills for Becoming a Wiser Practitioner: Tools, Techniques and Reflections for Building Practice Wisdom.* London: Jessica Kingsley Publishers.

Factor, R. and Rothblum, E.D. (2007) 'A study of transgender adults and their non-transgender siblings on demographic characteristics, social support, and experiences of violence.' *Journal of LGBT Health Research 3*, 3, 11–30.

Fausto-Sterling, A. (1999) 'Is Gender Essential?' In M. Rottnek (ed.) *Sissies and Tomboys: Gender Nonconformity and Homosexual Childhood.* New York: New York University Press.

Feinberg, L. (1996) *Transgender Warriors: Making History from Joan of Arc to Rupaul.* Boston, MA: Beacon Press.

Feldman, S.S. and Aschenbrenner, B. (1983) 'Impact of parenthood on various aspects of masculinity and femininity: A short-term longitudinal study.' *Developmental Psychology 19*, 2, 278–289.

Fiering, C., Taska, L., and Lewis, M. (2002) 'Adjustment following sexual abuse discovery: The role of shame and attribution style.' *Developmental Psychology* 38, 1, 79–92.

Fischer, A.H., Rodriguez-Mosquera, P.M., van Vianen, A.E.M., and Manstead, A.S.R. (2004) 'Gender and culture differences in emotion.' *Emotion 4*, 1, 87–94.

Fleming, J. and Benedek, T. (1983) *Psychoanalytic Supervision: A Method of Clinical Teaching.* New York: International Universities Press.

Foucault, M. (1972) *The Archaeology of Knowledge* (Trans. by A.M. Sheridan Smith). London: Routledge.

Foucault, M. (1988) 'Technologies of the Self.' In L.H. Martin, H. Gutman, and P.H. Hutton (eds) *Technologies of the Self: A Seminar with Michel Foucault.* Cambridge, MA: MIT Press.

Foucault, M. (1998) *The Will to Knowledge: The History of Sexuality.* Volume 1 (Trans. by R. Hurley). London: Penguin Books.

Foucault, M. (2000a) 'Sexuality and Solitude.' In P. Rabinow (ed.) *Michel Foucault: Ethics, Subjectivity and Truth: Essential Works of Foucault 1954–1984.* Volume 1. London: Penguin Books.

Foucault, M. (2000b) 'The Subject and Power.' In J.D. Faubion (ed.) *Michel Foucault: Power: Essential Works of Foucault 1954–1984.* Volume 3. London: Penguin Books.

Foucault, M. (2000c) 'Truth and Juridical Forms.' In J.D. Faubion (ed.) *Michel Foucault: Power: Essential Works of Foucault 1954–1984.* Volume 3. London: Penguin Books.

Frederik-Goldsen, K.L., Cook-Daniels, L., Kim, H.J., Erosheva, E.A., Emlet, C.A., Hoy-Ellis, C.P., and Muraco, A. (2014) 'Physical and mental health of transgender older adults: An at-risk and underserved population.' *The Gerontologist 54*, 488–500.

Freud, S. (1922) *Group Psychology and the Analysis of the Ego* (Trans. by J. Strachey). London: Hogarth Press.

Freud, S. (2001) 'Leonardo da Vinci and a Memory of His Childhood.' In J. Strachey (ed.) *The Standard Edition of the Complete Psychological Works of Sigmund Freud, Volume 11: Five Lectures on Psycho-Analysis, Leonardo da Vinci and Other Works.* London: Vintage.

Frommer, M.S. (2002) 'Listening to the erotic: Commentary on paper by Eric Sherman.' *Psychoanalytic Dialogues 12*, 4, 675–686.

Frosh, S., Phoenix, A., and Pattman, R. (2002) *Young Masculinities.* Basingstoke: Palgrave Macmillan.

Gale, J., Liljenstrand, A., Pardieu, J., and Nebeker, D.M. (2002) 'Executive Summary – Coaching: Who, What, When, Where, and How.' Unpublished manuscript, California School of Organizational Studies, Alliant International University, CA.

Garofalo, R., Deleon, J., Osmer, E., Doll, M., and Harper, G.W. (2006) 'Overlooked, misunderstood, and at-risk: Exploring the lives and HIV risk of ethnic minority male-to-female transgender youth.' *Journal of Adolescent Health 38*, 230–236.

Gehi, P.S. and Arkles, G. (2007) 'Unraveling injustice: Race and class impact of Medicaid exclusions of transition-related health care for transgender people.' *Journal of Sexual Research and Social Policy 4*, 7–35.

Gehring, D. and Knudson, G. (2005) 'Prevalence of childhood trauma in a clinical population of transsexual people.' *International Journal of Transgenderism 8*, 1, 23–30.

Gergen, K.J. (1991) *The Saturated Self.* New York: Basic Books.

Gerhardt, S. (2004) *Why Love Matters: How Affection Shapes a Baby's Brain.* Hove: Routledge.

Gilbert, P. (1998) 'What is Shame? Some Core Issues and Controversies.' In P. Gilbert and B. Andrews (eds) *Shame: Interpersonal Behavior, Psychopathology, and Culture.* New York: Oxford University Press.

Gilbert, P. (2002) 'Body Shame: A Biopsychosocial Conceptualisation and Overview with Treatment Implications.' In P. Gilbert and J. Miles (eds) *Body Shame: Conceptualisation, Research and Treatment.* Hove: Routledge.

Gilbert, P. (2011) 'Shame in Psychotherapy and the Role of Compassion Focused Therapy.' In R. Dearing and J. Tangney (eds) *Shame in the Therapy Hour.* New York: Guilford Press.

Gilbert, P. (2013) *The Compassionate Mind.* London: Constable and Robinson.

Gilbert, P. and McGuire, M. (1998) 'Shame, Status, and Social Roles: Psychobiology and Evolution.' In P. Gilbert and B. Andrews (eds) *Shame: Interpersonal Behavior, Psychopathology, and Culture.* New York: Oxford University Press.

Gilbert, S.C. and Thompson, J.K. (2002) 'Body Shame in Childhood and Adolescence: Relations to General Psychological Functioning and Eating Disorders.' In P. Gilbert and J. Miles (eds) *Body Shame: Conceptualisation, Research and Treatment.* Hove: Routledge.

Glick, P., Wilkerson, M., and Cuffe, M. (2015) 'Masculine identity, ambivalent sexism, and attitudes toward gender subtypes: Favoring masculine men and feminine women.' *Social Psychology 46*, 4, 201–217.

Goffman, E. (1963a) *Behavior in Public Places.* New York: Free Press.

Goffman, E. (1963b) *Stigma: Notes on the Management of Spoiled Identity.* New York: Simon and Schuster.

Goffman, E. (1967) *Interaction Ritual.* New York: Anchor.

Good, G., Gilbert, L., and Scher, M. (1990) 'Gender Aware Therapy: A synthesis of feminist therapy and knowledge about gender.' *Journal of Counseling and Development 68*, 4, 376–380.

Gopaldas, A. (2013) 'Intersectionality 101.' *Journal of Public Policy and Marketing 32*, 90–94.

Goss, K. and Gilbert, P. (2002) 'Eating Disorders, Shame and Pride: A Cognitive Behavioural Functional Analysis.' In P. Gilbert and J. Miles (eds) *Body Shame: Conceptualisation, Research and Treatment*. Hove: Routledge.

Gottlieb, R. (2016) 'Leaps of Faith: Trainees' Experiences of Not Knowing in Psychotherapy.' Doctoral dissertation, Duquesne University, Pittsburgh, PA. Retrieved from: http://ddc.duq.edu/etd/33 (accessed 06 December 2017).

Gramsci, A. (1971) *Selections from Prison Notebooks*. London: New Left Books.

Granato, S.L., Smith, P.N., and Selwyn, C.N. (2015) 'Acquired capability and masculine gender norm adherence: Potential pathways to higher rates of male suicide.' *Psychology of Men and Masculinity 16*, 3, 246–253.

Grant, J.M., Mottett, J.D., Tanis, J., Min, D., Herman, J.L., and Keisling, M. (2010) *National Transgender Discrimination Survey Report on Health and Health Care: Findings of a Study by the National Center for Transgender Equality and the National Gay and Lesbian Task Force*. Retrieved from: www.thetaskforce.org/static_html/downloads/resources_and_tools/ntds_report_on_health.pdf (accessed 8 January 2018).

Greenspan, J.D. and Traub, R.J. (2013) 'Gender Differences in Pain and Its Relief.' In S. McMahon, M. Koltenburg, I. Tracey, and D. Turk (eds) *Wall and Melzack's Textbook of Pain: Expert Consult-Online and Print* (Sixth edition). Amsterdam: Elsevier.

Griffith, D.M., Ober-Allen, J., and Gunter, K. (2011) 'Social and cultural factors influence African American men's medical help seeking.' *Research on Social Work Practice 21*, 337–347.

Grossman, A.H. and D'Augelli, A.R. (2006) 'Transgender youth: Invisible and vulnerable.' *Journal of Homosexuality 51*, 111–128.

Grossman, A.H. and D'Augelli, A.R. (2007) 'Transgender youth and life-threatening behaviors.' *Suicide and Life Threatening Behavior 37*, 5, 527–537.

The Guardian (2015) 'Female athletes often face the femininity police – especially Serena Williams.' 14 July. Retrieved from: www.theguardian.com/commentisfree/2015/jul/14/serena-williams-female-athletes-femininity-police (accessed 06 December 2017).

The Guardian (2016a) 'Omar Mateen: Orlando killer's ex-wife says he beat her and held her hostage.' 13 June. Retrieved from: www.theguardian.com/us-news/2016/jun/13/orlando-massacre-omar-mateens-ex-wife-says-he-beat-her-and-held-her-hostage (accessed 06 December 2017).

The Guardian (2016b) 'Nice attack bewilders Mohamed Lahouaiej-Bouhlel's relatives.' 16 July. Retrieved from: www.theguardian.com/world/2016/jul/16/nice-attack-bewilders-mohamed-lahouaiej-bouhlel-relatives (accessed 06 December 2017).

The Guardian (2017) 'Boys' jobs and girls' jobs – so who returns the Asos package?' 10 May. Retrieved from: www.theguardian.com/lifeandstyle/shortcuts/2017/may/10/theres-mays-girl-jobs-and-boy-jobs-but-who-buys-the-online-sex-toys (accessed 06 December 2017).

Haines, B.A., Ajayi, A.A., and Boyd, H. (2014) 'Making trans parents visible: Intersectionality of trans and parenting identities.' *Feminism and Psychology 24*, 238–247.

Hanshaw, J. (2016) *Why I'm Not Afraid to be Called Feminine,* 17 October. Retrieved from: www.verygoodlight.com/2016/10/17/black-hypermasculinity (accessed 06 December 2017).

Harrison, J., Grant, J., and Herman, J.L. (2012) *A Gender Not Listed Here: Genderqueers, Gender Rebels, and Otherwise in the National Transgender Discrimination Survey.* Los Angeles, CA: eScholarship, University of California.

Hartley, R.E. (1959) 'Sex role pressures and the socialization of the male child.' *Psychological Reports 5*, 457–468.

Hausman, B.L. (1995) *Changing Sex: Transsexualism, Technology, and Ideas of Gender.* Durham, NC: Duke University Press.

Healy, D. (2006) 'The latest mania: Selling bipolar disorder.' *PLoS Med 3*, 4, 441–444.

Henry, P.C. (2005) 'Social class, market situation, and consumers' metaphors of (dis)empowerment.' *Journal of Consumer Research 31*, 4, 766–778.

Herman, J.L. (1994) *Trauma and Recovery.* London: Pandora.

Hill, D. and Willoughby, B. (2005) 'The development and validation of the genderism and transphobia scale.' *Sex Roles 53*, 7–8, 531–544.

Hilton, L., Hempel, S., Ewing, B.A., Apaydin, E., Xenakis, L., Newberry, S., Colaiaco, B., Ruelaz Maher, A., Shanman, R.M., Sorbero, M.E., and Maglione, M.A. (2017) 'Mindfulness meditation for chronic pain: Systematic review and meta-analysis.' *Annals of Behavioral Medicine 51*, 2, 199–213.

HM Courts and Tribunals Service (2016) *The General Guide for All Users (Gender Recognition Act 2004) (T455).* Retrieved from: http://hmctsformfinder. justice.gov.uk/HMCTS/GetLeaflet.do?court_leaflets_id=2825 (accessed 06 December 2017).

HM Government (2011) *Advancing Transgender Equality: A Plan for Action.* Retrieved from: www.gov.uk/government/uploads/system/uploads/ attachment_data/file/85498/transgender-action-plan.pdf (accessed 06 December 2017).

Hollis, J. (1993) *The Middle Passage: From Misery to Meaning in Midlife.* Toronto: Inner City Books.

House, R. (2003) 'Beyond the medicalisation of "challenging behaviour": Or protecting our children from "Pervasive Labelling Disorder" – Part 1.' *The Mother Magazine 4–6*, 2.

Hubbard, P. (2001) 'Sex zones: Intimacy, citizenship and public space.' *Sexualities 4*, 1, 51–71.

Il'iyink, S.A. (2012) 'Masculinity and femininity: Interpretation in terms of the gender theory.' *Sociology*, October. Retrieved from: https://research-journal.org/en/2012-en/issue-october-2012/masculinity-and-femininity-interpretation-in-terms-of-the-gender-theory/?lang=en (accessed 06 December 2017).

Irigaray, L. (1981) 'This Sex Which is Not One.' In E. Marks and I. de Courtivron (eds) *New French Feminisms* (Trans. by C. Reeder). Brighton: Harvester.

Israel, G. and Tarver, D.E. (1997) *Transgender Care: Recommended Guidelines, Practical Information, and Personal Accounts.* Philadelphia, PA: Temple University Press.

James, A.L. (2012) *Fifty Shades of Grey.* London: Arrow.

Jeffreys, S. (2005) *Beauty and Misogyny: Harmful Cultural Practices in the West.* New York: Routledge.

Joel, D., Tarrasch, R., Berman, Z., Mukamel, M., and Ziv, E. (2013) 'Queering gender: Studying gender identity in "normative" individuals.' *Psychology and Sexuality 5,* 291–321.

Johnson, S.M. (1987) *Humanizing the Narcissistic Style.* New York: W.W. Norton.

Jung, C.G. (1969) 'Archetypes of the Collective Unconscious.' In G. Adler and R.F.C. Hull (eds and trans.) *The Archetypes and the Collective Unconscious,* Volume 9(I) (Second edition). Princeton, NJ: Princeton University Press.

Kabat-Zinn, J. (1982) 'An out-patient program in behavioral medicine for chronic pain patients based on the practice of mindfulness meditation: Theoretical considerations and preliminary results.' *General Hospital Psychiatry 4,* 33–47.

Kabat-Zinn, J. (1990) *Full Catastrophe Living: Using the Wisdom of Your Body and Mind to Face Stress, Pain and Illness.* New York: Delacorte.

Kabat-Zinn, J. (1993) 'Mindfulness Meditation: Health Benefits of an Ancient Buddhist Practice.' In D. Goleman and J. Gurin (eds) *Mind/Body Medicine.* Yonkers, NY: Consumer Reports Books.

Kabat-Zinn, J. (1994) *Wherever You Go, There You Are: Mindfulness Meditation in Everyday Life.* New York: Hyperion.

Kaili, M. (2014) 'Self-disclosure of queer identity: Exploring therapist perspectives.' *Dissertation Abstracts International: Section B: The Sciences and Engineering 74,* 7–B(E).

Katz-Wise, S.L., Reisner, S.L., Hughto, J.W., and Keo-Meier, C.L. (2016) 'Differences in sexual orientation diversity and sexual fluidity in attractions among gender minority adults in Massachusetts.' *Journal of Sex Research 53,* 1, 74–84.

Kaufman, G. (1985) *Shame: The Power of Caring.* Rochester, VT: Schenkman Books.

Kaufman, G. (1989) *The Psychology of Shame: Theory and Treatment of Shame-Based Syndromes.* New York: Springer.

Kernis, M.H. and Goldman, B.M. (2006) 'A multicomponent conceptualization of authenticity: Theory and research.' *Advances in Experimental Social Psychology 38,* 283–357.

Kimmel, M.S. (1996) *Manhood in America: A Cultural History.* New York: Free Press.

Kimmel, M.S. (2007) 'Masculinity as Homophobia: Fear, Shame, and Silence in the Construction of Gender Identity.' In N. Cook (ed.) *Gender Relations in Global Perspective: Essential Readings.* Toronto: Canadian Scholars' Press Inc.

Kimmel, M.S. (2008) *Guyland: The Perilous World Where Boys Become Men: Understanding the Critical Years between 16 and 26.* New York: HarperCollins.

Kimmel, M.S. and Messner, M. (2007) 'Introduction.' In M.S. Kimmel and M. Messner (eds) *Men's Lives*. London: Allyn and Bacon.

Kite, M.E. (1994) 'When Perception Meets Reality: Individual Differences in Reactions to Lesbians and Gay Men.' In B. Greene and H.M. Herek (eds) *Lesbian and Gay Psychology: Theory, Research, and Clinical Applications*. Thousand Oaks, CA: Sage.

Klein, K., Holtby, A., Cook, K., and Travers, R. (2015) 'Complicating the coming out narrative: Becoming oneself in a heterosexist and cissexist world.' *Journal of Homosexuality 62*, 3, 297–326.

Kochanek, K.D., Murphy, S.L., Xu, J., and Tejada-Vera, B. (2016) 'Deaths: Final data for 2014.' *Centers for Disease Control and Prevention: National Vital Statistics Reports 65*, 4, 1–122. Retrieved from: www.cdc.gov/nchs/data/nvsr/ nvsr65/nvsr65_04.pdf (accessed 08 January 2018).

Koken, J.A., Bambi, D.S., and Parson, J.T. (2009) 'Experience of familial acceptance rejection among trans women of color.' *Journal of Family Psychology 23*, 853–860.

Kopala, M. and Keitel, M. (eds) (2005) *Handbook of Counseling Women*. Thousand Oaks, CA: Sage.

Korobov, N. (2005) 'Ironizing masculinity: How adolescent boys negotiate hetero-normative dilemmas in conversational interaction.' *Journal of Men's Studies 13*, 2, 225–246.

Kristeva, J., Jardine, A., and Blake, H. (1981) 'Women's time.' *Signs 7*, 1, 13–35.

Kronner, H.W. and Northcut, T. (2015) 'Listening to both sides of the therapeutic dyad: Self-disclosure of gay male therapists and reflections from their gay male clients.' *Psychoanalytic Social Work 22*, 2, 162–181.

Kugler, P. (2012) *Jungian Perspectives on Clinical Supervision*. Einsiedeln: Daimon.

Kuper, L., Nussbaum, R., and Mustanski, B. (2012) 'Exploring the diversity of gender and sexual orientation identities in an online sample of transgender individuals.' *Journal of Sex Research 49*, 2–3, 244–254.

Kurtz, S. (1983) *The Art of Unknowing: Dimensions of Openness in Analytic Therapy*. Northvale, NJ: Jason Aronson.

Law Society (2015) *Working with Transgender Employees: A Practice Note*. Retrieved from: www.lawsociety.org.uk/support-services/advice/practice-notes/working-with-transgender-employees (accessed 06 December 2017).

Leeming, D. and Boyle, M. (2004) 'Shame as a social phenomenon: A critical analysis of the concept of dispositional shame.' *Psychology and Psychotherapy: Theory, Research and Practice 77*, 375–396.

Lehman, P. (2000) 'A Validity Study of the Femininity Ideology Scale.' Unpublished Master's thesis, Florida Institute of Technology, Melbourne, FL.

Lenihan, P., Kainth, T., and Dundas, R. (2015) 'Trans Sexualities.' In C. Richards and M.J. Barker (eds) *The Palgrave Handbook of the Psychology of Gender and Sexuality*. Basingstoke: Palgrave Macmillan.

Leo, L., Robyn, R., Geldenhuys, M., and Gobind, J. (2014) 'The inferences of gender in workplace bullying: A conceptual analysis.' *Gender and Behaviour 12*, 1, 6059–6069.

Lev, A.S. (2004) *Transgender Emergence: Therapeutic Guidelines for Working with Gender-Variant People and Their Families.* Binghamton, NY: Haworth Clinical Practice Press.

Levant, R.F. (1996) 'The new psychology of men.' *Professional Psychology 27,* 259–265.

Levant, R.F. (1998) 'Desperately Seeking Language: Understanding, Assessing, and Treating Normative Male Alexithymia.' In W.S. Pollack and R.F. Levant (eds) *New Psychotherapy for Men.* New York: John Wiley and Sons.

Levant, R.F., Alto, K.M., McKelvey, D.K., Richmond, K.A., and McDermott, R.C. (2017) 'Variance composition, measurement invariance by gender, and construct validity of the Femininity Ideology Scale-Short Form.' *Journal of Counseling Psychology 64,* 6, 708–723.

Levant, R.F., Richmond, K., Cook, S., House, A.T., and Aupont, M. (2007) 'The Femininity Ideology Scale: Factor structure, reliability, convergent and discriminant validity, and social contextual variation.' *Sex Roles 57,* 373–383.

Lewins, F. (1995) *Transsexualism in Society: A Sociology of Male-to-Female Transsexuals.* South Melbourne: Macmillan.

Lewis, H.B. (1971) *Shame and Guilt in Neurosis.* New York: International Universities Press.

Lewis, M. (1995) *Shame: The Exposed Self.* New York: Free Press.

Lewis, M. (1998) 'Shame and Stigma.' In P. Gilbert and B. Andrews (eds) *Shame: Interpersonal Behavior, Psychopathology, and Culture.* New York: Oxford University Press.

Linehan, M.M. (1980) 'Supervision of Behaviour Therapy.' In A.K. Hess (ed.) *Psychotherapy Supervision: Theory, Research and Practice.* New York: Wiley.

Loewenthal, D. and Snell, R. (2003) *Post-Modernism for Psychotherapists: A Critical Reader.* Hove: Routledge.

Lombardi, E.L., Wilchins, R.A., Priesing, D., and Malouf, D. (2002) 'Gender violence: Transgender experiences with violence and discrimination.' *Journal of Homosexuality 42,* 1, 89–101.

Macdonald, J. (1998) 'Disclosing Shame.' In P. Gilbert and B. Andrews (eds) *Shame: Interpersonal Behavior, Psychopathology, and Culture.* New York: Oxford University Press.

Macgillivray, I.K. (2008) 'Religion, sexual orientation, and school policy: How the Christian Right frames its arguments.' *Educational Studies 43,* 29–44.

Madsen, D. (1995) 'A biochemical property relating to power seeking in humans.' *American Political Science Review 79,* 448–457.

Mahalik, J.R., Good, G.E., and Englar-Carlson, M. (2003) 'Masculinity scripts, presenting concerns, and help seeking: Implications for practice and training.' *Professional Psychology: Research and Practice 34,* 123–131.

Mahalik, J.R., Good, G.E., Tager, D., Levant, R.F., and Mackowiak, C. (2012) 'Developing a taxonomy of helpful and harmful practices for clinical work with boys and men.' *Journal of Counseling Psychology 59,* 4, 591–603.

Mahalik, J.R., Locke, B.D., Ludlow, L.H., Diemer, M.A., Scott, R.P., Gottfried, M., and Freitas, G. (2003) 'Development of the conformity to masculine norms inventory.' *Psychology of Men and Masculinity 4*, 1, 3–25.

Manafi, E. (2010) 'Existential-Phenomenological Contributions to Counselling Psychology's Relational Framework.' In M. Milton (ed.) *Therapy and Beyond: Counselling Psychology Contributions to Therapeutic and Social Issues.* Chichester: John Wiley and Sons.

Martin, E. (1999) 'The egg and the sperm: How science has constructed a romance based on stereotypical male–female roles.' *Signs 16*, 3, 485–501.

Martinez, L.R., Sawyer, K.B., Thoroughgood, C.N., Ruggs, E.N., and Smith, N.A. (2016) 'The importance of being "me": The relation between authentic identity expression and transgender employees' work-related attitudes and experiences.' *Journal of Applied Psychology 27*, 455–466.

Mass, A., Cadinu, M., Guarnieri, G., and Grasseli, A. (2003) 'Sexual harassment under social identity threat: The computer harassment paradigm.' *Journal of Personality and Social Psychology 85*, 853–870.

McCall, L. (2005) 'The complexity of intersectionality.' *Signs: Journal of Women in Culture and Society 30*, 1771–1800.

McCormack, M. (2012) *Declining Significance of Homophobia: How Teenage Boys are Redefining Masculinity and Heterosexuality.* Oxford: Oxford University Press.

McCullough, L., Kuhn, N., Andrews, S., Kaplan, A., Wolf, J., and Hurley, C.L. (2003) *Treating Affect Phobia: A Manual for Short-Term Dynamic Psychotherapy.* New York: Guilford Press.

McDermott, R.C. and Schwartz, J.P. (2013) 'Toward a better understanding of emerging adult men's gender role journeys: Differences in age, education, race, relationship status, and sexual orientation.' *Psychology of Men and Masculinity 14*, 2, 202–210.

McGuire, M. (1988) 'On the possibility of ethological explanations of psychiatric disorders.' *Acta Psychiatrica Scandinavica 77*, Suppl., 7–22.

McGuire, M. and Troisi, A. (1987a) 'Physiological regulation-disregulation and psychiatric disorders.' *Ethology and Sociobiology 8*, 95–125.

McGuire, M. and Troisi, A. (1987b) 'Unrealistic wishes and psychological change.' *Psychotherapy Psychomatics 47*, 82–94.

McIntosh, P. (1989) 'White privilege: Unpacking the invisible knapsack.' *Peace and Freedom Magazine July/August*, 10–12.

McKee, K.J. and Gott, M. (2002) 'Shame and the Ageing Body.' In P. Gilbert and J. Miles (eds) *Body Shame: Conceptualisation, Research and Treatment.* Hove: Routledge.

McKelley, R.A. and Rochlen, A.B. (2007) 'The practice of coaching: Exploring alternatives to therapy for counseling-resistant men.' *Psychology of Men and Masculinity 8*, 1, 53–65.

McNeil, J., Bailey, L., Ellis, S., Morton, J., and Regan, M. (2012) *Trans Mental Health Study 2012.* Retrieved from: www.scottishtrans.org/wp-content/uploads/2013/03/trans_mh_study.pdf (accessed 06 December 2017).

Metro Youth Chances (2014) *Youth Chances Summary of First Findings: The Experiences of LGBTQ Young People in England*. London: Metro.

Meyerowitz, J. (2009) *How Sex Changed: A History of Transsexuality in the United States*. Boston, MA: Harvard University Press.

Milk, H. (2013) *An Archive of Hope: Harvey Milk's Speeches and Writings*. Edited by J.E. Black and C.E. Morris III. Berkeley: University of California Press.

Mills, M. (2001) *Challenging Violence in Schools: An Issue of Masculinities*. Buckingham: Open University Press.

Mills, M. and Stoneham, G. (2017) *The Voice Book for Trans and Non-Binary People: A Practical Guide to Creating and Sustaining Authentic Voice and Communication*. London: Jessica Kingsley Publishers.

Mills, S. (1992) 'Negotiating discourses of gender.' *Journal of Gender Studies 1*, 3, 271–285.

Milton, M., Coyle, A., and Legg, C. (2002) 'Lesbian and Gay Affirmative Psychotherapy: Defining the Domain.' In A. Coyle and C. Kitzinger (eds) *Lesbian and Gay Psychology: New Perspectives*. Oxford: Blackwell.

Mizock, L. and Hopwood, R. (2016) 'Conflation and interdependence in the intersection of gender and sexuality among transgender individuals.' *Psychology of Sexual Orientation and Gender Diversity 3*, 1, 93–103.

Money, J. (2016) *Gendermaps: Social Constructionism, Feminism and Sexosophical History*. London: Bloomsbury.

Moolchaem, P., Liamputtong, P., O'Halloran, P., and Muhamad, R. (2015) 'The lived experiences of transgender persons: A meta-synthesis.' *Journal of Gay and Lesbian Social Services 27*, 143–171.

Moon, L. (2008) 'Queer(y)ing the Heterosexualization of Emotion.' In L. Moon (ed.) *Feeling Queer or Queer Feelings? Radical Approaches to Counselling Sex, Sexualities and Genders*. Hove: Routledge.

Moradi, B. (2017) '(Re)focusing Intersectionality: From Social Identities Back to Systems of Oppression and Privilege.' In K.A. DeBord, A.R. Fischer, K.J. Bieschke, and R.M. Perez (eds) *Handbook of Sexual Orientation and Gender Diversity in Counseling and Psychotherapy*. Washington, DC: American Psychological Association.

Moradi, B., van den Berg, J.J., and Epting, F.R. (2009) 'Threat and guilt aspects of internalised anti-lesbian and gay prejudice: An application of personal construct theory.' *Journal of Counseling Psychology 56*, 1, 119–131.

Munt, S. (2007) *Queer Attachments: The Cultural Politics of Shame*. Hampshire: Ashgate.

Murdoch, E. (2013) 'Introduction: Overview of Coaching Supervision.' In E. Murdoch and J. Arnold (eds) *Full Spectrum Supervision: 'Who You Are, is How You Supervise'*. St Albans: Panoma Press.

Nadal, K.L. (ed.) (2017) *The Sage Encyclopedia of Psychology and Gender*. Thousand Oaks, CA: Sage.

Nathanson, D. (1992) *Shame and Pride: Affect, Sex, and the Birth of the Self*. New York: Norton.

The New York Times (2012) 'Not diseases, but categories of suffering.' 30 January. Retrieved from: www.nytimes.com/2012/01/30/opinion/the-dsms-troubled-revision.html?mcubz=0 (accessed 06 December 2017).

The New York Times (2017a) 'The universal phenomenon of men interrupting women.' 14 June. Retrieved from: www.nytimes.com/2017/06/14/business/women-sexism-work-huffington-kamala-harris.html (accessed 06 December 2017).

The New York Times (2017b) 'Women's voices are still not being heard.' 18 June. Retrieved from: www.nytimes.com/2017/06/18/opinion/women-sexism-work-huffington-kamala-harris.html?mcubz=1 (accessed 06 December 2017).

Newsweek (1993) 'Lesbians: What are the limits of tolerance?' 21 June.

NHS England (2013) *Interim Gender Dysphoria Protocol and Service Guidelines 2013/14.* Retrieved from: www.england.nhs.uk/wp-content/uploads/2013/10/int-gend-proto.pdf (accessed 06 December 2017).

Nixon, D. and Givens, N. (2007) 'An epitaph to Section 28? Telling tales out of school about changes and challenges to discourses of sexuality.' *International Journal of Qualitative Studies in Education 20*, 4, 449–471.

Nuttbrock, L., Rosenblum, A., and Blumenstein, R. (2002) 'Transgender affirmation and mental health.' *International Journal of Transgenderism 6*, 4, 33–37.

O'Neil, J.M. (1981) 'Male sex role conflicts, sexism and masculinity: Psychological implications for men, women and the counseling psychologist.' *Counseling Psychology 9*, 61–80.

O'Neil, J.M. (2008) 'Summarizing 25 years of research on men's gender role conflict using the Gender Role Conflict Scale: New research paradigms and clinical implications.' *Counseling Psychologist 36*, 358–445.

O'Neil, J.M., Helms, B.J., Gable, R.K., David, L., and Wrightsman, L.S. (1986) 'The Gender Role Conflict Scale: College men's fear of femininity.' *Sex Roles 14*, 335–350.

Oriah Mountain Dreamer (2001) *The Dance.* San Francisco, CA: HarperONE.

Osherson, S. and Krugman, S. (1990) 'Men, shame and psychotherapy.' *Psychotherapy 27*, 327–339.

Paechter, C. (2010) 'Tomboys and girly-girls: Embodied femininities in primary schools.' *Discourse: Studies in the Cultural Politics of Education 31*, 2, 221–235.

Parker, I. (1999) 'Deconstructing Diagnosis: Psychopathological Practice.' In C. Feltham (ed.) *Controversies in Psychotherapy and Counselling.* London: Sage.

Pavey, J. (2014) *This Mum Runs: 10,000 Metre Gold Medallist at 40.* London: Yellow Jersey Press.

Pe, R. (2016) 'Yes, Asia is obsessed with white skin.' *Business Inquirer.* 1 October. Retrieved from: http://business.inquirer.net/215898/yes-asia-is-obsessed-with-white-skin (accessed 06 December 2017).

Penny, L. (2014) *Unspeakable Things: Sex, Lies and Revolution.* London: Bloomsbury Press.

Pleck, J.H. (1981) *The Myth of Masculinity.* Cambridge, MA: MIT Press.

Plummer, K. (1995) *Telling Sexual Stories: Power, Change, and Social Worlds.* London: Routledge.

Pollack, W. (1998) *Real Boys: Rescuing Our Sons from the Myths of Boyhood.* New York: Henry Holt.

Prosser, J. (1998) *Second Skins: The Body Narratives of Transsexuality.* New York: Columbia University Press.

Rachlin, K. (1997) 'Partners in the journey: Psychotherapy and six stages of gender revelation.' Paper presented at the Second Congress on Sex and Gender, 19–22 June, King of Prussia, PA.

Rachlin, K. (2002) 'Transgender individuals' experiences of psychotherapy.' *International Journal of Transgenderism 6*, 1. Retrieved from: www.researchgate.net/publication/288078302_Transgender_individuals%27_experiences_of_psychotherapy (accessed 08 January 2018).

Raj, R. (2002) 'Towards a transpositive therapeutic model: Developing clinical sensitivity and cultural competence in the effective support of transsexual and transgendered clients.' *International Journal of Transgenderism 6*, 2. Retrieved from: http://itgl.lu/wp-content/uploads/2015/04/IJ-TRANSGENDER-Towards-a-Transpositive-Therapeutic-Model_-Developing-Clinical-Sensitivity-and-Cultural-Competence-in-the-Effective-Support-of-Transsexual-and-Transgendered-Clients.pdf (accessed 08 January 2018).

Rasmussen, M.L. (2004) 'The problem of coming out.' *Theory into Practice 43*, 144–150.

Raymond, J. (1980) *The Transsexual Empire.* London: Women's Press.

Reilly, D. and Neumann, D. (2013) 'Gender role differences in spatial ability: A meta-analytic review.' *Sex Roles 68*, 9–10, 521–535.

Richards, C. and Barker, M. (2013) *Sexuality and Gender for Mental Health Professionals: A Practical Guide.* London: Sage.

Richards, C., Pierre Bouman, W., Seal, L., Barker, M.J., Nieder, T.O., and T'Sjoen, G. (2016) 'Non-binary or genderqueer genders.' *International Review of Psychiatry 28*, 1, 95–102.

Richards, M. and Bedi, R.P. (2015) 'Gaining perspective: How men describe incidents damaging the therapeutic alliance.' *Psychology of Men and Masculinity 16*, 2, 170–182.

Rizq, R. (2006) 'Training and disillusion in counselling psychology: A psychoanalytic perspective.' *Psychology and Psychotherapy: Theory, Research and Practice 79*, 4, 613–627.

Robbins, C.K. and McGowan, B.L. (2016) 'Intersectional perspectives on gender and gender identity development.' *New Directions for Student Services 154*, 71–83.

Robertson, J.M. and Williams, B.W. (2010) '"Gender Aware Therapy" for professional men in a day treatment center.' *Psychotherapy Theory, Research, Practice, Training 47*, 3, 316–326.

Rochlen, A.B. and Rabinowitz, F.E. (eds) (2013) *Breaking Barriers in Counseling Men. The Routledge Series on Counseling and Psychotherapy with Boys and Men.* New York: Routledge.

Rochlin, M. (1972) *The Heterosexual Questionnaire.* Retrieved from: www.uwgb. edu/pride-center/files/pdfs/Heterosexual_Questionnaire.pdf (accessed 06 December 2017).

Roscoe, W. (1998) *Changing Ones: Third and Fourth Genders in Native North America.* New York: St. Martin's Press.

Rose, N. (1996) 'Power and Subjectivity: Critical History and Psychology.' In C.F. Graumann and K.J. Gergen (eds) *Historical Dimensions of Psychological Discourse.* Cambridge: Cambridge University Press.

Rosenberg, K.L., Tangney, J.P., Denham, S., Leonard, A.M., and Widmaier, N. (1994) *Socialization of Moral Affect-Parent of Children Form (SOMA-PC).* Fairfax, VA: George Mason University.

Royal College of Psychiatrists (RCP) (2013) *Good Practice Guidelines for the Assessment and Treatment of Adults with Gender Dysphoria.* Retrieved from: www. rcpsych.ac.uk/files/pdfversion/CR181_Nov15.pdf (accessed 06 December 2017).

Rutherford, A. and Pettit, M. (2015) 'Feminism and/in/as psychology: The public sciences of sex and gender.' *History of Psychology 18,* 3, 223–237.

Ryan, C., Russell, S.T., Huebner, D., Diaz, R., and Sanchez, J. (2010) 'Family acceptance in adolescence and the health of LGBT young adults.' *Journal of Child and Adolescent Psychiatric Nursing 23,* 205–213.

Safran, J.D. and Muran, J.C. (2003) *Negotiating the Therapeutic Relationship: A Relational Treatment Guide.* New York: Guilford Press.

Samaritans (2017) *Suicide Statistics Report 2017.* Retrieved from: www.samaritans. org/sites/default/files/kcfinder/files/Suicide_statistics_report_2017_ Final%282%29.pdf (accessed 06 December 2017).

San Francisco Bay Times (1993) 'Dykeweek.' 1 July, 1.

Sanchez, F.J. and Vilain, E. (2009) 'Collective self-esteem as a coping resource for male-to-female transsexuals.' *Journal of Counseling Psychology 56,* 202–209.

Sanderson, C. (2015) *Counselling Skills for Working with Shame.* London: Jessica Kingsley Publishers.

Scaturo, D.J. (2005) *Clinical Dilemmas in Psychotherapy: A Transtheoretical Approach to Psychotherapy Integration.* Washington, DC: American Psychological Association.

Scheff, T. (1988) 'Shame and conformity: The deference-emotion system.' *American Sociological Review 53,* 395–406.

Schore, A.N. (1994) *Affect Regulation and the Origin of the Self: The Neurobiology of Emotional Development.* New York: Erlbaum.

Schore, A.N. (2003a) *Affect Regulation and Repair of the Self.* New York: W.W. Norton.

Schore, A.N. (2003b) *Affect Dysregulation and Disorders of the Self.* New York: W.W. Norton.

Schug, J., Alt, N.P., Lu, P.S., Gosin, M., and Fay, J.L. (2015) 'Gendered race in mass media: Invisibility of Asian men and Black women in popular magazines.' *Psychology of Popular Media Culture 6,* 3, 222–236.

Sedgwick, E.K. (1990) *Epistemology of the Closet.* Berkeley, CA: University of California Press.

Sevelius, J.M. (2013) 'Gender affirmation: A framework for conceptualizing risk behavior among transgender women of color.' *Sex Roles 68,* 675–689.

Shepard, D.S. and Rabinowitz, F.E. (2013) 'The power of shame in men who are depressed: Implications for counsellors.' *Journal of Counseling and Development 91,* 451–457.

Shepherd, C.B. and Rickard, K.M. (2011) 'Drive for muscularity and help-seeking: The mediational role of gender role conflict, self-stigma and attitudes.' *Psychology of Men and Masculinity 13,* 4, 379–392.

Sherman, E. (2005) *Notes from the Margins: The Gay Analyst's Subjectivity in the Treatment Setting.* Hillsdale, NJ: Analytic Press.

Singh, A.A. (2013) 'Transgender youth of color and resilience: Negotiating oppression and finding support.' *Sex Roles 68,* 690–702.

Singh, A.A. and dickey, l.m. (2016) 'Implementing the APA guidelines on psychological practice with transgender and gender nonconforming people: A call to action in the field of psychology.' *Psychology of Sexual Orientation and Gender Diversity 3,* 2, 195–200.

Smith, J.T. (1902) *The Art of Disappearing.* New York: Benziger Brothers.

Soloway, J. (Producer) (2014) Transparent [TV Series]. United States: Amazon Video.

Sprott, R.A. and Berkey, B. (2015) 'At the intersection of sexual orientation and alternative sexualities: Issues raised by *Fifty Shades of Grey.*' *Psychology of Sexual Orientation and Gender Diversity 2,* 4, 506–507.

Stone, S. (1991) 'The Empire Strikes Back: A Posttranssexual Manifesto.' In J. Epstein and K. Straub (eds) *Body Guards: The Cultural Politics of Gender Ambiguity.* New York: Routledge.

Strokoff, J., Halford, T.C., and Owen, J. (2016) 'Men and Psychotherapy.' In Y.J. Wong and S.R. Wester (eds) *APA Handbook of Men and Masculinities.* Washington, DC: American Psychological Association.

Stryker, S. (1994) 'My words to Victor Frankenstein about the village of Chamounix performing transgender rage.' *GLQ: A Journal of Lesbian and Gay Studies 1,* 3, 227–254.

Stryker, S. (2006) '(De)subjugated Knowledges: An Introduction to Transgender Studies.' In S. Stryker and S. Whittle (eds) *The Transgender Studies Reader.* New York: Routledge.

Sue, D. and Sue, D.M. (2008) *Foundations of Counselling and Psychotherapy: Evidence-Based Practices for a Diverse Society.* Hoboken, NJ: John Wiley and Sons.

Tangney, J. and Dearing, R. (2002) *Shame and Guilt.* New York: Guilford Press.

Tantam, D. (1998) 'The Emotional Disorders of Shame.' In P. Gilbert and B. Andrews (eds) *Shame: Interpersonal Behavior, Psychopathology, and Culture.* New York: Oxford University Press.

Taylor, G. (1996) 'Guilt and Remorse.' In R. Harre and G. Parrott (eds) *The Emotions: Social, Cultural and Biological Dimensions.* London: Sage.

Taywaditep, K. (2001) 'Marginalisation among the marginalised: Gay men's anti-effeminacy attitudes.' *Journal of Homosexuality 42*, 1, 1–28.

Tee, N. and Hegarty, P. (2006) 'Predicting opposition to the civil rights of trans persons in the United Kingdom.' *Journal of Community and Applied Social Psychology 16*, 70–80.

The Telegraph (2016) 'Meet Jo Pavey, the 42-year-old mum on the way to her fifth Olympics.' 14 July. Retrieved from: www.telegraph.co.uk/women/family/ meet-jo-pavey-the-42-year-old-mum-on-the-way-to-her-fifth-olympi (accessed 06 December 2017).

Tharinger, D.J. (2008) 'Maintaining hegemonic masculinity through selective attachment, homophobia, and gay-baiting in schools: Challenges to intervention.' *School Psychology Review 37*, 2, 221–227.

Thomas, A., Hammond, W.P., and Kohn-Wood, L.P. (2015) 'Chill, be cool man: African American men, identity, coping, and aggressive ideation.' *Cultural Diversity and Ethnic Minority Psychology 21*, 3, 369–379.

Thoreau, H.D. (1908) *Walden, or, Life in the Woods.* London: J.M. Dent. (Originally published in 1854.)

Total Jobs (2016) *Trans Employee Experiences Survey.* Retrieved from: www. totaljobs.com/insidejob/wp-content/uploads/2016/04/160407_TJ_ Trans_Report.pdf (accessed 06 December 2017).

Travers, R., Bauer, G., Pyne, J., Bradley, K., Gale, L., and Papadimitriou, M. (2012) *Impacts of Strong Parental Support for Trans Youth: A Report Prepared for Children's Aid Society of Toronto and Delisle Youth Services.* Retrieved from: http://transpulseproject.ca/research/impacts-of-strong-parental-support- for-trans-youth (accessed 08 January 2018).

UK Trans Info (2016) *Current Waiting Times and Patient Population for Gender Identity Clinics in the UK.* Retrieved from: https://uktrans.info/attachments/ article/341/patientpopulation-oct15.pdf (accessed 06 December 2017).

van Anders, S.M. (2015) 'Beyond sexual orientation: Integrating gender/sex and diverse sexualities via sexual configurations theory.' *Archives of Sexual Behavior 44*, 1177–1213.

van Caenegem, E., Wierckx, K., Elaut, E., Buysse, A., Dewaele, A., van Nieuwerburgh, F., and T'Sjoen, G. (2015) 'Prevalence of gender nonconformity in Flanders, Belgium.' *Archives of Sexual Behavior 44*, 5, 1281–1287.

Vandello, J.A. and Bosson, J.K. (2013) 'Hard won and easily lost: A review and synthesis of theory and research on precarious manhood.' *Psychology of Men and Masculinity 14*, 101–113.

Veale, D. (2002) 'Shame in Body Dysmorphic Disorder.' In P. Gilbert and J. Miles (eds) *Body Shame: Conceptualisation, Research and Treatment.* Hove: Routledge.

Velez, B.L., Moradi, B., and DeBlaere, C. (2015) 'Multiple oppressions and the mental health of sexual minority Latina/o individuals.' *Counseling Psychologist 43*, 7–38.

Vogel, D.L., Heirmerdinger-Edwards, S.R., Hammer, J.H., and Hubbard, A. (2011) '"Boys Don't Cry": Examination of the links between endorsement of masculine norms, self-stigma and help-seeking attitudes for men from diverse backgrounds.' *Journal of Counseling Psychology 58*, 3, 368–382.

Watkins, C.E. (1997) 'Defining Psychotherapy Supervision and Understanding Supervisor Functioning.' In C.E. Watkins Jr. (ed.) *The Handbook of Psychotherapy Supervision*. New York: John Wiley and Sons.

Watts-Jones, D. (2010) 'Location of self: Opening the door to dialogue on intersectionality in the therapy process.' *Family Process 49*, 3, 405–420.

Webb, J., Schirato, T., and Danaher, G. (2002) *Understanding Bourdieu*. London: Sage.

Weber, G. (2008) 'Using to numb the pain: Substance use and abuse among lesbian, gay, and bisexual individuals.' *Journal of Mental Health Counseling 30*, 1, 31–48.

West, C. and Zimmerman, D. (2009) 'Accounting for doing gender.' *Gender and Society 23*, 1, 112–122.

Wexler, D. (2009) *Men in Therapy: New Approaches for Effective Treatment*. New York: W.W. Norton.

White, M. (1995) *Re-authoring Lives: Interviews and Essays*. Adelaide: Dulwich Centre Publications.

White, M. and Epston, D. (1990) *Narrative Means to Therapeutic Ends*. New York: W.W. Norton.

Whittle, S. (2000) *The Transgender Debate: The Crisis Surrounding Gender Identities*. Berkshire: Garnett and Ithaca Press.

Whittle, S. (2006) 'Foreword.' In S. Stryker and S. Whittle (eds) *The Transgender Studies Reader*. New York: Routledge.

Whittle, S., Turner, L., and Al-Alami, M. (2007) *Engendered Penalties: Transgender and Transsexual People's Experiences of Inequality and Discrimination*. London: Equalities Review.

Wilchins, R.A. (1997a) *Read My Lips: Sexual Subversion and the End of Gender*. New York: Firebrand.

Wilchins, R.A. (1997b) *The First National Survey of Transgender Violence: GenderPAC 2*. Waltham, MA: University of Michigan.

Winnicott, D.W. (1969) 'The use of an object.' *International Journal of Psychoanalysis 50*, 711–716.

Winter, W. and Udomsak, N. (2002) 'Gender stereotype and self among transgenders: Underlying elements.' *International Journal of Transgenderism 6*, 2. Retrieved from: www.atria.nl/ezines/web/IJT/97-03/numbers/symposion/ijtvo06no02_02.htm (accessed 08 January 2018).

Wittig, M. (1980) 'The straight mind.' *Feminist Issues 1*, 1, 103–111.

Wolf, N. (1990) *The Beauty Myth*. New York: Morrow.

Wonderlich, S.A., Brewerton, T.D., Jocic, Z., Dansky, B.S., and Abbott, D.W. (1997) 'Relationship of childhood sexual abuse and eating disorders.' *Journal of the American Academy of Child and Adolescent Psychiatry 36*, 1107–1115.

Wood, A., Linley, P., Maltby, J., Baliousis, M., and Joseph, S. (2008) 'The authentic personality: A theoretical and empirical conceptualization and the development of the authenticity scale.' *Journal of Counselling Psychology 55*, 3, 385–399.

Worell, J. and Remer, P. (2003) *Feminist Perspectives in Therapy: Empowering Diverse Women* (Second edition). New York: Wiley.

World Health Organization (WHO) (2015) 'Transsexualism.' *International Statistical Classification of Diseases and Related Health Problems (Version 10: 2015, ICD-10)*. Geneva: WHO, F64.0. Retrieved from: http://apps.who.int/classifications/icd10/browse/2016/en#/F64.0 (accessed 05 February 2018).

World Professional Association for Transgender Health (WPATH) (2011) *Standards of Care for the Health of Transsexual, Transgender, and Gender Nonconforming People*. Retrieved from: www.wpath.org/site_page.cfm?pk_association_webpage=3926&pk_association_webpage_menu=1351 (accessed 08 January 2018).

Woskett, V. (1999) *The Therapeutic Use of Self: Counselling Practice, Research and Supervision*. Abingdon: Routledge.

Woskett, V., Page, J., and Page, S. (2002) 'The Cyclical Model of Supervision: A Container for Creativity and Chaos.' In M. Carroll and M. Tholstrup (eds) *Integrative Approaches to Supervision*. London: Jessica Kingsley Publishers.

Xavier, J., Bradford, J., Hendricks, M., Safford, L., McKee, R., Martin, E., and Honnold, J.A. (2012) 'Transgender health care access of Virginia: A qualitative study.' *International Journal of Transgenderism 14*, 3–17.

Zahn-Waxler, C., Cole, P.M., and Barrett, K.C. (1991) 'Guilt and Empathy: Sex Differences and Implications for the Development of Depression.' In J. Garber and K.A. Dodge (eds) *The Development of Emotion Regulation and Dysregulation*. Cambridge: Cambridge University Press.

SUBJECT INDEX

AUTHOR INDEX